Commonwealth of Compromise

Commonwealth of Compromise

Civil War Commemoration in Missouri

Amy Laurel Fluker

UNIVERSITY OF MISSOURI PRESS
COLUMBIA

University of Missouri Press, Columbia, Missouri 65211
Printed and bound in the United States of America
 First printing, 2020.

Library of Congress Cataloging-in-Publication Data

Names: Fluker, Amy Laurel, author.
Title: Commonwealth of compromise : Civil War commemoration in Missouri / Amy Laurel Fluker.
Description: Columbia : University of Missouri Press, 2020. | Includes bibliographical references and index.
Identifiers: LCCN 2019053539 (print) | LCCN 2019053540 (ebook) | ISBN 9780826222084 (hardcover) | ISBN 9780826274441 (ebook)
Subjects: LCSH: Missouri--History--Civil War, 1861-1865--Historiography. |
Memorialization--Missouri--History . | Collective memory--Missouri.
Classification: LCC F465.2 .F55 2020 (print) | LCC F465.2 (ebook) | DDC 977.8/03--dc23
LC record available at https://lccn.loc.gov/2019053539
LC ebook record available at https://lccn.loc.gov/2019053540

™ This paper meets the requirements of the
American National Standard for Permanence of Paper
for Printed Library Materials, Z39.48, 1984.

Typefaces: Old Standard and Adobe Caslon Pro

For Steven and Irene Fluker

In Memory of John R. Neff

Contents

Illustrations

Acknowledgments

Nothing has ever preserved me better, given me more strength, than the enthusiasm born within me when I talk about the people of Missouri.

—Major General Benjamin M. Prentiss (USA),
Macon, April 17, 1895

IN MANY WAYS, THIS PROJECT began in my childhood. Growing up in Jefferson City, Missouri, my parents indulged my interest in the past with endless weekend trips to local historic sites in Pilot Knob, St. Charles, Hermann, Arrow Rock, Lexington, Liberty, and Kearney—places few outside the state have ever heard of, but places steeped in nineteenth-century history. Our soundtrack on these adventures was often *Johnny Whistletrigger*, an album by folk musicians Bob Dyer, Dave Para, and Cathy Barton of songs from and about the Civil War era in Missouri. It was through this music that I first learned about Franz Sigel, Nathaniel Lyon, William Clarke Quantrill, Jo Shelby, and the Civil War on the western border. Since then, in the words of Major General Benjamin M. Prentiss, "Nothing has ever preserved me better, given me more strength, than the enthusiasm born within me when I talk about the people of Missouri." In short, the task of writing *Commonwealth of Compromise* has been tremendously rewarding, both personally and professionally. And, although its shortcomings are no one's fault but my own, it could not have been completed without the assistance of numerous people, particularly my colleagues, friends, and family.

Thank you, first of all, to the staff at the State Historical Society of Missouri, the Missouri State Archives, and the Missouri Historical Society. Thank you to the numerous colleagues who offered input on this project including Miller W. Boyd, III, April Holm, Kelly Mezurek, Jeremy Neely, Sheila Skemp, Jodi Skipper, Ann L. Tucker, Anne S. Twitty, and Noell

Wilson. Their guidance was extremely valuable in shaping the final direction of this work.

Commonwealth of Compromise reflects the support of the faculty, staff, and students at Youngstown State University, particularly in the Department of History, College of Liberal Arts and Social Sciences, Maag Library, and Office of Research. Graduate student Alysha Schall lent meticulous and invaluable research assistance. Brian Bonhomme, Donna DeBlasio, Jacob Ari Labendz, and Martha I. Pallante shared their wisdom and extended their collegiality. Thank you for making my move to Youngstown so satisfying.

Finally, the most tremendous debt of gratitude I owe is to my friends and family. I am especially thankful to have been part of my graduate student cohort at the University of Mississippi. A more accomplished and affirming group of historians it would be difficult to find. Amanda M. Myers I owe thanks as both my dear friend and as a fellow Civil War scholar. Amanda provided insightful suggestions for revisions and entertained endless brainstorming sessions about border states, Missouri, and memory. *Commonwealth of Compromise* is a better book for her input. Tiffany Eggleston, my best friend and companion of many amazing adventures, helped me keep life and work in perspective. Dianna Townsand, one of the hardest-working and most supportive women I know, encouraged me to have confidence in what I do. Meghan Kobza's contagious passion for history inspired me to maintain my initiative. Laura Jacoby and Emily Vonderahe, my wonderful cousins and lifelong friends, turned research trips to Missouri into special occasions. Last, but certainly not least, a thank you to my parents. Thank you for nurturing my love of history from that first trip to Pilot Knob to today. You set me on my course but let me find my own way. This is for you.

In closing, I wish to further dedicate this book to the memory of Dr. John R. Neff. I was blessed to call John my teacher, mentor, colleague, and friend. John was judicious, patient, profoundly wise, and incredibly generous. The more I came to know him, the more I saw him not only as the kind of historian and educator I aspired to be, but also as a kindred spirit who shared my interests in art, literature, music, and film. The many hours I spent in his company, whether seeking his advice or simply chatting, were among the most enriching of my life. It was a pleasure, Dr. Neff. I will never be able to thank you enough.

Abbreviations

EMM	Enrolled Missouri Militia
GAR	Grand Army of the Republic
KKK	Ku Klux Klan
LGAR	Ladies of the Grand Army of the Republic
MSM	Missouri State Militia
OR	*The War of the Rebellion: A Compilation of the Official Records of the Union and Confederate Armies*
SCV	Sons of Confederate Veterans
UCV	United Confederate Veterans
UDC	United Daughters of the Confederacy
USCT	United States Colored Troops
WRC	Woman's Relief Corps

Commonwealth of Compromise

Introduction

The deeds we have done are a part of ourselves, and we can never shake them off.

—Judge James B. Gantt (CSA), Kansas City, May 30, 1902

LATE IN THE MORNING OF February 11, 1897, an excited buzz filled the Missouri statehouse. The Senate was nearing a vote to determine whether the government would assume control of the state's two privately operated homes for Civil War veterans—the Missouri Confederate Home in Lafayette County and the Federal Soldiers' Home in Phelps County. As the first state to establish homes for both Union and Confederate veterans, Missouri's proposed legislation was unprecedented, and the symbolic importance of the measure was not lost on anyone present that day. As word spread that Henry H. Hohenschild, the young Democratic senator from Phelps County, had risen to introduce the bill on behalf of the Federal Home, legislators, state officers, and visitors crowded into the senate chamber.[1] There, Hohenschild delivered a speech later described as "one of the most beautiful orations . . . heard in that historic chamber for years."[2]

Still in his early thirties, Hohenschild was too young to remember the Civil War himself. While his parents were German immigrants and might be assumed to have been sympathetic to the Union, no one in his immediate family served in either army. Nevertheless, Hohenschild came of age in a state still fractured by wartime allegiances, and he was sensitive to these peculiar circumstances. Those fractures were particularly evident in the efforts of white Missourians to build and maintain two separate homes for Civil War veterans. Both the Missouri Federal Soldiers' Home, which had opened the previous October, and the Confederate Home, dedicated in 1893, were the result of private fundraising initiatives on the part of Missouri's men and women to establish care for the state's veterans. Persistent financial difficulties, however, threatened the operations of both homes. Their respective managers proposed state adoption as the only realistic means of remaining open. It was a pragmatic move, born of necessity, but a highly symbolic one nevertheless.

Hohenschild's colleagues in the General Assembly were primed to be receptive to the measure. In 1897, Missouri and the nation were riding a high tide of reconciliationist feelings. Facing a potential conflict with Spain over Cuban independence, white Americans reveled in remembrances of the Civil War that fostered national solidarity as opposed to sectionalism. In so doing, white Missourians also recalled an older, local tradition of compromise and conciliation, reaching back to Missouri's statehood crisis. Indeed, in the week following Hohenschild's speech, hundreds of Civil War veterans attended the funeral of one of Missouri's most famous Confederates, General Joseph O. "Jo" Shelby. Once the embodiment of the unreconstructed rebel, Shelby fled to Mexico in 1865 rather than surrender to the United States. He returned to his home state just two years later, however, and ended his days as a federal employee—the U.S. marshal for the western district of Missouri. In a eulogy for Shelby, Union veteran Judge John Phillips observed that in mourning the general's death, Union and Confederate Missourians "looked each other in the face, heart answering heart, tear to tear, with one flag, one destiny, one hope, one country."[3]

It was this pervasive spirit of reconciliation that Hohenschild sought to invoke in his address before the eager crowd in the statehouse. For the government to assume joint responsibility for the administration of the homes, he argued, would facilitate healing in what had been a particularly divisive theater of the Civil War. "The passion of the bloody Civil war will be rapidly extinguished by the adoption of these bills," he promised. Although Hohenschild specifically represented Union veterans, he understood reconciliation required the cooperation of both sides. Gathering momentum, he declared, "Here in this historic old Capitol today, standing on Missouri soil, beneath a Missouri sky, I would excite no partisan prejudice, no sectional bitterness; I would see a peace as deep and as broad and as beautiful as the love of the great God pervade every section of our great state." In Missouri, he recognized, peace was a difficult proposition. "Missouri was a border state during that unpleasantness," Hohenschild reminded his rapt audience; "her sons were divided, one against the other." Rather than serving as an obstacle to reconciliation, however, Hohenschild viewed this tumultuous past as the essential foundation of an amicable future. "As Missouri contributed brave soldiers to both armies," he explained, "she will . . . set an example to her sister states by taking under her sheltering care these homes." If passed, the legislation would serve "as an enduring record of what this present generation deemed most worthy to be honored." The adoption of the homes, he insisted, would offer testimony to the harmonious spirit of Missouri's people rooted in their shared past, common values, and future aspirations. "May the dawn of the twentieth century," Hohenschild concluded, "break on no more wondrous scene than the people of Missouri . . . forever banded by the indissoluble links of friendship, love and patriotism, to differ never more."[4]

Hohenschild's speech encapsulated the peculiar mood of Civil War commemoration in Missouri. It was a carefully framed appeal designed to negotiate a complicated set of circumstances unique to the border state. Despite the state's political tradition of compromise, stemming from its statehood crisis, the war rent Missouri along partisan, sectional, and racial lines. The situation was further complicated by Missouri's unique position as a border state not only between the North and South but between the East and West as well. The deeply contentious nature of the Civil War in Missouri meant that Missourians emerged from the conflict without a mutual understanding of what it had been about. These divisions persisted into the postwar period and throughout the life of the Civil War generation, as Missourians confronted a new racial dynamic and learned to live and work alongside their former foes.

Missourians were not alone in their struggle to come to terms with the legacy of the Civil War. Indeed, the Civil War holds a place of profound importance in American memory—that is, in how Americans have interpreted the past, imbued it with meaning, and imparted that meaning to future generations.[5] Usually, the development of commemorative traditions serves to consolidate group culture, unifying disparate communities around their shared past.[6] But in the late nineteenth-century United States, a nation fractured from the national down to the most intimate, familial level, acts of Civil War commemoration accentuated Americans' differences and made it difficult for them to move on. In the words of Civil War veteran James Gantt, "The deeds we have done are a part of ourselves, and we can never shake them off."[7]

Remembrances of the Civil War, therefore, often proved fractious. As Americans made provisions for their dead, erected monuments, founded veterans' associations, and hosted reunions, they ensured their wartime sacrifices would not be forgotten by posterity. But in the process, people cultivated competing interpretations of the war, reflecting conflicting regional, political, and racial perspectives. As a result, scholars have often observed that Civil War commemoration reveals less about the history of the war itself than it does about its contested legacy.

As cultural constructions, Civil War memories are complex, multifaceted, and defy simple categorization. Nevertheless, historians have condensed the complicated landscape of Civil War memory into four distinct narrative traditions: Unionist, emancipationist, Confederate, and reconciliationist.[8] Each tradition reflected the different wartime experiences of Americans on both sides of the conflict.

White Unionists, for example, remembered the war according to the Union Cause. They justified the war as the suppression of an illegal and traitorous rebellion. In victory, they celebrated the preservation of American democracy and the elimination of slavery as a source of disunion. Alternatively, African Americans embraced the Emancipation Cause. They regarded the Civil War as a fight to abolish slavery and grant freedom and citizenship to millions of people. African Americans, however, understood the Civil War as only part of a larger and longer campaign for racial equality. The gains won by black men on the battlefield served to inspire further political, social, and legal struggles.

Former Confederates, on the other hand, constructed their reminiscences of the war around the Lost Cause. The Lost Cause depicted the Civil War not as a struggle over slavery but as a defensive war against the supposedly tyrannical federal government. The Lost Cause also emphasized the bravery of Confederate soldiers who, it maintained, were not so much defeated as overwhelmed by the superior resources of the United States.

Lastly, as the nineteenth century drew to a close, white Americans increasingly embraced a reconciliationist memory of the Civil War. They sought to bridge wartime divisions by emphasizing the common bravery of white men and minimizing the importance of slavery and racism to the causes and consequences of the conflict. Although reconciliation never entirely superseded the other strains of Civil War memory, it did help rejuvenate patriotic feelings at a time when the United States was becoming a competitor on the world stage.

Even within the Unionist, emancipationist, Confederate, and reconciliationist traditions, however, endless variations of Civil War memory existed. This was particularly true in Missouri where, as in other centrally located states, national, sectional, and regional identities collided.[9] Useful as these categories are for making sense of Americans' responses to the war, therefore, they can serve to flatten important "regional variations."[10] As historian Anne Marshall rightly points out: "Civil War memory was not always geographically defined. . . . It was pluralistic and subject to myriad nuanced interpretations, and, most important, it was, and still is, greatly contested."[11] On their own, none of the accepted traditions entirely encapsulates Civil War commemoration in Missouri.

Understanding Missouri's place in the history and memory of the Civil War presents a particular challenge. As a slaveholding Union state on the western frontier, Missouri's Civil War experience placed it at odds with each of the standard traditions of Civil War memory. Living in a formerly slaveholding Union state, Missourians often clashed with one another even as they worked to mend the scars of an intensely divisive conflict. In an eastern context, the efforts of white Americans to celebrate northern victory or to mourn Confederate defeat existed largely independently of one another. While both sides were aware of their former enemies' attempts to construct Civil War memories, white Americans rarely intruded on one another's activities. Missourians, on the other hand, encountered unique difficulties as they undertook commemorative projects because they faced competition from their neighbors and skepticism on the part of many easterners—most of whom regarded Missouri as either too Confederate or too Unionist to suit their particular commemorative traditions. Missouri's especially complicated Civil War history threatened to undermine the foundations that provided meaning to the Civil War in the minds of many northerners and southerners.

As an indication of their muddled involvement in the Civil War, Missourians constructed competing memories of the conflict. White Unionists in the state found themselves compelled to defend their loyalty against a conviction held by many northerners that Missouri was a breeding ground for treacherous slaveholders and unreconstructed Democrats. The loyalty of African American Missourians was far more generally accepted, but they faced widespread discrimination in their efforts to channel Union victory and emancipation into racial uplift. Finally, former Confederates struggled to situate themselves within the Lost Cause. They argued that due to Missouri's position as a border state, they sacrificed more and suffered more for the Confederacy than many southerners. Their efforts were not particularly successful, but then neither Union nor Confederate Missourians established an uncontested memory of the Civil War in the state.

While each of these factions concentrated on their separate commemorative traditions, white Missourians nevertheless made earnest overtures toward reconciliation. As border westerners, they felt a special appreciation for the divisiveness of the war and also for the immediate economic, political, and social necessity of reconciliation. While resigning themselves to the bitter feelings engendered by the war, white Missourians constructed a reconciliationist memory shaped by a variety of influences: their marginalization from the dominant national narratives of Civil War memory; their strong sense of local identity; and a spirit of fraternalism strengthened by racism, nationalism, and gender. They cooperated in care for the war dead, built economic and political alliances, worked to distinguish Missouri's contributions to the Civil War, and redefined the relationship between Missouri's veterans and the state.

A wealth of scholarship spanning the last half-century has effectively situated Missouri at the center of the issues that fractured Civil War America, rather than on the periphery.[12] And yet, it has not fully explicated Civil War memory in the state. Much of this work followed the publication of Michael Fellman's seminal history of Missouri's guerrilla war, *Inside War*.[13] While Fellman can certainly be credited with attracting widespread scholarly attention to Missouri, the result has been a disproportionate emphasis on the guerrilla war and on the state's cultural and political ties to the South.[14] This has also impacted histories of Civil War memory in Missouri, resulting in studies that have focused predominantly on the development of the Lost Cause in the state.[15] This approach has invited comparisons between Civil War memory in Missouri and its sister border state Kentucky, which, as historian Anne Marshall has persuasively demonstrated, embraced the Lost Cause and exaggerated its wartime commitment to the Confederacy.[16] Adopting a similar argument, historian Aaron Astor claims that as newly freed African Americans made increasing demands for political and social equality in central Missouri, white conservative Unionists chose to "'forget' their whole service to the Union." "These belated Confederates," Astor claims, "helped legitimize the construction of a southern regional identity in the postwar border states."[17] Racism, southern identity, and the Lost Cause, however, are not mutually exclusive. While racism is firmly entrenched in the mythology of the Lost Cause, racism is not confined to the states of the former Confederacy.

In fact, the pervasive racism and conservatism that marked Missouri's culture and politics were far more in keeping with the "Loyal West," as historian Matthew E. Stanley has termed it. In Ohio, Indiana, and Illinois, he argues, a distinctly western identity took root. Like Missouri, the states of the Loyal West represented "a politically and culturally pragmatic middle space where conservative Unionism predominated, resulting in various forms of compromise politics and a nonbinary posture of Civil War memory." Key to the politics and culture of this region was white supremacy.[18] And while the inhabitants of the region demonstrated a growing sympathy for reconciliation with former Confederates, they stubbornly and persistently celebrated their role in the preservation of the Union.

Thus, nineteenth-century Missouri far more embodied the characteristics of the West than the South. In the years following its statehood, Missouri emerged as the heartland of the growing United States, a "middle ground," or as historian Stephen Aron describes it, part of the "American confluence"—the hub of the Mississippi, Missouri, and Ohio Rivers and "the place where north, south, east, and west connected."[19] The appeal of the mythic West as a place of unbounded opportunity positioned Missouri as the "Gateway to the West" but muddied its relationship to the Civil War. As a pro-Union, proslavery state situated on the western frontier, Missouri lacked a unified response to the war and its commemoration.[20]

Until recently, historians did not typically associate the West with the study of the Civil War. When it comes to Civil War scholarship, Elliott West notes, "It's as if there are two independent historical narratives, and because the one that is set in the East and centered on the Civil War has been tapped as the defining story of its time, the one that is set out West seems peripheral, even largely irrelevant, to explaining America during a critical turn of its history."[21] The neglect of a western perspective on Civil War history can be attributed to the difficulty of defining the West and its place in the United States. The West may represent a geographic area, a process, and a culture all at once.[22] It is a fluid and complex space, a region where political categories, cultural groups, and geographic boundaries defy simple explanation.[23] Furthering this confusion, the West has continually expanded over the course of U.S. history and, depending on the era, might variously apply to Ohio, Missouri, or California—the lands west of the Appalachians, west of the Mississippi, or west of the Rockies. It is also a region of mythological proportions, encompassing not just a geographic space but also an ethos of egalitarianism, individualism, and American exceptionalism. In many ways, the West is a place more imagined than real, one that has dominated the American consciousness for more than a century.[24]

If the parameters of the West have proven difficult to define, so has its influence on identity and memory in the Civil War era. This is reflected in the scholarly literature on Missouri. Only two historians have seriously examined the link between Missouri's western identity and its Civil War memory. Christopher Phillips characterizes Missouri as part of the antebellum West but suggests Missouri ultimately became southern before the Civil War began.[25] Then, he says, in the aftermath of the war, white Missourians consolidated the transformation of their "former West" into the

"One South" by embracing the Lost Cause and opposing racial equality.[26] Matthew C. Hulbert, however, argues that the failure of Missouri's guerrillas to earn recognition in the Lost Cause prompted the "westernization of guerilla memory." This memory morphed pro-Confederate bushwhackers like Jesse James into the heroes of dime novels, Wild West shows, and western films.[27]

Commonwealth of Compromise seeks to understand how Missouri's unique regional identity dictated its course during the war and how that identity shaped the formation of Civil War memory in the state. In the process, this book expands on previous scholarship by taking a broad look at Civil War commemoration across the state and over a broad stretch of time from the conclusion of the war to the mid-twentieth century. While including the guerrillas as important players in the construction of Missouri's various Civil War memories, it also devotes equal attention to Union, African American, and Confederate commemoration.

It argues that Missourians never arrived at a complete consensus over the legacy of the Civil War in their state and that, unlike Anne Marshall's "Confederate Kentucky," the ways Missourians remembered the war largely reflected the ways they experienced it.[28] Just as there was no singular response to the war among Missourians, there was no singular interpretation of its legacy. Whereas Kentucky experienced a postwar identity shift, becoming even "more southern" than it was in the antebellum period, Civil War commemoration cemented Missouri's western identity. Most Missourians did not adopt the culture, politics, or Civil War memories of white southerners. While fundamental aspects of life in Missouri were forever altered by the war, particularly for African Americans, the character of the state remained largely unchanged. Missourians still exhibited profound racial and political divisions, but they continued to espouse pragmatism and favor compromise.[29]

Chapter 1 traces the origins of Missouri's western identity in the Civil War era. Situated at the heart of the Louisiana Purchase and the confluence of the nation's greatest rivers, Missouri was both the western frontier of the United States and the front line of westward expansion. In the antebellum period, white Missourians considered themselves to be westerners and embraced a political tradition of compromise and conservatism. As westward expansion precipitated violent and divisive controversies over slavery, white Missourians struggled to reconcile their interest in slaveholding to their commitment to the Union. At the outbreak of the Civil War, many white Missourians desired neutrality but soon found themselves on opposing sides of the conflict. Amid the chaos and confusion of the war, Missouri politicians instituted emancipation and ushered in a Radical Republican regime. In the process, they permanently severed Missouri from the "Solid South" and set the stage for future contestations over Civil War commemoration.

Examining how Missourians began to articulate their Civil War memories, chapter 2 considers the evolution of the Union Cause in Missouri through the work of the Department of Missouri Grand Army of the Republic (GAR) and its auxiliary, the Woman's Relief Corps (WRC). Both societies worked to commemorate the Union Cause in Missouri in the face of resistance from their Confederate neighbors and in spite of the dismissal of their eastern comrades. As far as many northerners were concerned, Missouri's history of slaveholding and Democratic politics threatened to undermine the foundations of Union memory that provided meaning to the Civil War. Despite these challenges, the Department of Missouri established an active and vibrant organization dedicated to perpetuating the Union Cause.

Chapter 3 provides an African American perspective on Civil War memory in Missouri. Often excluded from white commemorations of the Union Cause, black veterans organized both within and outside the ranks of the GAR, constructing their own unique interpretation of the war. In celebrating the Emancipation Cause, black Missourians linked Union victory and the abolition of slavery to the promise of citizenship and the project of racial uplift. In defiance of segregation and violent intimidation, they employed Civil War memory in order to secure African American manhood suffrage, establish the first public schools for African Americans in Missouri, and foster race pride.

The fourth chapter turns to Confederate commemoration. It explains the failure of the Lost Cause to gain an uncontested following in Missouri and details the efforts of the Missouri Division of the United Confederate Veterans (UCV) and the United Daughters of the Confederacy (UDC) to craft Confederate memory in Missouri. By appealing to Missouri's cultural ties to the South and to their state's wartime martyrdom under Union occupation, these groups hoped to demonstrate Missouri's legitimacy as a Confederate state. Ultimately, however, the Lost Cause could not easily accommodate Missouri because of its history of Unionism, its inescapable association with guerrilla warfare, the lack of organization among its Confederate veterans, and the determined opposition of local Unionists.

Chapter 5 demonstrates the unique cooperation that sometimes characterized Civil War commemoration among white veterans in Missouri. As westerners, white Missourians believed they had a special responsibility to set the standard for national reconciliation. At the same time, the realities of life in the border state made reconciliation an immediate and practical necessity. In response, former enemies in Missouri united with one another through joint commemorative undertakings—three, in particular. In Springfield, Union and Confederate veterans negotiated the incorporation of Confederate burials into the Springfield National Cemetery. In St. Louis and Kansas City, white veterans formed blue and gray societies to facilitate their particular economic and political agendas. Finally, this reconciliationist spirit was exemplified by the erection of a monument to Missouri's Union and Confederate soldiers at Vicksburg National Military Park. These accomplishments reflect the cultural, financial, and political traction of reconciliation among white veterans in Missouri. At the same time, they highlight the racial and gendered limits of reconciliation.

The final chapter further elaborates on the importance of reconciliation to Civil War commemoration in Missouri by chronicling the history of the state's two veterans' homes, the Missouri Confederate Home and the Federal Soldiers' Home. Although begun as private charities, both homes came under state control in 1897, making Missouri the first state to undertake such a complicated responsibility. These homes represented the culmination of Civil War commemoration in Missouri. Although burdened by administrative difficulties, financial challenges, and lingering wartime tensions, Missouri's veterans' homes facilitated the reconciliation of white Missourians by privileging the status of white veterans and their dependents as uniquely worthy of state benefits.

The epilogue briefly reviews the evolution of Civil War commemoration in Missouri after the passing of the Civil War generation. As Missourians entered the second half of the twentieth century, they remained divided over their tumultuous Civil War history. At the Civil War centennial, Missourians demonstrated a conflicted attitude toward the war and its history. In the new millennium, Missourians began the process of dismantling and contextualizing Confederate memorials, further disassociating Missouri from the South and the Lost Cause.

Before beginning, there are a couple of important terms that require clarification. First, in the context of this study, "Missourian" is liberally defined. A Missourian need not necessarily be a native of the state or even have lived there during the Civil War but is simply anyone residing in the state. It is perhaps worth adding that this definition of a "Missourian" is one the Civil War generation would have understood. Missouri's veterans' associations, their auxiliaries, and the veterans' homes also employed a liberal definition of "Missourian," requiring at most two years of residency in the state for eligibility. Of necessity, this work occasionally generalizes about the identity and feelings of Missourians, although it is essential to acknowledge their diverse individual, gendered, racial, ethnic, and political perspectives.

Second, it is important to be clear about the usage of "reconciliation" in this study of Civil War memory. In many ways, the painful legacy of the Civil War in Missouri remained evident for generations. Even so, a sincere movement toward reconciliation did exist in the state and made its mark on Civil War commemoration. In this context, therefore, reconciliation implies *acceptance* more than *forgiveness*. White Missourians *reconciled* to their differences, forged compromises through their shared regional identity, and cooperated in the service of their mutual interests. According to historian Jeremy Neely, this mentality was not foreign to the western border, particularly between Missouri and Kansas. "By encouraging the erosion of old antagonisms and the establishment of commercial, political, and social ties," Neely argues, "growth-minded citizens helped to refashion the state line, transforming the once-divisive boundary into a more benign relic of collective memory."[30]

Next, a brief word on sources and their limitations. The majority of the sources that make up this study were generated by Missourians, so they generally reflect how Missourians thought about themselves, their place in Civil War history, and their responses to its aftermath. *Commonwealth of Compromise* only engages with the perspectives of outsiders inasmuch as Missourians responded to how they believed others perceived them—whether it had a basis in truth or not. It also relies heavily on organizational and government sources, which privilege the perspectives of white Missourians. While African American newspapers offered valuable insight into Civil War commemoration in Missouri's black communities, there are still many gaps in this story.

Indeed, many of the nuances of Civil War memory in Missouri remain to be explored. Missourians engaged in a multitude of acts of Civil War commemoration, some of which only receive passing treatment here, including the organization of aid societies, literary and historical societies, memorial associations, and monument committees. Observations of Memorial and Decoration Day celebrations receive scant attention, as do the efforts of Union and Confederate associations to censor school textbooks. Although this work calls attention to the vital role of veterans' societies and their auxiliaries in shaping Civil War commemoration, it gives short shrift to the Military Order of the Loyal Legion of the United States, the Society of the Army of the Tennessee, the Ladies of the Grand Army of the Republic

(LGAR), the Sons of Union Veterans, and the Sons of Confederate Veterans (SCV). In short, there are many promising directions for the further study of Civil War memory in Missouri.

Despite its complications and contradictions, Missouri presents an excellent opportunity to explore the interplay between region and memory. Understanding Missouri requires looking beyond the North-versus-South dichotomy that has been central to the way the Civil War is talked about and studied. By interjecting a western perspective into the study of the Civil War era, it becomes evident how inflexible the accepted narratives of Civil War memory are and how they have served to marginalize the perspectives of a vast range of Americans—particularly westerners and moderates—on this watershed moment in history.

ONE

"Cradled in a Compromise"

Missouri in the Civil War Era

If it be the glorious mission of Missouri to aid in arresting the progress of revolution and in restoring peace and prosperity to the country; . . . she will but occupy the position for which nature designed her by giving her a central position. . . . And why should she not?—she was brought forth in a storm and cradled in a compromise.

—Hamilton Rowan Gamble, "Report and Resolutions of Committee on Federal Relations," Missouri State Convention, St. Louis, March 9, 1861

UPON RECEIVING WORD THAT MISSOURI would hold a state convention in late February 1861 to chart its course through the secession crisis, Hamilton Rowan Gamble left the comforts of retirement in Pennsylvania and returned to Missouri—his home of more than three decades—to be counted among the state's Unionists. Just a few weeks prior, delegates from the seceded states of South Carolina, Mississippi, Florida, Alabama, Georgia, and Louisiana had met in Montgomery, Alabama, to form the Confederate States of America. Resolutely Unionist, Gamble and many of his fellow Missourians watched in disbelief as the nation disintegrated before them. Steeped in a political tradition of moderation and compromise reaching back to statehood, white Missourians were among the last to accept that the secession crisis would not be resolved peacefully.

Gamble's personal history embodied the unpredictability of Missouri's response to the crisis. A native Virginian, Gamble moved to the Missouri territory to pursue a legal career. In 1827, he married fellow southerner Caroline J. Coalter of South Carolina. And, according to the 1850 slave schedule, he claimed ownership over six enslaved people.[1] As a conservative Unionist, Gamble believed the preservation of slavery was essential to the stability of the Union. He could not envision the multiracial civil society emancipation would inevitably usher in, favoring instead the colonization of freed people as the best means of preserving America's white republic. Still, he did not sympathize with proslavery extremism. In 1848, while serving as a judge on the Missouri supreme court, Gamble heard arguments in Dred Scott's famed freedom suit. When the court denied Scott's freedom, Gamble wrote the dissenting opinion. He warned the court against allowing popular unrest over slavery to disturb the precedent of "once free, always free." "Times may have changed, public feeling may have changed," he observed, "but principles have not and do not change."[2] Considering Gamble's personal ties to the South, slaveholding, and moderate politics, it would have been easy to assume the increasing sectionalism of antebellum America strained his commitment to the Union. Nothing could have been further from the truth.

Nevertheless, conservative Unionists like Gamble caused their northern and southern neighbors some consternation. Would a state settled by southern-born slaveholders adhere to the Union or succumb to dissolution? As a result, the Missouri state convention excited great interest, locally and nationally. As the delegates gathered in the Mercantile Library Hall in St. Louis, concerned citizens crowded in to listen to the proceedings. Much anxiety surrounded the presence of a delegation from Georgia, who presented an invitation from Missouri's sister slaveholding states to join the Confederacy. Their attendance was a reminder that while white Missourians avowed Unionism, the persistence of slaveholding made them an outlier among the majority of loyal states. It also served as further notice that even as these Missourians worked to find a compromise, the national crisis was only deepening.

So it was that after nine long days of debate, competing resolutions, and committee work, Gamble presented the convention's "Report and Resolutions of Committee on Federal Relations," which dictated the state's much-anticipated response to the secession crisis. In the report, Gamble decried the "morbid sensitiveness" on the part of northerners toward the institution of slavery. At the same time, however, he condemned secession as an illegitimate measure that amounted to nothing short of "revolution." Then, voicing the question on everyone's minds, he asked, "But what is now the true position for Missouri to assume?" Unswervingly committed to the Union yet sympathetic to his southern kindred, Gamble vowed Missouri would do whatever it could to forge compromise and secure peace. He said, "If it be the glorious mission of Missouri to aid in arresting the progress of revolution and in restoring peace and prosperity to the country; . . . she will but occupy the position for which nature designed her by giving her a central position. . . .

And why should she not?—she was brought forth in a storm and cradled in a compromise. She can resist the one and recommend the other."[3]

For Gamble and the convention delegates, compromise still seemed within reach. Yet within a month, the nation and the state would descend into civil war. Following the Confederate assault on Fort Sumter in April 1861, all hope of compromise evaporated and Missourians joined the ranks of the opposing armies. Even men who served together in the state convention found themselves at odds. By the summer of 1861, convention president Sterling Price was in command of the Missouri State Guard and in the thick of a military campaign to draw Missouri into the Confederacy. Hamilton Gamble, however, remained steadfast for the Union. All thoughts of retirement now entirely abandoned, Gamble accepted an appointment as the state's wartime governor. From this position, he continued to espouse compromise even as he consolidated Missouri's place in the Union.

The Civil War generation, who laid the foundation for Civil War commemoration in Missouri, worked within a contentious atmosphere borne of the complex social, cultural, political, and economic realities of the region. These circumstances dictated the response of Missourians to the Civil War and set the stage for the peculiar challenges they faced by undertaking Civil War commemoration. These challenges largely stemmed from the commitment of enfranchised Missourians to conservative Unionism, which countenanced both the defense of slavery and loyalty to the Union. This attitude emerged as a result of several unique characteristics of the state. First, its location on the western frontier and the diversity of its settlers. Second, was the recognition that these factors meant the approach of the Civil War presented Missourians with a more significant threat than most of the rest of the country. As mounting sectional tension threatened to fracture Missouri's diverse populace and jeopardize its slaveholdings, white Missourians embraced conservative Unionism as a means of preserving local and, by extension, national unity. Third, while this approach offered Missouri's best hope for peace, it produced misunderstandings. With the fate of slavery and the Union on the line, the determination of white Missourians to seek neutrality, compromise, and other conservative solutions read to outsiders on both sides as perfidy. Northerners and southerners alike regarded Missouri with distrust, a feeling that later dogged Missouri's efforts at Civil War commemoration. Finally, there was the nature of the Civil War in Missouri. When conservatism failed and with their interests and sympathies divided between the various regions of the nation, the Civil

War embroiled Missourians in a vicious, fratricidal conflict.[4] While participating in the regular armies of the Union and Confederacy, Missourians also negotiated a highly localized and violent guerrilla war. The chasms opened by the war remained intact well after the peace and even into the twentieth century, challenging the ability of Missourians to find meaning in the Civil War and its legacy.

Although it is not possible to provide a complete and detailed history of Missouri in these pages, it is important to establish some elements of Missouri's complex nineteenth-century history in order to adequately contextualize Civil War commemoration. Beginning with its acquisition from France in 1803, Missouri occupied a dynamic place in the antebellum United States. As the gateway to the Louisiana Purchase, the territory loomed large in the national vision of Manifest Destiny and in debates over the expansion of slavery into the West. Missouri emerged in the years following its addition to the Union as the heartland of the growing United States—the "American confluence," a geographic, social, cultural, and political crossroads.[5] From the earliest days of settlement, white Missourians envisioned their state as the gateway to a boundless new national destiny. They embraced both the pragmatic and mythic potential of the West. They imagined Missouri as the center of national commerce, anticipated opportunities for individual enterprise, and looked forward to the erasure of provincialism.

Race also played an important role in how white territorial Missourians thought about national expansion and the West. This was particularly evident in their treatment of Native Americans. Missouri was not only home to several tribes but also a destination for thousands of displaced Native Americans relocating to Indian Territory. Between 1804 and 1824, the removal of tribes from the eastern United States caused the Native American population of Missouri to balloon from around two thousand to eight thousand.[6] In this atmosphere, Missouri's character as a "middle ground" heightened, as Native American, formerly French, and American communities intermingled. As American settlers migrated into Missouri, however, they enjoined the federal government for assistance in driving Native Americans out. Forced on the Trail of Tears, the last groups of Native Americans had left Missouri by 1833. The common ground Missouri's white settlers forged on the "confluence" was rooted in white supremacy.

This mentality has often been attributed to the significant influence of white southern emigrants on the political, economic, and cultural life of early Missouri. Indeed, slaveholding became an important component of Missouri's nascent western identity. Even though many northern states still retained slaves in this period, all of them had implemented programs for gradual emancipation. Missouri, on the other hand, symbolized slaveholders' intent to grow and strengthen their peculiar institution. They viewed Missouri as an avenue through which they would secure the future of what they considered the most profitable enterprise of the era, maintain racial hegemony, and ensure the continued expansion of the nation.

White territorial Missourians regarded slaveholding as an important part of the process of civilization and progress on the frontier. They believed it helped to establish white racial and cultural superiority. According to historian Christopher Phillips, "Dominance of others filled the void created by the insecurity of distance that the West naturally forced upon its frightened inhabitants."[7] As a result, slavery scholar Diane Mutti Burke adds, "most Missourians supported slavery as a system of labor and of social and racial control."[8] This meant that enslaved people participated, however unwillingly, in the settlement of Missouri. Whether they came with individual owners or in traders' coffles, the West promised no opportunities for advancement for them; rather, migration increased the likelihood of forcible and painful separations from loved ones.[9]

Although slaveholdings in Missouri never approached the scale of those in the southern states, this was due rather to a consequence of geography than to a lack of ambition. Bordered both by free states and free territory, there were too many avenues of escape for enslaved people to establish a stable plantation society on the western frontier. Furthermore, Missouri's climate was not conducive to growing cotton, so white Missourians utilized enslaved labor in cultivating grains, tobacco, and hemp, and in raising livestock.

The mobility of western life and the nature of small-scale slaveholding contributed to economic diversification and made slavery in Missouri distinct.[10] Missouri was a critical outpost of the plantation South but not a slave society by those standards.[11] Still, white Missourians did aspire to their own kind of slave society. Along the western border of the state in particular, historian Kristen Epps argues, elite slaveholders commanded "significant cultural and political capital" and laid the foundations of an aspirational slave society.[12] Missouri's slaveholders were certainly not any less adept at exerting violent control over enslaved people than their southern neighbors. From its earliest territorial history, Missouri's slave codes defined enslaved people as chattel and denied them essential human and civil rights. White Missourians considered white supremacy and slavery as crucial to the development of their state and, thereby, the continued expansion of the nation. Racism and republicanism were not contradictions to them, even though those positions became increasingly difficult to reconcile as the nineteenth century wore on.

One of the moments where this contradiction first became evident was in the controversy over Missouri's application for statehood in 1819–1820. Missouri's proslavery constitution jeopardized the tenuous balance of power between free and slave states in Congress and threatened a national crisis over slaveholding in the republic. In Congress, various proposals sought to limit slavery in Missouri's statehood bill and even created programs for gradual emancipation. White Missourians resented the sectional bickering in Congress that delayed their statehood. They wanted their state to be admitted without restriction and on equal terms with every other one. After extensive debate, Congress finally arrived at the Missouri Compromise in 1820, a deal that admitted Maine as a free state and Missouri as a slave state but prohibited the formation of new slave states in the Louisiana Territory north of Missouri's southern border at the latitude of 36° 30'. Although the compromise ultimately proved only a temporary solution, it was a momentous occasion—one that heralded doom in the minds of slaveholders and put Missouri at the center of the national dilemma over slavery. Missouri's admission to the Union set an important precedent for the future of slaveholding in the United States and established a tradition of compromise in Missouri politics. This would later manifest itself through a pervasive strain of conservative Unionism. As the antebellum era wore on, white Missourians increasingly adopted a responsibility for tempering sectional ambitions and channeling them into a beneficial direction for the nation.

Even though slavery dominated the emergence of Missouri on to the national stage, slaveholding and a sense of southern sectional identity did not go hand in hand. While southern emigrants made up the majority of Missouri's white population, along the Kansas-Missouri border the overwhelming majority of residents had been born west of the Appalachian Mountains.[13] As a result, Phillips claims, "Early national Missourians . . . uniformly regarded themselves as Westerners."[14] Despite the proslavery politics of the state, many white Missourians understood themselves as distinct from their southern antecedents. Although this distinction was not always clear to contemporary outsiders, nor to modern scholars for that matter, white Missourians could be westerners and defend slavery just as ardently as southerners. The commitment of white Missourians to slavery notwithstanding, Missouri remained a western state with a distinctly western perspective throughout the Civil War era.

In the 1820s, Missourians encouraged white settlers from all across the nation, not just the South, to come to their new state. They envisioned Missouri as a place where sectional identities could be remade, a place that could heal the hostilities so evidenced in the tortured birth of their state.

The *Missourian* welcomed "intelligent freemen" of all stripes to the state and pledged "to assist the march of industrious enterprise to Missouri, from every country; to harmonise and conciliate local animosities into a bond of fraternal concord, and to melt down all distinctions into the enviable one of a 'Missourian.'"[15] "Emigration should be encouraged by every means in our power," the *Missourian* insisted. "Our state should be made the home of those whom enterprize or want or misfortune may induce to plant their future prospects among us. The misfortunes of the times have for two or three years checkered the growth and prospects of our state. . . . This evil, it is to be hoped, will be remedied. . . . Missouri, possessing such great advantages of soil, climate and navigation, cannot fail to reach exalted destinies." Furthermore, "We must explore and develope the resources of the state," the paper entreated its readers. "The west is filling with active and enterprizing people, good farmers and industrious artisans, and it behoves Missouri not to be an underling, a stinted shrub of the prairie, amidst the surrounding oaks of the forest."[16] The appeal of Missouri and the west as a place of opportunity did indeed attract a new flood of migrants. Missouri experienced exponential population growth: "nearly 600 percent between 1820 and 1840," according to historian Elliott West.[17] "Each year the tide of immigration grew larger," historian Ray Allen Billington explained, "attracted by the rising prosperity of the frontier state."[18] Time, distance, and prosperity, however, did not entirely erase the interest of adopted Missourians in their native regions. This necessitated the emphasis on conservatism and compromise in state politics.

Missouri's growth was built on the tide of Manifest Destiny sweeping the nation in the 1840s. White Americans felt inspired to expand, believing that it was their God-given duty to create an American empire stretching from coast to coast, bringing white hegemony, republicanism, and Christianity to the limitless and, in their minds, uncivilized West.[19] White Missourians in particular embraced this expansive national vision, eschewing sectional entrenchment. "To Missouri," one newspaper reflected with pride, "belongs the exalted privilege of disseminating the principles of the federal constitution over the vast regions west of the Mississippi: from her bosom will issue colonies of freemen to carry the stripes and stars of the union to the provinces of Spain, to the Pacific ocean, to the frozen realms of the north."[20]

Once the frontier itself, Missouri soon became the most westerly outpost of civilization. As the point of departure for the Santa Fe Trail, the Oregon Trail, and the California goldfields, Missouri was of central importance to the project of westward expansion. Drawn by the lure of Manifest Destiny, the trickle of adventurers that had long crossed the state became a tide, deepening Missouri's association with the West. St. Louis, in particular, became the largest city west of the Appalachians and the lynchpin uniting the Far West to the East. In 1847, the *Democratic Banner* proclaimed St. Louis "the *pride of the west*," and by 1849 St. Louis was known as the "Gateway to the West."[21]

White Missourians eagerly anticipated the wealth and power westward expansion would bring to their state. Missouri's politicians championed funding for internal improvements, including clearing the Mississippi and Missouri Rivers of snags and sawyers to allow steamboat traffic.[22] Such efforts, one paper hoped, "will give a new impetus to enterprise and improvement that must carry our citizens rapidly forward on the road to prosperity and wealth."[23] Missouri's leaders also encouraged the construction of new roadways and invested in railroads, which they believed were essential to further growth. As the *Western Union* put it, "Why lag behind our sister states in the noble race for greatness? Why strive to keep down internal improvement, and *drive* the emigrant from our shores to other and less desirable States?"[24] "Missouri is now on the high road to prosperity and true greatness," the *Hannibal Journal* added, "and with railroads and navigable rivers to every point of the compass—rich in mineral and agricultural resources—who can bespeak for her other than a glorious career."[25] Such initiatives were part of the larger transportation revolution that redefined culture and commerce in antebellum America. The enthusiasm of the press for this revolution illustrates its national, as opposed to sectional, vision. White Missourians' continued concern with remaining at the center of national trade was another important consideration behind their moderate politics.

Despite Missouri's diverse commercial interests, slaveholding continued to play a central role in state politics. As one of the westernmost slaveholding states, Missouri featured heavily in the ongoing debate over the future of slavery in America. In 1848, the controversy reached a new crisis when the conclusion of the Mexican War and the annexation of vast new territory in the Southwest brought the issue to the forefront of Missouri politics once more. As Congress debated the future of slaveholding in the territories, Democrats in the Missouri General Assembly rejected any attempt to limit the expansion of slavery into the Southwest. In a piece of legislation known as the Jackson Resolutions, proposed by future governor Claiborne Fox Jackson, Missouri Democrats voiced their belief that Congress had no power to legislate on the expansion of slavery and branded attempts to proscribe it as radical aggression against slaveholding states.[26] They also threatened to unite with the other slaveholding states in the interest of mutual protection if Congress imposed any further restrictions.[27]

It would be easy to read the passage of the Jackson Resolutions as an important break from the compromise tradition in Missouri politics. It might also be interpreted as a sign that Missouri's sense of regional identity was shifting away from the West and more toward the South. Perhaps the Jackson Resolutions were an early indication, as historian Christopher Phillips sees it, of how western individualism, which resisted government interference in local affairs, merged with "proslavery militancy" in Missouri, drawing the state more firmly into line with the South.[28]

The Jackson Resolutions, however, did not stand unopposed. Although the General Assembly backed the Jackson Resolutions, an emerging group of conservative Unionists, led by Saline County representative George Caleb Bingham and revered U.S. senator Thomas Hart Benton, were convinced they "did not represent the will of the people." In 1849, they wrote the Bingham Resolutions in response. In stark contrast to the Jackson Resolutions, the Bingham Resolutions spoke for Missouri's moderates. They acknowledged that Congress did have the authority to legislate over slavery in the territories but not over slavery where it already existed, maintaining the rights of citizens to control the "internal policy" of their respective states. Nevertheless, the resolutions recognized that Missouri's prosperity depended on its position at the nation's confluence, not solely on its allegiance to the slaveholding section of the country. For that reason, the Bingham Resolutions stressed the importance of the preservation of the Union at all costs. "We deem it our most sacred duty," they declared, "to cherish an immovable attachment to the National Union; to watch for its preservation with jealous anxiety, to discountenance even the suggestion, that it could in any event be abandoned, and indignantly to frown upon the first dawning of every attempt to alienate any portion of the country from the rest."[29] The Bingham Resolutions clearly illustrated white Missourians' concern with preserving the Union as well as their continued commitment to slavery. Benton canvassed the state, championing these resolutions as evidence "that the people of Missouri love the Union, and are in favor of maintaining it at all hazards." Along the way, he made important converts, including the very governor, Democrat Austin King, who ratified the Jackson Resolutions. The Jackson Resolutions had been a victory for Democrats, but their power was precarious. In fact, Bingham, Benton, and their allies maneuvered the General Assembly into a repudiation of the Jackson Resolutions in 1853.[30] The conservative approach once more carried the day.

Taken together, the Jackson and Bingham Resolutions demonstrated that white Missourians viewed slavery as central to the Union and to the project of national expansion. The ultimate success of the Bingham Resolutions, however, indicated Missouri was no more closely aligned with the South than it had been before. In fact, Missouri's population was now dramatically more diverse than even in its territorial days. "By 1860," historian Diane Mutti Burke writes, "the foreign-born population of Missouri reached 12 percent; as early as 1850, half of St. Louis residents were immigrants, mostly German and Irish. On the eve of the Civil War, nearly 17 percent of state legislators were natives of northern states or foreign countries, more so than in any other slaveholding state."[31] This demographic diversity proved a stumbling block to partisan extremism and kept the state's pragmatic, conservative political tradition alive.

The arrival of German immigrants, in particular, spoke to Missouri's continuing appeal as a part of the "mythic West"—a place of opportunity and prosperity, where provincial identities gave way to overarching "Americanness." German immigrant Carl Schurz, who later became a leading Missouri politician, explained, "Especially did I long to breathe the fresh air of that part of the Union which I imagined to be the 'real America,' the great West," as he called it, of Illinois, Wisconsin, and Missouri. "This was something of the America that I had seen in my dreams; a new country, a new society almost entirely unhampered by any traditions of the past; a new people produced by the free intermingling of the vigorous elements of all nations, . . . with almost limitless opportunities open to all, and with equal rights secured by free institutions of government." Schurz's visit to St. Louis confirmed his perception of the fluidity of western life, with one important qualification. "There the existence of slavery," he observed, "with its subtle influence, cast its shadow over the industrial and commercial developments of the city, as well as over the relations between the different groups of citizens."[32] Like most German immigrants, Schurz was antislavery. To him, slavery felt incompatible with the egalitarian spirit of the West.

Schurz's observation was quite important. While the scale of slaveholding in Missouri paled in comparison with that in the Deep South, its controls remained every bit as rigid, oppressive, and violent. Missouri law prohibited enslaved people from testifying in court, applying for marriage licenses, owning property, traveling without permission, and accessing education. Missouri law also placed restrictions on free African Americans, prohibiting them from attending school or gathering for religious services without white supervision.[33] State law further required free African Americans to obtain a license for residency.

In 1855, Missouri garnered national attention as a result of a murder case that served to reinforce the status of enslaved people as human chattel while bringing the "moral dilemmas" of slavery into sharp focus. A Missouri court convicted Celia, a nineteen-year-old enslaved woman, of murdering her enslaver, Robert Newsom. Celia's attorney argued this was a case of self-defense, as it was known in the local community that Newsom regularly sexually assaulted Celia. Under Missouri law, the sexual assault of "any woman" was a criminal offense.[34] Yet, the court advised the jury that Celia was not a woman—she was property. As such, the only crime that could be committed upon her would be trespass. In the eyes of the court, it was not possible for Newsom to trespass on his own property. Celia was executed by hanging. While white Missourians did not overwhelmingly identify with the South, they were as disinclined to accept the personhood of enslaved African Americans as the planters of the cotton states.

Slavery also continued to have a profound impact on state politics. Missouri returned to the center of the national debate over slavery during the controversy surrounding the passage of the Kansas-Nebraska Act in 1854. Because the new law allowed popular sovereignty to determine the expansion of slavery, repealing the Missouri Compromise, proslavery Missourians favored the bill. Already bordered by free states to the east and north, they feared restrictions on the spread of slavery. Proslavery Missourians were concerned not only with the survival of the institution but also with maintaining (if not expanding) the power of slaveholding states in Congress. Following California's admission as a free state in 1850, this was particularly imperative if the slave states wished to regain their longstanding majority in congressional representation. Furthermore, proslavery Missourians regarded the expansion of slavery as essential to the continued momentum of westward expansion. Missourians were concerned, Phillips explains, "that if Kansas should not become a slave state, Missouri would become the first and only slave state bordering a free state to its west, effectively sealing slavery from further ingress and changing forever the complexion of westward expansion."[35] Alongside the conviction that the expansion of slavery would help establish white supremacy in the West, proslavery Missourians believed the labor of enslaved people was essential to civilizing the frontier and realizing its commercial potential. Finally, they believed westward expansion offered slavery a crucial "safety valve" by which the widespread diffusion of slavery would ease sectional tension.[36] In other words, these Missourians believed slavery was essential to the vitality of the Union and to their place in it.

The escalating tension along the Missouri-Kansas border throughout the mid-1850s frightened many Missourians and gave them a glimpse into the catastrophe that full-scale war would bring to their region. In the aftermath of the Kansas-Nebraska Act, Missourians watched the influx of settlement into the territory with trepidation. "The roads are filled with people all bound for the new Territories," the *Glasgow Weekly Times* reported. "A determined effort is to be made to introduce slavery into Kansas," it continued, "while there is a general disposition to let Nebraska be free. . . . Much excitement, violence and bloodshed is anticipated."[37]

Fearing the influence of abolitionist immigrants in Kansas, hordes of proslavery Missourians poured across the border to vote in the territorial elections and defend the expansion of slavery. The immediate consequence was the affair known as Bleeding Kansas—"violence and bloodshed" between proslavery Missourians and antislavery Kansans. It was only the prelude of the much longer and exponentially more bloody conflict to come. The Kansas-Nebraska Act "not only brought civil war upon Kansas," Missouri senator Edward Bates fretted, "but is likely to bring civil war upon the whole country."[38] Indeed, historian Stephen Aron writes, "Historically the place where north, south, east, and west connected, the American confluence looked more and more like it would be the site at which the United States divided."[39] As the 1850s came to a close, white Missourians became increasingly attuned to this frightening potential. A terrifying realization dawned on them about what civil war would mean for their region. Bleeding Kansas powerfully demonstrated both the brutality of civil conflict and its potential to jeopardize the stability of slavery on the western border. Many white Missourians felt slavery must be defended but that civil war likewise must be avoided at all costs.

The defense white Missourians mounted on behalf of proslavery politics reflected their continued reliance on the institution in the antebellum era. Proportionally speaking, however, the numbers of enslaved Missourians did not keep pace with the burgeoning free population. By 1860, enslaved people made up less than 10 percent of the state's population.[40] Yet, according to historians Christopher Phillips and Kristen Epps, that percentage obscures important facts. "Despite the proportional decline of the slave population in Missouri during the final antebellum decades," Phillips argues, "raw numbers of slaves in Missouri actually increased during the same period, and they did so dramatically. Between 1830 and 1850, Missouri's slave population more than tripled to 87,422; by 1860, that number had increased by another third to 114,931, an all-time high."[41] "It cannot be argued that slavery was being strengthened in Missouri," Epps adds, "but neither can it be argued that—barring the events of Bleeding Kansas—the system faced its impending demise."[42] Still, the institution of slavery in Missouri remained small-scale and the comparatively greater mobility of enslaved people, as well as the diversity of their modes of labor, meant that its conditions in Missouri differed from plantation-style slavery. This gave Missouri, Schurz observed, "much more of the elasticity of Western life than any of the larger . . . slave-holding States."[43] Such circumstances should not imply that the legal and violent controls exercised over enslaved people loosened. Chattel slavery remained as entrenched as ever. In spite of persistent resistance on the part of enslaved people, antislavery voices among the state's white population remained muted.[44]

Even with the institution of slavery threatening to tear the nation apart, many of Missouri's slaveholders staunchly defended the Union because they believed it offered the best protection for slavery. They feared secession would lead to war, the disruption of which would jeopardize their slaveholdings. The federal government offered security as it consistently protected the property rights of slaveholders. "It is well known that slave property is timid in Missouri," one individual acknowledged, "and as it is my fortune to be one of the largest slaveholders in this part of the State, I would earnestly ask gentlemen who have no direct interest in this matter, to desist in protecting my interest after the fashion of [William Lowndes] Yancey and his disunion followers, feeling assured as I do, that if their councils prevail, Missouri will not be a slaveholding State many years."[45] So while white Missourians had a stake in protecting slavery, that did not necessarily lead them to sympathize with secession. In fact, many of the state's most prominent slaveholding politicians, including Thomas Hart Benton; Francis P. Blair, Sr.; and James S. Rollins, were also the most vocal critics of disunion.

These men and others like them embodied the rise of conservative Unionism in the state. The appeal of this ideology in Missouri stemmed from both the state's diverse population and its longstanding commitment to slavery. In the decade before the Civil War, however, conservative Unionism became a fully articulated political identity. Representing a conglomeration of partisan identifications, including some Democrats, Republicans, and Constitutional Unionists, conservative Unionists stood for moderation and compromise. At the heart of this philosophy, however, was straightforward pragmatism—or, as historian Aaron Astor describes it, "practical concerns with protecting a slave-based economy and society in the face of serious, but not unreasonable, threats." They warned against "the twin heresies of abolitionism and secession."[46]

In tune to the lessons of Bleeding Kansas, conservative Unionists feared sectional extremism would pull their region into the heart of a devastating civil war with the potential to unleash unprecedented destruction and destabilize their slaveholdings. Conservative Unionists urged their fellow Americans to recall their shared commitment to republican government and decried any measure that might weaken it. As a result, they lionized great American statesmen like Andrew Jackson, Daniel Webster, and Henry Clay. While these men had oppositional policies and would not have necessarily considered themselves allies, they had each acted to forestall crises that threatened the Union.[47] To conservative Unionists, their achievements were to be emulated.

White Missourians, in particular, used the legacy of the Missouri Compromise for guidance in the face of the brewing sectional conflict. As the presidential election of 1860 drew near, however, neither southern Democrats nor northern Republicans knew what to make of this conservative approach. Southerners felt the slaveholding border state had abandoned its region and regarded it with suspicion. Northerners worried that border state Republicans were effectively a fifth column, intent on undercutting the more radical antislavery elements of the party.[48] This mistrust from both sides toward Missouri persisted well into the war years and beyond, and ultimately colored how outsiders perceived Civil War commemoration in the state.

Missourians understood the tremendous stakes of the coming presidential election in 1860 and anticipated its complicated regional implications. The local press generally condemned both southern Democrat John C. Breckinridge and Republican Abraham Lincoln as sectional candidates. Many white Missourians embraced Unionism but regarded the Republican Party as a strictly northern party and found its antislavery platform worrying. Some clearly feared the Republicans sought not only emancipation but racial equality. One Missouri newspaper, for example, warned its readers about Republican efforts in Pittsburgh, Pennsylvania, to promote universal suffrage by recruiting black men into the Wide Awakes, a paramilitary club. It advised its readers to "calmly reflect what the Republican party is doing, and what it is bringing us to."[49] The German population of St. Louis, however, saw little to fear in the prospect of a Republican victory. "Every day we hear what the South will do or have done if we elect Lincoln as president," the German-language newspaper *Anzeiger des Westens* observed. "But we are much more interested in what shall become of the North and the West. . . . The shirt is closer to us than the coat, and if Lincoln's election supports the interests of the North and the West, then we are only sad at second hand that the South might suffer for it."[50]

Ultimately, Missourians overwhelmingly voted as conservative Unionists in the election of 1860. Northern Democrat Stephen Douglas carried the state with Constitutional Unionist candidate John Bell trailing closely behind.[51] The election was a testament to the strength of Missouri's Unionism. White Missourians remained proslavery, but they were not secessionists. "The people of this State are Union-loving law-abiding people and have repudiated [secessionists]," the *Weekly Jefferson Inquirer* proclaimed. "What a withering and lasting rebuke this is to disunion," it concluded.[52]

While the 1860 election reiterated the commitment of white Missourians to the Union as it was, it also highlighted their discomfiture with sectional antagonism over slavery. Although disappointed by Lincoln's victory, most Democratic Missourians did not regard his election in and of itself as grounds for secession. "Mr. Lincoln is elected," the *Daily Missouri Republican* lamented. "It is no fault of ours that he was not beaten, for we took some pains to do it." Still, the paper continued, "We say that no good citizen of Missouri ought to take any step, nor do any act, which looks to the destruction of the Union."[53] "We have no doubt he will make us a good President," the *Weekly Jefferson Inquirer* stated, "at least we hope so. Although elected entirely as a sectional candidate, it is his duty to so shape his course as to make his administration national."[54] There was no reason to expect anything less. After all, Lincoln consistently promised not to interfere with slavery where it existed. The *Weekly California News* reassured its readers that even if Lincoln broke his promises, Congress would prevent him from harming the interests of slaveholders. "There are conservative men enough North to see that our rights shall be preserved," the paper determined.[55] "The enlightened world will not look upon the election of Lincoln as a cause for the secession of a State or States," one contributor to the *Weekly Jefferson Inquirer* concluded. Disunion could not be countenanced as long as slavery remained secure. "Wait until something is done real and tangible against the property, liberty, or life of the people of the South," another writer urged.[56] As much as it recognized its minority status as a Republican, antislavery paper, the *St. Joseph Weekly Free Democrat* observed confidently that "Missouri is for the Union, and that there is no real disapprobation of the election of Lincoln."[57]

The election, however, was only the first test of Missouri's loyalty. As the secession crisis unfolded, the nation watched Missouri's next move with interest. Missouri's compromise tradition, diverse population, unique regional identity, and adherence to slavery made it a question mark. The *New York Tribune*, in a story reprinted in the *St. Joseph Weekly Free Democrat*, expressed optimism about Missouri's place in the Union. It considered voters' marginal support for Lincoln and success of Douglas as evidence that the "slave power" was in decline in Missouri. The election "represents the apparent neutrality and actual transition which characterizes at this moment the position of Missouri," it commented. "Not yet advanced enough to act with that party which, in Missouri, is the emancipation party, it has yet cut loose from that which represents the Pro-Slavery conservatism of the South."[58] The New York paper was not entirely off-base. In the local press, Missourians vowed they would not march in lockstep with southern secessionists. "It would be well to remember that it is a fallacy to say that the south demands [secession]," the *Daily Missouri Republican* sniped, "if by this equivocal term it is meant that the fifteen slave States demand it. . . . It is unjust to Missouri, and Kentucky, and Tennessee, and Maryland, and North Carolina, and nearly all of the Slave States, to characterize them as faithless to the Union, because one State has threatened to break up the Confederacy for no better reason than that an election did not terminate to please them."[59] The German-language *Anzeiger des Westens* asserted, "Obviously the fire-eaters of the cotton states have nothing to expect from Missouri."[60] Whatever steps Missouri took next, the state would dictate its own course. "South Carolina acted . . . for and by herself," the *Randolph Citizen* remarked. "Missouri has equally weighty interests at stake, and sound sense, policy, conservatism, and practical statesmanship, plainly require that she should act for herself." "If the Union is to be hopelessly destroyed," it went on, "we believe it the will of our people that no action of Missouri shall tend to produce that misfortune."[61]

All too often, however, Missouri's assurances of loyalty were accompanied by expressions of sympathy for its fellow slaveholding states. In a report of resolutions from a Union meeting in Randolph County, the *Randolph Citizen* confessed, "We are unwilling to surrender the Union, yet, at the same time, we do not wish it inferred that we do not know our rights, and intend to maintain them even at the cannon's mouth."[62] "We have been asked the question," the *Weekly Jefferson Inquirer* commented, "'to which section of the Union will you go should a dissolution take place?' . . . *We are for the Union at all hazards.—We believe the people of the State of Missouri are for the Union.*"[63] "But if the Union be permanently disrupted," the same paper continued weeks later, "there can be no doubt of the destiny of Missouri. . . . Missouri would go with the South, *if she must go anywhere*; and it is equally clear that her citizens will acquiesce in no attempt to coerce the cotton States into submission."[64] Another Democratic paper, the *Weekly California News* agreed: "We believe the patriotic sons of Missouri, should dissolution become inevitable, would rally to the standard of her sisters of the South. Duty and interest alike, would dictate this course. If we cannot get our rights *in* the Union, then we should insist upon having them *out* of it."[65] These seemingly contradictory perspectives speak to the pervasiveness of conservative, in this case conditional, Unionism. Most white Missourians remained committed to slavery. They were not prepared to accede to disunion, but neither could they imagine a future for their state without slavery.

Despite expressing sympathy with the plight of other slaveholders, many white Missourians faced the prospect of a civil war with dread. As the secession crisis deepened, they became ever more acutely aware of the danger of their geographic position on the border between slavery and freedom. Their state's location on the "middle ground," which brought them dynamic growth and prosperity, now seemed a frightening liability. As the *St. Joseph Weekly Free Democrat* observed, "Missouri, in addition to the great national considerations which attach her with unflinching fidelity to the Union, has a peculiar and local interest in its preservation which is not felt by the Southern States that are situated with the Gulf on one side of them and a tier of slave States upon the other." It was obvious to Missourians of all political stripes that war would place Missouri and its slaveholdings in peril. "The permanent continuance of slavery in Missouri depends upon the continuance of the Union," the *Free Democrat* stated.[66] "Hers, indeed, it is a pivotal position as regards not only the North and the South, but also the East and the West," the *Weekly Jefferson Inquirer* agreed. "She is the great half-way house of the four extremes and her interests are intimately identified with all." These conflicting interests, the paper predicted, would inevitably put Missouri at the frontlines of the war, and the well-being of the state, particularly the institution of slavery, would hang in the balance. "Missouri, in the event of a sectional war," the *Inquirer* anticipated, "will be more exposed, and has more to lose than any other State in the Union. She is therefore more interested in the maintenance of the Union than any other State—much more than any other slave State; will suffer more in the destruction and loss of property; more in the loss of social amity; more of orphanage and widowhood, and will sacrifice more of future prosperity and greatness."[67] Even the staunchly

Republican German-language *Mississippi Blätter* concurred. "Missouri is the most exposed of all the slave states," it noted, suggesting that enslaved people would take advantage of the chaos of secession to emancipate themselves. "Who is not able to see that this property (which is endowed with understanding and its own will) becomes *ten times more insecure* on the day Missouri withdraws from the Union?"[68] The *Randolph Citizen* warned that secession and civil war would jeopardize Missouri's slaveholdings and the safety of its white residents as well. "We would be exposed to all the outrages between the North and South," it warned, "and that our fields would be the common battle grounds."[69] However much white Missourians identified with the plight of their fellow slaveholders in the South, they understood they occupied a region apart and faced very different dangers.

For the sake of self-preservation, then, Missouri's conservatives attempted to distance themselves from both northern and southern extremism. Rather than choosing between the two sides, some Missourians felt they should forge an alliance with either their fellow border states or with the West and leave the sectional squabbling to the North and South.[70] The *Anzeiger des Westens* hoped for a prompt resolution to the secession crisis, "but if this is not the case," it suggested, "then the Germans in the Western states—to which Missouri belongs—must take their stand on freedom and right and oppose this state entering the *Southern* confederation. . . . If the Union falls to pieces and Missouri cannot stay with the North, then a *Central States League* to which Germans and border slave states would gravitate would not be impractical or unrealistic."[71] "Our State," Representative John W. Reid wrote in the *Weekly Jefferson Inquirer*, "from the character of her people, the nature of her productions, and her interior and central position, has many interests, which bind her to the people of both sections of the country. . . . My opinion is, that she will attach herself neither to . . . the North or the South, but make herself the centre of a great Western Republic, upon which the stomachs of both the others will be dependent."[72]

More often white Missourians felt a responsibility as westerners and as the inheritors of the Missouri Compromise to act as arbitrators.[73] Missouri's German population also embraced this role. Reprinting a translated excerpt from the German-language newspaper *Tages Chronik*, the *Daily Missouri Republican* reported, "We believe that Providence has assigned to us a peculiar task at this critical juncture of affairs. We believe that, being most numerous and powerful in the centre of the Union—such States as Pennsylvania, Ohio, Indiana, Illinois and Missouri—we are destined to interpose a conservative influence between the extremists of both sections of the Union and the aims to which they aspire."[74] The Missouri Compromise had prevented one national crisis over slavery. Perhaps another such measure could be crafted. "What ever position Missouri may take," the *Weekly Jefferson Inquirer* remarked, "we hope to see her act in the spirit of conservatism—to act cautiously."[75] Two weeks later it continued, "Missouri is the child of compromise, and her people will ever be found ready to make any compromise not inconsistent with her honor."[76] Thus, the memory of the Missouri Compromise guided the response of Missourians to the secession crisis. While the hope of compromise ultimately proved futile, it remained important to how white Missourians thought about their place in the origins of the Civil War, even long after it was over.

Nevertheless, Missouri still had its share of secessionists. Chief among them was Claiborne Fox Jackson, author of the Jackson Resolutions and now governor of the state. Although elected as a moderate Democrat and avowed Unionist, Jackson changed his colors after the election of 1860. In his inaugural address, he justified secession and blamed the current crisis on northern antagonism, as manifested by the Republican Party and President Lincoln. Lincoln's election, Jackson claimed, posed a serious threat to slaveholders, and he appealed to Missourians to stand by the South. "The destiny of the slaveholding States of this Union is one and the same," he said. Jackson acknowledged that Missourians were "devoted to the Union" but insisted that Missouri would "stand by her sister slaveholding States, in whose wrongs she participates and with whose institutions and people she sympathizes." The governor concluded by advising the state militia to arm itself in preparation for war.[77]

As the secession crisis deepened, the Missouri General Assembly called for a state convention to meet on February 28, 1861, in order to decide how the state would respond. Missourians understood that the outcome of this convention had important implications not only for Missouri but for the nation and for posterity. At least one correspondent to the *Weekly Jefferson Inquirer* feared such a convention would serve as a ploy to coerce Missouri out of the Union. "If any Union man favors the call of a convention," the author remarked, "he is deceived, deluded, cheated, swindled, outrageously so." "Missouri is either disunion or not," the writer continued. "If disunion, let her act like other disunion States, and call a convention; if not, let her act unlike the disunion States, call no convention, and concentrate all her powers in aiding the Federal Government in the execution of the laws."[78]

The convention having been decided upon, the St. Louis *Anzeiger des Westens* begged its readers to elect Union men to serve:

> Preserve this state in the Union and no one will dare to apply to *it* the word *treason*, and then we will have the right to arbitrate in the great struggle that now divides the land. For just as the two great systems of labor encounter one another on a large scale in the Union, so also they encounter one another within our state on a smaller scale. If Missouri decides to resolve this struggle peacefully by itself and without civil war, and if it sees its way to a better existence *within the Union alone* despite all of its supposed difficulties, then the bridge will have been built over which the South and the North will approach one another and join hands.

The paper concluded, "Never permit the slander to sully the pages of the history of this state: *Missouri, too, betrayed its mother, the Union!*"[79]

The German population of St. Louis need not have worried. The delegates elected to the convention highlighted the diverse origins of the state's white population but also evinced their commitment to conservative Unionism and compromise. Like Hamilton Gamble, the delegates were overwhelmingly southern-born. In fact, of the 104 men in attendance, 87 hailed from slaveholding states and only 13 from free states. The remaining 4 were born abroad. Drawn from vastly different corners of the state—from the cities, farmlands, mountainous Ozarks, and slaveholding river counties—they were all resolutely Unionist. No doubt echoing the sentiments of many of his fellow delegates, James O. Broadhead declared, "I stand here not as a Southern man, but as a Missourian and an American citizen. Born at the South, I think I know something of my duty to the South as well as to the Constitution of my country."[80]

The convention first assembled in the courthouse in Jefferson City before decamping to more spacious headquarters at the Mercantile Library Hall in St. Louis. The convention proceedings give the impression that, at times, the deliberations were heated. As a raucous crowd gathered to observe the convention, the delegates found it necessary to close the doors to the general public. Only as many spectators as would fit in the available seating could remain in the hall; the rest of the crowd listened from the lobby. They occasionally became so disruptive that the delegates appointed a doorkeeper and sergeant-at-arms to keep them at bay. The convention authorized the sergeant-at-arms to eject particularly rowdy spectators from the building.

In the course of the convention, there was extensive debate over the constitutionality of secession. The delegates blamed the crisis on antislavery fanaticism but insisted there were no grounds on which secession could be justified. Following Gamble's presentation of the report from the Committee on Federal Relations, the convention applauded the spirit of the Crittenden Compromise, then under deliberation in Congress, which promised to restore the Missouri Compromise and create stronger fugitive slave laws. To preserve the peace, the delegates also resolved to petition the federal government to withdraw garrisons from all forts within the seceded states.

The other main business of the convention was to consider when and how Missouri would respond in case of a civil war. While the delegates swore slaveholding Missourians would never willingly surrender their human chattel, they expressed considerable reluctance over fighting for its defense. Gamble, for example, cautioned the convention about the risk of military conflict for Missouri. Speaking on behalf of the Committee on Federal Relations, he said, "But what is now the true position for Missouri to assume? Evidently that of a State whose interests are bound up in the maintenance of the Union, and whose kind feelings and strong sympathies are with the people of the Southern States, with whom we are connected by ties of friendship and of blood." Although he recognized the strength of these ties, he urged the convention to act with caution. "In a military aspect," he warned, "secession and a connection with a Southern confederacy is annihilation for our State. . . . Emigration must cease. No Southern man owning slaves would come to the frontier State; no Northern man would come to this foreign country avowedly to battle his native land. Our slave interest would be destroyed, because we would have no better right to recapture a slave found in a free State than we now have in Canada."[81]

Several delegates shared Gamble's opinion that remaining within the Union would best protect Missouri's interests—slave and otherwise. Broadhead expressed his certainty that "slavery would not exist ten years after Missouri joined a Southern Confederacy. As she stands now," he assured the convention, "she is protected." Delegate Sample Orr went even further. Missouri's "only salvation for the institution of slavery," he insisted, "is her adherence to the Government that pro[t]ects slavery"—the United States. As Broadhead reminded the convention, in the case of civil war, Missouri stood to lose far more than its stake in slavery. "I am a slave owner myself," he admitted, "but I am not willing to sacrifice other interests to the slave interest, or say that it is the peculiar institution of Missouri, when we know that it is not true." He cited Missouri's investment not only in agricultural enterprises but also in mining, manufacturing, and trade. These industries were more important to Missouri than the institution of slavery, Broadhead argued, and it would be foolish to sacrifice them by joining arms with the Confederacy. He continued,

> Where are we to get men to open our fertile prairies? Where are we to get the men to work in our mines, in our workshops, and to carry on our commercial business, if it is not from the overcrowded Eastern States and Europe? . . . If you make Missouri a member of the Southern Confederacy, with but a small slave population, you can see at once that all this population is driven off. Men will not . . . come to Missouri for the purpose of engaging in these pursuits, when they know that, so far as our political power is concerned, we shall be subjected to the cotton lords of South Carolina and Louisiana.[82]

Broadhead recognized that Missouri owed its prosperity to its power to attract immigrants from every corner of the country—even the world—to the West. He saw no advantage to be gained by siding with the South.

As westerners, the delegates expressed a great deal of uncertainty about their place in the brewing sectional conflict. Some seemed to think it had a little to do with Missouri at all. "We stand like the rock in the ocean," one man declared, "rolling back from us the waves that come from the North and the South." "Missouri is an integral part of the great West," delegate James McFerran insisted, "and declares her fealty and attachment to her own interests and section, and invites her sister States of the West to ignore the dogmas of New England on the one hand, and the Gulf States on the other; and at once inaugurate a Western policy, loyal to the Federal Constitution and the Union of the States." "Missouri," he went on, "is emphatically a Western State."[83] The path that McFerran and many Missourians like him sought was one of neutrality.

Other delegates believed they had a central role to play in the conflict. As westerners, they felt ideally situated to facilitate compromise between the North and South. "I hold it especially to be the duty of Missouri to be calm, prudent and wise in this emergency," one delegate advised. "She should occupy a middle ground in the temperate zone of politics, which she occupies in a geographical point of view. . . . The office of Missouri is that of a pacificator."[84] "Missouri entered the Union at the close of an angry contest on the subject of slavery," Gamble said. "Her geographical position, the variety of the branches of industry to which her resources point, her past growth and future prospects, combine to demand that all her counsels be taken in the spirit of sobriety and conciliation." "Missouri," another delegate succinctly concluded, "is for peace, compromise, concession, conciliation and settlement of all the questions involved."[85]

On the whole, the proceedings of the convention exemplified the conservative Unionism that had long characterized the politics of white Missourians. They understood themselves to be a part of the West, with prerogatives distinct from both the North and South. Their devoted commitment both to the national Union and to slaveholding made sense in their context, though by the spring of 1861, the two propositions seemed increasingly irreconcilable to outsiders. While Missouri's moderates pled for neutrality and worked to manufacture a compromise, Confederates opened fire on the federal garrison at Fort Sumter in South Carolina and initiated the Civil War. This was not the moment for a noncommittal response. To both Unionists and Confederates, Missouri's hesitancy to take sides read as duplicitous. This perception of Missouri persisted throughout the war and into its aftermath, profoundly influencing how Missourians made sense of their place in its history.

Unfortunately, Missouri could not long remain outside of the conflict. As the clouds of war gathered, deep political and social divisions wracked Missouri as both the United States and Confederate States vied for Missouri's allegiance. Within the state, the opposing sides marshaled armed forces but continued to profess a desire for neutrality. On May 10, 1861, events came to a crisis in St. Louis when home guard troops organized by the U.S. Army arrested southern-sympathizing militiamen during what became known as the Camp Jackson affair. Even though the militiamen had not yet taken direct action, they seemed poised to attack a nearby federal arsenal. As the home guard marched the arrested men through the streets of the city, a riot broke out. In the end, twenty-eight civilians were killed. Camp Jackson inaugurated the Civil War in Missouri.[86]

In the aftermath of Camp Jackson, the Confederacy worked to secure Missouri's allegiance. They believed Governor Jackson supported their cause—with good reason. Jackson refused Lincoln's call for 75,000 troops to subdue the rebellion and mobilized the Missouri State Guard. Recognizing this as a threat to federal authority, the Union Army moved on the capital city and Jackson fled. While in exile in southwest Missouri, Jackson convened the legislature and passed an illegitimate ordinance of secession.[87] The Confederate States accepted it, however, and welcomed delegates from

Missouri to the Confederate Congress. Jackson ultimately reestablished his government in Marshall, Texas, where it remained for the duration of the war. Missouri's rogue Confederate government would ultimately present an interesting challenge to the commemoration of the Lost Cause in Missouri. Although the state received representation in the Confederate Congress, because it never really seceded, it could not claim to have popularly supported the Confederacy.

Nevertheless, local opposition to the Union continued in the form of Missouri's notorious guerilla war. While Missouri played an important role in the Civil War and even served as the scene of several major battles, those points have often been overshadowed—then as now—by the guerrilla warfare that wracked the state.[88] To those outside Missouri, the persistent perception of Missouri's disloyalty seemed justified by the brutal guerrilla fighting that spread throughout the state. Due to the Confederate Army's neglect of the Missouri theater, and in the face of stringent Union control, southern-sympathizing Missourians sometimes turned "bushwhacker" and proceeded to conduct their own private war with a vengeance. Perhaps the most feared of these bushwhackers followed William Clarke Quantrill. Quantrill considered himself a partisan ranger, or Confederate auxiliary, authorized to disrupt Union operations and terrorize loyal civilians. "There was hardly any form in which treason to country, treachery to friends, faithlessness to obligations, and disregard of all law, . . . that was not exhibited daily, for years, in this unhappy State," St. Louis attorney Charles D. Drake remembered.[89] Ironically, far from reinforcing Missouri's ties to the Confederacy, guerrilla activity amplified the federal presence in the state and led to the implementation of increasingly severe measures to subdue irregular warfare. Ultimately, the guerrillas never had the organization or strength to dislodge the Union Army, who remained in firm control of Missouri throughout the war. Still, the guerrillas tarnished Missouri's reputation among the loyal states at least until the end of the nineteenth century.

This became a source of much hand-wringing for Missourians in the aftermath of the war, particularly among white Unionists, who understood that the actions of the guerrillas were not representative of Missouri's larger participation in the war. Missouri's contributions were not confined to the local or to the "abyss of undifferentiated guerrilla attacks," as historian Louis S. Gerteis describes it.[90] Missourians served in both the western and the eastern theaters of the war, in all the major campaigns, and under all the famed leaders. Indeed, Missouri sent troops to both regular armies but fielded far more Union than Confederate soldiers: perhaps 100,000 Union soldiers, including more than 8,000 African American troops, and as few as 30,000 Confederates.[91] This meant the Unionists enjoyed a significant majority by any reasonable rubric. Still, the presence of that Confederate minority could not be wished away—nor would it be easily overlooked by later-day Americans reflecting on the Civil War in the state. The notorious exploits of the guerrillas during and after the war dominated popular perceptions of Civil War Missouri for generations.

In the meantime, faced with the disintegration of the elected government, the delegates from the February state convention acted as the interim governing body. In July 1861, they appointed new officials to fill the offices vacated by Jackson and his secessionist allies and established a provisional wartime government.[92] On August 1, 1861, the delegates appointed Hamilton Gamble as the new governor of Missouri. Working in close cooperation with the Lincoln administration, Gamble's government sought to stem the chaos left in Jackson's wake with a return to conservative Unionism.[93] In particular, Gamble expressed a commitment to preserving Missouri's slave property. In the light of Jackson's secession measure, however, the federal government remained generally uneasy about the loyalty of white Missourians, especially considering their unwavering commitment to slavery.

Although the provisional government sought to limit outside intervention in Missouri in the early stages of the war, the federal government could not rest safely on the strength of conservative Unionism in the state. Historian Richard S. Brownlee explains the government's predicament in relation to Missouri:

> There were numerous people disloyal to the Union throughout the State, and there were even more, who if forced to take sides, would become disloyal. There was the baffling question as to the definition of loyalty itself. . . . There was the vexing riddle of the various types and shades of disloyalty, and the matter of measures to be taken against men in each instance. There was the problem of guilt; guilt by active resistance to authority; . . . guilt by blood relationship and marriage, and guilt suggested by informers or by mischievous or revengeful people. . . . To further complicate the situation, the Union command also had as its responsibility a very large population that was loyal to the Union. This population had to be protected, supported where possible.[94]

In the interest of caution, the federal government assumed an extensive degree of disloyalty among the population of the slave state that did not necessarily exist—with tremendous implications for wartime Missourians. "Missouri was . . . unquestionably opposed to the secession of the State," one

Missourian later remembered. "But so closely was she identified with the South by reason of her institutions as well as the origin of a large portion of her inhabitants that she became an object of suspicion and of prompt military occupation by the troops of the United States."[95] This action was both prompted by and helped perpetuate a widespread and persistent mistrust of Unionism in Missouri.

On August 30, 1861, U.S. major general John C. Frémont placed the state under martial law.[96] This measure, perhaps even more than the secession crisis, tested Missouri's loyalty. White Missourians sometimes found their civil liberties sacrificed to wartime necessity. The provisional government mandated all public officials and anyone suspected of disloyalty take what became known as "test oaths," avowing their allegiance to the federal government.[97] Provost marshals enforced the oaths with arbitrary power. They seized property, suspended the writ of habeas corpus, and arrested citizens.[98] Frémont also vowed to confiscate and free enslaved people belonging to known rebels.[99] This measure prompted intense debate, and President Lincoln quickly rescinded it out of fear it would drive Missouri's conservative Unionists into the arms of the Confederacy. Nevertheless, Frémont's actions alienated many white Missourians, and the imposition of martial law put them in an unenviable position—they "remained loyal to the Union," historian Michael Fellman argues, "yet deeply resentful of Federal force."[100] When white Missourians criticized violations of their civil liberties, regardless of the support they furnished to the Union, they gave northerners reason to doubt the sincerity of their loyalty.

Among Missouri's diverse and conflicted populace, however, federal authorities discovered that there were some Missourians whose loyalty they need not question: African Americans. In fact, the U.S. Army depended heavily on enslaved people to enforce martial law. "In a reversal of decades of Missouri law that would not allow for the testimony of slaves against whites," historian Diane Mutti Burke writes, "the provost marshals used the testimony of slaves as they built cases against white Missourians accused of disloyalty."[101] In 1863, federal officials also authorized the recruitment of black Missourians into the U.S. Army. While African American Missourians faced a greater likelihood of violent reprisals for their commitment to the Union than their white neighbors, their loyalty was not questioned to the same extent as white Missourians. This interesting distinction would later have important ramifications for Civil War commemoration in Missouri's African American communities. Black Missourians were far less preoccupied than their white comrades with insisting on their faithfulness to the Union war effort.

Enslaved Missourians also found that the Civil War presented them with opportunities for resistance. When the federal government failed to endorse Frémont's proposal for limited emancipation, many enslaved people emancipated themselves. In their efforts to attain freedom, they could not always rely on Union officials for support. Although Frémont's successor, Major General Henry Halleck, had the authority to liberate enslaved people whose owners forced them to work in aid of the Confederacy, he ultimately banned fugitive slaves from entering Union lines. Furthermore, while Union policy dictated that federal troops would not act as slave-catchers, the loyal Missouri militias did.[102]

Despite these obstacles, enslaved people fled Missouri by the thousands, many to the neighboring free states of Kansas, Iowa, and Illinois.[103] Some took up arms with antislavery Unionist Jayhawkers in neighboring Kansas and participated in raids across the border to liberate their families and other enslaved people in Missouri. Such actions invoked the memory of John Brown's raid on Harpers Ferry and stoked fears of a race war. In an exposé intended for Congress, state treasurer George Caleb Bingham reported with unmitigated outrage that Jayhawkers had recently arrived in Missouri alongside "a company composed, exclusively, of negroes, armed, uniformed and mounted as soldiers of the United States, and headed by a slave, who had been enticed from a master of widely known and unwavering loyalty!"[104] In a private letter, Bingham said the execution of Jayhawker chieftain Colonel Charles Jennison "would do more for the Union cause in Missouri, than the defeat of a Rebel army."[105]

The provisional state government demanded and received federal assistance in subduing these emancipatory raids, but the disintegration of Missouri's slaveholdings continued. In July 1862, the Second Confiscation Act granted freedom to enslaved people belonging to Confederate sympathizers, empowering them to inform against their disloyal enslavers.[106] Although federal authorities often tried to constrain the law in order to appease Unionist slaveholders, confiscation seriously destabilized the institution of slavery in Missouri. The passage of the Emancipation Proclamation in early 1863 signaled its demise. Although Missouri remained within the Union and was therefore exempt from the proclamation, it further invigorated resistance among the enslaved and forced the provisional government to begin reckoning with the future of slavery in the state.

By the summer of 1862, in part because of their ineffectiveness at curbing guerrilla violence, Missourians became increasingly vexed with the conservatism of Gamble's provisional government, and a cadre of Radical Republicans emerged in opposition.[107] War-weary white Missourians seemed receptive to their new agenda and increasingly so to emancipation. Missouri's compromise tradition gave way to support for more radical measures. As leading Radical Republican Charles Drake observed, "As well attempt to roll back the Mississippi to its source, as to stem the mighty swell of that enfranchised opinion, which, throughout Missouri, presses home upon S[l]avery all the woes and tears, the ravages and dismay, which have made those two years hideous and insufferable to her people."[108]

Under pressure from Drake and his growing number of supporters, Gamble called a convention in July 1863 to discuss emancipation.[109] As antebellum Missourians predicted, the Civil War destabilized slavery in Missouri to the point where emancipation seemed possible. The delegates devised a program for gradual emancipation, which would free enslaved people between the ages of twelve and forty on July 4, 1870. Enslaved children under twelve years of age would attain freedom in 1876, while those born before July 4, 1830, would remain enslaved for life.[110] It also proposed to soften the blow to loyal slaveholders by suspending any further tax payments on slave property. This disappointed the Radicals, who wanted immediate emancipation. "It was," Drake complained, "for any good to this generation, about equivalent to declaring [emancipation] in the next century."[111]

Drake found an opportunity to initiate more dramatic changes after Governor Gamble died suddenly from pneumonia in 1864. Following his death, Missouri increasingly came under the sway of Republicans. Emerging from their stronghold among the German population of St. Louis, the Republicans also took advantage of the circumstances of the war. Many conservatives had grown frustrated with the provisional government, and with the security of slavery irreversibly undermined, Republicans extended their base of support. In addition, thousands of Confederate-sympathizing refugees abandoned the state—some voluntarily, others under force—allowing the Republicans to gain significant traction.

As a testament to the rising popularity of the Republicans, Lincoln tidily carried Missouri in the 1864 election. As a further demonstration of their ascendancy, Radical Republicans soon filled the majority of state offices. Although, as historian Christopher Phillips is careful to point out, 40 percent fewer Missourians voted in 1864 than in 1860, a consequence of the imposition of the test oath and dislocations produced by the war.[112] Even at this late hour, with Union victory ever more certain, Missouri's loyalty seemed conditional. The success of the Republican Party did not reflect a change of heart on the part of local Confederates; rather, they had relinquished the state.

The Civil War in Missouri ended with little fanfare. In 1864, Confederate general Sterling Price made a last-ditch effort to reclaim the state. He anticipated a great uprising of sympathetic Missourians would join his ranks and drive out the Union Army, but no such response materialized.[113] His famous "Great Raid" was ultimately unsuccessful, and Missouri remained under the control of the Union Army. After Price's withdrawal from the state, the Confederates recognized their cause in Missouri was lost.

At the end of the war, however, guerrilla violence only underwent a brief hiatus. With many of the Union troops in Missouri either dispatched to the East as reinforcements or demobilized following the Confederate surrender, there was no one left to keep the guerrillas in check. Former guerrillas reemerged from hiding and mounted a new resistance fueled by wartime bitterness, economic distress, and resentment against the Radical Republicans. Rampant vigilante violence plagued the state for decades. The exploits of these outlaws, especially Jesse James and his gang, made Missouri infamous.[114] For outsiders, it also served as evidence that their long-held suspicion of Missourians was warranted. These were not the actions of loyal citizens.

The Civil War era was a complicated period for the state of Missouri as its inhabitants forged their regional identity against a backdrop of contentious debates over slavery and disunion. Although Missouri entered the Union as a slave state, many of its people linked their destiny to the West and to the Union rather than to the South. White Missourians embraced their state's identity as the "Gateway to the West," espousing conservative politics to unite their heterogeneous population. The Civil War forced Missouri's moderates to take sides. As a result, the war years were incredibly disrupting for Missourians. The Civil War strained the commitment of white Missourians to compromise, turned its diverse population against itself, and marred Missouri's reputation among the loyal states. Enslaved Missourians astutely navigated these complicated internal dynamics and made the Civil War a war for liberation—despite the determined opposition of their enslavers, both loyal and secessionist, and the vacillations of federal authorities.

In the aftermath of the war, black and white Missourians struggled to come to terms with their new relationships to one another and to the reunited nation. The second half of the nineteenth century would bring still further change to Missouri as a result of political upheaval and significant postwar in-migration. It is worth remembering, however, that the generation who began the long and fraught process of commemorating the Civil War also experienced it firsthand.[115] Although the war brought profound changes, antebellum attitudes vaunted by white Missourians—including their western regional identity and political traditions of conservatism and compromise—reasserted themselves in the realm of Civil War commemoration.

TWO

"Poor Old Missouri"

Redeeming Missouri's Union Cause

> **Any claim now made by any one, . . . that Missouri ever belonged in sentiment to the South is an unmerited slander, promulgated only by those who are . . . densely ignorant of the glorious history of our great commonwealth. "Poor Old Missouri" she is not and never was. Union Missouri she was, is and always will be.**
>
> —Captain George S. Grover (USA), "Civil War in Missouri," Warrensburg, November 4, 1893

AS UNION VETERANS DISEMBARKED FROM trains in Lexington, Missouri, in May 1904 to attend the annual meeting, or encampment, of the Department of Missouri Grand Army of the Republic (GAR), they had reason to wonder about the welcome they would receive. Situated in Lafayette County just west of Kansas City, Lexington lay at the heart of "Little Dixie"—a unique region of Missouri marked by its longstanding cultural, political, and economic ties to the South. In the territorial period, Little Dixie attracted slaveholders who cultivated tobacco and hemp in its prime lands along the Missouri River bottoms. As a result, Little Dixie became the hub of the state's antebellum slave-based economy.[1] During the Civil War, Little Dixie served as a hotbed of Confederate sentiment and a hunting ground for the state's notorious guerrillas. Long after the war, one contributor to the *National Tribune*, the Union veteran's newspaper of choice, remembered Lafayette County as "the hottest hole of rebellion" in Missouri and possibly "the hottest place on God's green earth for loyal and patriotic people to exist in (except Charleston, S. C.)."[2]

In 1861, Lexington was also the site of one of the state's few major battles. That September, the pro-Confederate State Guard under the command of Sterling Price led an assault on a desperately outnumbered garrison of federal soldiers entrenched around the city's Masonic College. After two days of fierce, back-and-forth fighting, a group of State Guardsmen turned the tide of the battle when they discovered a quantity of hemp bales stored in a nearby warehouse. Using the man-sized bales as moving breastworks, they crept close enough to the Union fortifications to launch a charge and force their surrender. As a result, Missourians christened the siege at Lexington the "Battle of the Hemp Bales."[3]

Now, forty years after their ignominious retreat from the city, hundreds of Union men returned to Lexington to attend the GAR encampment. They were looking forward to two full days of festivities, including speeches, music, dancing, and a parade.[4] Whatever their apprehensions about the sympathies of the locals, all initial signs promised a harmonious reception. In anticipation of the encampment, citizens festooned their homes and businesses with patriotic bunting. As the event got underway, the city's mayor, Oswald Winkler, offered the veterans a friendly welcome to Lexington. He apologized for the rough condition of the city streets but joked that the lack of civic improvement would afford the veterans a chance to relive the past. "The ruin of your shot and shell are yet to be seen," he told them, "and you should be proud of the glory of marching the same old streets and seeing the same old mud holes with here and there an old canteen to remind you of the past." Mayor Winkler noted with appreciation the names of former Confederates among the participants in the encampment program and promised that the locals would receive the GAR with nothing but hospitality and respect.[5]

With Winkler's assurance from the morning's ceremonies no doubt still ringing in their ears, the veterans assembled at 3:30 that afternoon for their parade. They marched down Main Street to the battlefield on College Hill. Along the route, however, the men encountered a provocative sight: some women defiantly flying a Confederate flag from the porch of a home. Due to the age and gender of these particular unreconstructed rebels, it is unlikely the veterans directly confronted them. Still, the episode cast enough of a pall over the GAR men to merit a departmental report that was not only recorded in their annual proceedings but printed in the local newspaper as well. According to the report,

> The boys in blue looked at [the flag] with curiosity and interest as they marched by, but not with any disposition to disturb it. With equal interest they gazed at the white haired old ladies who sat beside it, and thought of the care with which they had treasured that relic . . . so as to preserve it for exhibition forty years after its use had ceased; and they thought of the mother's love which may have been entwined with its preservation, but they thanked the God of Battles . . . that every citizen of Lexington

joined with them in loyalty to one flag and to one country, and holding themselves a little more erect they marched on with a little firmer step, and the incident closed.[6]

After running a copy of the GAR report, the *Lexington Intelligencer* concluded its coverage of the encampment, remarking without a hint of irony: "The welcome given the G. A. R. was in every respect cordial, and seemed to be received in a spirit of lively appreciation."[7]

It hardly seems likely the GAR men appreciated being taunted by a Confederate flag at the site of one of the most notorious Union defeats in the state. All things considered, however, they had little choice but to be magnanimous. The tone of the report reflected a sensitivity on the part of the GAR to the contentious atmosphere of the state and highlighted the particular tension that attended the efforts of Missouri's Unionists to commemorate the Civil War. In Missouri, embracing the Union Cause was complicated by the state's tumultuous politics and its persistent internal divisions. Clashes over memory were unavoidable in such a deeply divided state, where both Confederates and Unionists lived in close quarters. Out of necessity, Missouri's Unionists conceded space to former Confederates. In no sense, however, did they abandon the cause. Missouri's Unionists formed large, long-lived, and active societies that kept Union memory alive. Although they occasionally fraternized with their former enemies, they condemned the defeated Confederacy and fought for more widespread recognition of Missouri's contributions to the Union war effort.

In the scope of Civil War memory, the Union Cause is surprisingly problematic and elusive. Variously referred to as the "Union Cause," "Treasury of Virtue," "Cause Victorious," "Triumphant Cause," and "Won Cause," it has defied neat categorization.[8] In contrast to the Lost Cause, which evoked a romanticized memory of the Civil War embraced by white southerners, the Union Cause was much more nebulous. It had to accommodate the perspectives of antislavery Unionists, unconditional Unionists, radicals, conservatives, white Americans, African Americans, and immigrants. Race, in particular, was a critical obstacle to building a unified Union Cause. Rather than embracing African Americans as coequal citizens, Unionists, as historian David Blight argues, reconciled with former Confederates in service of the politics of white supremacy and forgot their wartime commitment to emancipation.[9] Perhaps as a result of these conflicting perspectives, Union commemoration has sometimes been characterized as "more muted," "amorphous and obscure," "less active," or "weak" compared to that of former Confederates.[10] In part this is because the history of the United States, unlike that of the Confederacy, extended beyond the Civil War era. According to historian Caroline E. Janney, "Loyalty to the Union became enveloped in the national allegiance and patriotism of all Americans, and it was all but impossible to separate the United States of 1861–65 from the United States of the 1880s or 1920s."[11] The Union survived the Civil War and went on to face further perils and win more laurels, making that conflict only a part of its unfolding national history.

Acknowledging the conflicting perspectives that marked the Union Cause, Union commemoration of the Civil War nevertheless emphasized a few key themes. First and foremost, the Union Cause upheld the preservation of the Union as the most important accomplishment of the war. It cast the war as a traitorous slaveholder's rebellion that threatened not only the United States but also the principles of republicanism more generally. Union victory saved the United States and, in so doing, ensured the survival of the great experiment in representative government won by the American Revolution and enshrined in the Constitution. The war had been a trial, but it had not derailed the unique mission of the United States to model the virtues of republican government. Second, the Union Cause celebrated the demise of slavery, if not always for the sake of enslaved people themselves. Many white Unionists regarded slavery as a destructive force, chiefly responsible for the sectional tension that produced the Civil War. Finally, with this wellspring of disunion eliminated, the Union Cause anticipated the complete reunification and reconciliation of Union and Confederate Americans.[12] According to historian Peter S. Carmichael, "Northern soldiers' strong convictions in the notion of Union as both a philosophical position and political goal would have been betrayed if they had not extended a respectful hand toward their enemies in the name of peace and reunion."[13]

As a slaveholding border state, Missouri occupied an uneasy place within the Union Cause. Unionist Missourians embraced many of its primary tenets but had a twofold task: challenging the Confederate counternarrative and trying to assert their own legitimacy within the Union. At the same time, Missouri's complicated history and complex politics threatened to undermine the principles that gave the war meaning in the minds of many northerners. For example, far from regarding slavery as a source of disunion, Missouri's conservatives viewed the Union as essential to its survival. Considering the preservation of slavery was the main impetus for the formation of the Confederacy—the very "corner-stone" on which its government was established, according to Confederate vice president Alexander H. Stephens—slaveholding gave northerners cause to doubt Missouri's loyalty.[14] Given Missouri's rogue Confederate government, representation in the Confederate Congress, and the persistence of irregular resistance, the United States believed its loyalty could only be secured through military occupation.

Slavery, however, was not the only issue that left Missourians out of step with the Union Cause, for it also hinged on the belief that Union victory accomplished an immediate reconciliation and that the Union was stronger than ever. The persistence of Confederate commemoration in Missouri revealed that the full and complete reconciliation of the nation had not yet been achieved. Even worse, the eventual return of former Confederates and Democrats to political power in Missouri suggested Union victory had been deliberately undermined. This set of circumstances led historian Aaron Astor to brand Missouri's Unionists "belated Confederates" who chose to "'forget' their whole service to the Union" and embrace the white supremacist politics of the South.[15] He writes, "They yielded public space to former Confederates and made little or no effort to present a pro-Union narrative in response."[16] Nonetheless, conservatism did not necessarily equate to Confederate sympathies. White Missourians celebrated the Union Cause but remained largely disinterested in racial equality and longed for an end to the hostilities in their state. They learned the value of moderation and embraced their legacy of compromise. It was a strategy not unlike that adopted by other conservative regions of the West.[17] Far from abandoning the Union Cause, Missouri's Unionists simply operated in a different geographic, cultural, social, and political context. Indeed, the fortunes of the Union Cause in Missouri cannot be understood apart from its politics. With Radical Republicans firmly in charge of Missouri at the end of the Civil War, it was inevitable that they would be first to shape the legacy of the war in Missouri. On the whole, however, Radicalism hampered Union commemoration in the state by alienating conservatives. Many Missourians could not endorse the agenda of the Radicals or a legacy of Union victory that seemed destined to further antagonize a badly divided people.

In order to make sense of the influence of Republican politics on Civil War commemoration, it is necessary to briefly revisit the war years. Moderation, conservatism, and compromise characterized Missouri's wartime provisional government. This remained true until late in the war. The Republicans, still under the leadership of Charles Drake, won a remarkable victory in the state elections of 1864. They attained the governor's office and swept the General Assembly, giving them complete control of Missouri's government. Flushed with success, the Radicals passed an ordinance of immediate and unconditional emancipation, effective January 11, 1865. They also drafted a new state constitution, nicknamed the Drake Constitution. As a loyal state exempt from Reconstruction, the changes the Radicals imposed in Missouri nevertheless amounted to just that. Their success, particularly in accomplishing emancipation, promised to finally align the state firmly with the Union Cause. While slaveholding had been significantly undermined by the resistance of enslaved people and by the prosecution of the war, Missourians took the unique step for a border state of abolishing the institution themselves. The Radicals could be proud that they had achieved emancipation not under force of arms but through a fair, democratic process. In so doing, they made emancipation one of the most important legacies of the Union Cause in their state.

The proposed Drake Constitution of 1865 went even further toward establishing a foundation for Union memory in Missouri. It included what became known as the Iron Clad Oath—a measure intended to disenfranchise former Confederates and southern sympathizers. The oath demanded that all voters and all persons serving in public office, including elected officials, lawyers, jurors, educators, and clergymen, swear they had never committed treason against the United States. The constitution deemed as traitors all veterans of the Confederate Army and Navy, as well as former guerrillas and anyone else who had "ever given aid, comfort, countenance, or support" to the nation's enemies. It condemned any person who "by act or word manifested his . . . sympathy with those engaged in exciting or carrying on rebellion against the United States." Anyone who failed to take the oath within sixty days would not only be banned from voting and removed from public office but might also face fines or imprisonment. Finally, the constitution barred anyone who would be unable to vote under its new provisions from voting for its ratification.[18]

Radicals defended the Drake Constitution and the Iron Clad Oath as the necessary first steps toward their goals of solidifying Missouri's place among the loyal states and securing its future prosperity within the reunited nation. By curbing the political power of former Confederates, the Radicals divested the state from the political ties it long held with the South and made an important statement. Missouri nurtured no sympathy for slaveholders or traitors to the Union. It would not cling to the antebellum order but would instead resume its place at the forefront of national expansion. "The world is attentively and anxiously observing our progress," the *Missouri State Times* advised its readers. "With a free State Constitution, and the adoption of a policy that will speedily and effectively eradicate the disloyal element from amongst us, Missouri will be regarded as the emigrant's haven of rest.

Reject the proposed Constitution and our State will be flooded with rebels, and those seeking homes in the West will shun us as a community of semi-barbarians."[19] In the aftermath of the Civil War, Missouri did indeed record a 45.6 percent population increase.[20] As many as 95 percent of the new migrants came from other Union states.[21] These demographic changes helped consolidate Republican power and further removed Missouri from the southern homogeneity of its early territorial days.

Missourians ratified the Drake Constitution by a slim majority, and it went into effect on the Fourth of July 1865. Some of the Drake Constitution's most outspoken proponents were members of the Soldiers' Leagues, the earliest Union veterans' organizations in Missouri. In order to gain support for the new constitution, the Soldiers' Leagues mobilized the memory of the late war by employing the kind of tactics that would later be described as "waving the bloody shirt." They branded their opponents "copperheads" and, according to historian William E. Parrish, "admonished the eligible soldier electorate to vote as they shot" and prevent former Confederates from returning to public office.[22] They warned that if Radicals were defeated, "The graves of our comrades, mouldering in the Southern sand, would be desecrated; the rebel soldiers would receive pensions and bounties out of the Federal treasury; the rebel debt would be paid; the Union declared bankrupt; our cripples would be outcasts; our families abandoned to the bitterest misery, and we ourselves would be insulted and ridiculed."[23] Soldiers' League gatherings infused the Union Cause with Radical politics. For example, on May 10, 1866, at a rally celebrating the anniversary of Camp Jackson, the soldiers carried a banner reading "Loyal men shall rule, not rebels."[24]

The longest-lasting and most prolific Union veterans' organization in Missouri, however, was the Grand Army of the Republic. Founded in 1866, at the height of Radical power in Missouri, the GAR was a national fraternal society for any honorably discharged Union veteran, whether white or African American. Missouri established its first chapter in 1867. First and foremost, the GAR was a social club that allowed veterans to keep alive the camaraderie of the war years. It also served as a charitable society, dedicated to assisting needy comrades—as its members called themselves—and vowing to uphold the memory of Union soldiers by ensuring dignified burials and participating in Memorial Day ceremonies.[25] Finally, the GAR acted as a political lobby; it fought for pensions and patriotic education, and advocated for political rights for African American veterans.[26]

In the first phase of the organization in Missouri, despite its claims to being nonpartisan, the GAR was overtly linked to the Radical Republican Party. According to the *Missouri Democrat*, "ninety-nine out of every hundred of the G.A.R. are staunch Republicans."[27] The GAR's association with Radicalism was troubling to many of Missouri's conservatives. While the Radicals found support during the chaos of war, peace brought a renewed desire for moderation. Just as Missourians had alike condemned northern and southern fanaticism before the war, they now drew little distinction between Radicals and unreconstructed rebels. They considered both groups as hostile to the peaceful and productive reconciliation of their state and of the nation. According to historian James N. Primm, "The *Missouri Republican* issued a bitter denunciation of the G.A.R. as a 'Praetorian Guard' which threatened to undermine the Constitution and liberties of the people."[28] On another occasion, Primm continues, "The *Republican* likened the Grand Army to the Ku Klux Klan, and on another . . . an armed band of Radicals, 'revolutionary bandits' who would start a civil war if [not] foiled in their dark plots."[29] "Far from denying such accusations," Primm argues, "the [*Missouri*] *Democrat* advertised the Grand Army as the military and vigilante wing of the Radical party."[30] The fears of Missouri's conservatives were realized when the GAR unanimously adopted a resolution offering "the services of fifty thousand Missouri Grand Army veterans 'to carry out the action of Congress'" and remove President Andrew Johnson from office.[31] By threatening Johnson, the GAR closed ranks with the Radical Republicans in Congress. This overtly political move alienated Missouri's white conservatives and precipitated the collapse of the GAR in Missouri after 1868.

Although its association with Radicalism proved the GAR's undoing, the stint of Radical dominance in which it originated had tremendous implications for the development of the Union Cause in Missouri. Emancipation, the Drake Constitution, northern emigration, and the disenfranchisement of former Confederates distanced Missouri from other former slave states. The Radicals had accomplished a self-imposed version of Reconstruction in Missouri. In so doing, they severed their state from the Solid South. As time passed, however, significant opposition to the Radical regime grew within Missouri, particularly among former Confederates and white conservatives, both of whom blamed the Radicals for stoking wartime hostilities into political capital. As much as Unionist Missourians desired to lay claim to Union victory and take part in the future growth of the reunited nation, the path charted by the Radicals was too narrow for white Missourians to walk together.

The Radicals swept the state elections again in 1868, but an opposition began to form. Carl Schurz, elected that year to the U.S. Senate, emerged as the chief challenger to Drake and his Radical regime. As a GAR member and a Republican himself, Schurz understood that wartime animosities heavily colored Missouri's political context. "Republicanism in Missouri was in one respect somewhat different from Republicanism elsewhere," he later explained. "In Missouri a large part of the population had joined the rebellion. The two parties in the Civil War had not been geographically divided. The Civil War had therefore the character of a neighborhood war—not only State against State or district against district, but house against house. . . . The bitter animosities of the civil conflict survived in Missouri much longer than in the Northern States."[32] Schurz encouraged Missourians to "endeavor to close up the distracting agitations which have sprung from our civil conflict" and believed he could help make that happen.[33] Still, he recognized that he would need the support of former Confederates.

At the 1868 national Republican convention in Chicago, Schurz introduced a resolution to modify the party platform in favor of "equal suffrage for all," including African Americans and former Confederates.[34] "We highly commend the spirit of magnanimity and forbearance with which men who have served in the rebellion . . . are received back into the communion of the loyal people," Schurz's resolution read, "and we favor the removal of the disqualifications and restrictions imposed upon the late rebels."[35] Although the convention adopted Schurz's proposal, he found his Republican colleagues unwilling to repeal the Iron Clad Oath in Missouri. To Schurz, however, it was clear the disenfranchisement of ex-Confederates served no purpose beyond keeping the Radicals in power. In an 1870 address to his fellow Missourians, Schurz asked,

> Is the peace reigning in Missouri not an undeniable fact, as clear as sunlight? Is it not the obvious interest of all classes of society in the State that odious distinctions, calculated to keep alive the heartburnings of past conflicts, should without delay be abolished? Is it not time, at last, to open to all the prospect of a common future, so that all may devote their energies to the problems we have in common to solve? . . . Is it not time for them to prove to the world that in establishing those disqualifications they were not actuated by feelings of hate or desires of revenge, but compelled by the necessities of the situation, and that after the cessation of those necessities, they are happy to show a spirit of peace and good-will to all men?[36]

In 1870, outraged by the Radicals' unflagging defense of the Iron Clad Oath, Schurz broke with his party and proclaimed himself a Liberal Republican. The central plank of the new party's platform was political equality for freed people and former Confederates alike. On behalf of the

Liberals, Schurz declared, "We desire peace and good will to all men. . . . We desire the questions connected with the Civil War to be disposed of forever, to make room as soon as possible for the new problems of the present and the future."[37] For Schurz and his growing number of followers, such a proposal did not sound a retreat from the Union Cause—it was its consummation. For the Union Cause to be well and truly won, former Confederates had to be brought back into the fold and all petty sectional jealousies forgotten. Only then would the salvation of the Union be complete.

Considering the complexities of Missouri's geographic, social, cultural, and political position, it made perfect sense that the Liberal Republican movement originated in the state. Many white Missourians regarded compromise as one of the central aspects of their identity. They believed compromise had served them well in the past and that it would secure their future. In this atmosphere, as Parrish explains, "old animosities" only "proved a hindrance to communication and a needless burden."[38] Schurz's Liberal Republican Party promised to unite white Missourians from both ends of the political spectrum and build a coalition of former conservative Unionists and Democrats. This did not mean, however, that Schurz or other Liberals intended to become Confederate apologists. "We are accused of desiring the support of Democrats," Schurz wrote. "We have abandoned no principle to secure it. . . . And if there are Democrats who . . . frankly recognize the great results of the civil war as accomplished and irreversible facts, and unite with us in promoting upon that basis the common welfare—is it not well that they should do so?"[39] In other words, he expected Democrats and former Confederates to convert to the Liberal way of thinking. Such conversion was possible, the Liberals believed, because the American spirit of liberty and individualism would triumph over special interests. The Liberals' early success in Missouri, combined with their emphasis on liberty and individualism—traits increasingly associated with the mythic West—helped cement Missouri's identity as a western state and as a place where a new, reunified national culture would take root.[40] Of course, the Liberals enjoyed a more pragmatic appeal as well. They offered white Missourians, including the Democrats, the opportunity to consolidate a majority to undermine the Radicals.[41]

Thus, white Missourians celebrated reconciliation as part of the Union Cause and embraced its practical outcomes. The Liberals hoped to secure reconciliation, but it proved perhaps more difficult than they imagined. With Schurz at their head, the Liberal Republicans consolidated their success in 1870 when Missourians elected their candidate, B. Gratz Brown, as governor and voted to repeal the Iron Clad Oath. The Liberal press celebrated the demise of the Radical faction. "Liberal men are going to rule Missouri," the *St. Louis Democrat* boasted to the Radicals, "and your part in its future is ended."[42] The success of the Liberals' third-party movement was, however, short-lived. While the Liberals won the gubernatorial contest, Democrats were gaining ground in the General Assembly. Perhaps, as author T. J. Stiles suggests, former Confederates took advantage of the idealism of the Liberals to regain their vote. That achieved, they returned to the ranks of the Democrats and worked to subvert the Radicals' legacy. With the repeal of the Iron Clad Oath, former Confederates returned to the polls in 1872 and voted the Democrats back into power.[43] Even Schurz, who had so fervently fought for the restoration of Confederates' voting rights, lost his 1874 Senate reelection campaign to Confederate veteran Francis Cockrell. Cockrell held his Senate seat for the next thirty years, and Democrats controlled state offices well into the first decade of the twentieth century.[44]

On the surface, the return of the Democrats threatened to undermine the Union Cause in Missouri. Their triumph was inescapably linked to the restoration of the political power of former Confederates, who now seemed poised to dismantle the gains of the Republican era. Indeed, Missouri's Unionists had cause to fear how Democratic hegemony might reverse their progress toward reconciliation. The *St. Louis Dispatch*, for example, issued the Republicans an unequivocal warning:

> *It is impossible . . . for the Missouri Democracy to forget within the next twenty years the remorseless persecution that was its lot from 1862 to 1870. . . .* When the millennium comes, indeed, and the lion and the lamb lie down together, the new party, born of a race that has neither wrongs to remember nor monuments to build, may come into Missouri as a plant likely to find root and growth, and bear fruit meet for the repentance of its followers. Until then, Democracy in the state will remain as now—the Gibralter of the continent.[45]

It would be too simple, however, to suggest that the success of the Democrats represented a wholesale repudiation of Missouri's wartime Unionism. In fact, Parrish notes, the Democrats "sought to keep off their ticket anyone 'who was not thoroughly identified with the Government during the rebellion.'"[46] Although the election of renowned Confederates like Cockrell and General John Sappington Marmaduke undercuts this claim, it generally holds up. For example, even though Marmaduke made no attempt to distance himself from his Confederate service during his 1885 campaign for the governorship, he strongly disavowed the claim that he was still a "rebel."[47]

Marmaduke proclaimed that he "never waved the bloody shirt" in his pursuit of political office and vowed "to take care of all the interests of the people of Missouri, both republican and democrat, white and black."[48] According to the *Butler Weekly Times*, "All veteran soldiers know the difference between war and peace, but few, however, better than General Marmaduke. Since the late conflict ended few men, of either army, have done more than he to establish permanent and lasting reconciliations."[49] Marmaduke's moderate approach was in keeping with the temperature of Missouri politics. Of the first six Democrats elected governor after the Civil War, one had adamantly opposed secession, two were Union veterans, and another served in the pro-Union Missouri State Militia (MSM). Although postwar party politics in Missouri, as elsewhere, were aligned with wartime allegiances, Democrats did not dismantle the legacy of the Union Cause in Missouri. Many had been Unionists and remained committed to moderation, in opposition to the antagonistic practices of the Radicals.[50]

Nevertheless, Republicans at the local and national levels lamented the loss of Missouri, taking up the refrain of "Poor Old Missouri" in the press. It was a call-back to wartime questions about Missouri's loyalty and cast doubts upon its commitment to the Union Cause. Here was a loyal state with self-defeating tendencies—chief among them a refusal to follow the party line. Throughout the late 1880s, any time the failings of Democratic rule were contemplated—when a new saloon was built, when public education stagnated, or when the mosquitoes were particularly noxious—Republican papers reported it to the tune of "Poor Old Missouri." "It has been called 'Poor Old Missouri' so long," the *Butler Weekly Times* complained, "that it is not easy to convince people that we have here one of the greatest states in the Union."[51] Indeed, the epithet tarnished Missouri's national reputation. For example, the *Omaha Daily Bee* warned that "although the state has excellent resources and natural advantages, the quality of its population does not seem to be up to the standard of modern civilization."[52] Many Missourians bristled at the slander and blamed the Republican press for the problem. As the *Chariton Courier* put it:

> For many years the *Globe-Democrat* . . . has cried "poor old Missouri" until it has actually succeeded in giving the state a bad name all over the country. As law abiding as any commonwealth in the Union, strangers have been afraid to pass through "poor old Missouri" lest they be robbed, or shot down, or both. . . . It would seem that considerations of home pride would have inspired a big newspaper to efforts in behalf of its own state, especially

> when that state was absolutely the best field for the investment of capital, affording the best homes for immigrants, settled already by the best people and enjoying the best government to be found anywhere in the far West.[53]

Contrary to popular imagination, they argued, "there is no more law-abiding, religious, peace-loving people in all the land."[54] Just as they had during the 1860s, white Missourians found themselves on the defensive, asserting their loyalty in the face of local opposition and national skepticism.

Rather than derailing Union commemoration in Missouri, however, the resurgence of the Democrats coincided with its heyday. Missouri's Unionists remained committed to preserving the memory of the Union Cause, even in the face of persistent challenges. In 1879, the GAR reorganized in St. Louis.[55] But the GAR's earlier association with Radicalism initially made recruitment difficult. According to Department Commander William Warner, in 1881 the organization claimed 9 posts and 596 members. By June 1882, it had 14 posts and 777 members—only 181 new members in a year. "This, I confess, was a poor showing for the great state of Missouri," Warner observed.[56] Warner felt that in order for the department to grow, it would have to distance itself from Radicalism. "There seemed to be a feeling that the organization was, in some way, political in its tendencies," he noted. In response, he ordered the printing of circulars which explained the GAR's commitment to nonpartisanship. Warner also stressed the "spirit of soldierly fraternity and charity," which guided the society's efforts, aligning it more firmly with the conciliatory, reconciliationist bent of the Union Cause in Missouri. To further its appeal and in a clear break from Radicalism, Warner promised the GAR's fraternalism even extended to former Confederates. "We clasp hands with those who wore the grey across the grave of the buried rebellion," he said, "that while we cherish the memories of the past, it is not that these memories may be an element of discord, but on the contrary, that they may be 'an ever-living influence for good in all our hearts.'"[57]

This emphasis on fraternalism and bipartisanship was not unique to the Department of Missouri but reflected the principles of the national organization more generally.[58] Still, it had particular relevance in Missouri. Departmental leadership waited to see if their new tactics would pay off. "For months it seemed to be a struggle for existence," one veteran remembered, "a fight to dispel prejudice as to its objects and purposes, many associating it with . . . an earlier organization of the Grand Army of the Republic in this state, which stranded upon the tempestuous shores of politics."[59] "Missouri was slow to appreciate the importance and advantages of a union of its veterans in a fraternal society," Department Commander Leo Rassieur later confessed, "but when her citizens fully recognized the merits of the organization, they took upon themselves the duty of placing their Department where their State stood during the War of the Rebellion, among the first upon the list of the faithful, strong and reliable."[60]

This turn from Radicalism to moderation boosted GAR membership across the country and in Missouri as well. By 1883, the enrollment of the Department of Missouri reached 2,594. Among the border states, Missouri enjoyed the best representation in the GAR. The Department of Maryland was the next largest with 1,984 members, while the Department of Kentucky claimed only 520.[61] Comrade Egbert E. Kimball proudly proclaimed, "The Grand Army . . . has now entered upon an era when it needs no excuse for its existence, or apology of any sort. We need no longer to stand before the people with tears in our eyes, and our hands upon our hearts, to convince them that our purpose is a peaceful one."[62] "There were 'doubting Thomases' there," Warner recalled, "there were some weak-kneed representatives that thought that the Grand Army of the Republic would not flourish and prosper upon the soil of Missouri; I believed then to the contrary, and what I expected then has been more than realized by the years that have passed."[63]

Figure 1. Members of the Department of Missouri Grand Army of the Republic and the Modern Woodmen of America gathered for Memorial Day, Boonville, May 30, 1900. Courtesy of Charles van Ravensway Photograph Collection (P0014). 000708. The State Historical Society of Missouri, Photograph Collection

Confident in the strength of Missouri's Unionism, the GAR anticipated reaching still greater heights. "Let the good work go forward," one officer encouraged his comrades, "and let us not relax our efforts until every worthy honorably discharged Union soldier in the State is enrolled in the ranks of the Grand Army of the Republic."[64] By 1891, the Department of Missouri reached its peak strength with 21,028 members in 437 posts located all across the state—including Little Dixie. Even considering that Missouri had a larger overall population, the representation of the other border states in the GAR paled in comparison. In that year the Department of Kentucky, the second largest border state organization, had only 5,789 members.[65] The strength of Missouri's numbers also contributed to the election of three Missourians to the rank of national commander in chief of the GAR, namely William Warner, Leo Rassieur, and Charles Germman Burton.

Another testament to the strength of Missouri's Unionism was the organization of two local women's auxiliaries to the GAR, the Ladies of the Grand Army of the Republic (LGAR) and the Woman's Relief Corps (WRC). Although the rosters of the two societies often overlapped, membership in the LGAR only extended to blood relatives of GAR men and it was generally less active. The Department of Missouri WRC organized in 1885 and acted as the official auxiliary of the GAR. The WRC admitted army nurses and all loyal women, including African Americans, whether or not they claimed relatives in the GAR. Compared to the GAR, the WRC remained small with a peak enrollment of 2,244 in April 1893.[66] Still, the WRC's Department of Missouri was larger than any of the organizations in its fellow border states. Maryland, for example, had the next largest membership with only 683. Kentucky, whose total population more closely approximated Missouri's, had 505 members.[67]

In Missouri and across the country, the WRC vowed to support the GAR, honor the Union dead, and provide aid to needy Union veterans as well as their widows and orphans.[68] Although they were an auxiliary society committed to honoring the wartime service of men, the WRC also operated as a women's organization *for* women. Among their achievements, the WRC believed they had "contributed largely in making this a Woman's Age, an age in which woman, in her proper sphere, extends to the old, respect and gratitude; to the young, encouragement and sympathy."[69] The WRC embodied the ethos of the clubwoman movement of the late nineteenth century. In the decades before the United States enacted woman's suffrage, organizations like the WRC allowed women the opportunity to practice civic engagement, usually directed at social welfare efforts. The WRC, for example, took a leading role in establishing veterans homes—including the Missouri Federal Soldiers' Home.

While the organization of the Department of Missouri GAR and WRC provided a strong foundation for Union commemoration in the state, a combination of local and national problems presented challenges to their work on behalf of the Union Cause. Although the Department of Missouri GAR enjoyed extensive membership, it still represented only a fraction of the eligible Union veterans in the state. Even more troubling, the membership declined every year after 1891. "Why our Department should run from fourteen to fifteen thousand when we ought to have from twenty-five to thirty thousand," Department Commander John P. Platt mused in 1898, "is the question which . . . I have tried to solve."[70] A number of different issues no doubt frustrated their recruitment and retention efforts, including the 1897 depression. The economic crisis hit rural Americans hardest, so few Missourians had the extra money to pay organizational dues or travel to reunions. "Hard times and scarcity of money may account for a part of the loss," Department Commander Thomas B. Rodgers acknowledged, "but the main cause may be found in the increasing age and infirmities of the comrades, many of whom find it difficult to keep up their interest in the Order by attending Post meetings and thus become suspended."[71]

Missouri's divided loyalties presented another complication. In Missouri, it was not always clear which Union veterans were eligible for membership in the GAR. This was particularly problematic for veterans of the Unionist state militias, which included the MSM, Enrolled Missouri Militia, Home Guards, Provisional Militia, and the Paw Paw Militia. Under the rules of the GAR, veterans of state regiments were only eligible if they served under U.S. officers and had never taken up arms against the government.[72] Because the Missouri provisional government conscripted many men into the militia, not to mention that the Paw Paw Militia recruited their men from the ranks of paroled Confederates, many regarded the loyalty of the militia as suspect. Department Commander Nelson Cole recognized this difficulty. He explained that Missouri was

> different from any other Department, having been a battle ground, in many localities equally divided, where of necessity all bore arms, and while many who were in these organizations, and who wore the blue, had little or no sympathy for our cause, but sought them either from policy or because they were compelled to espouse one side or the other, still others entered

> this service through pure love of country and a feeling of loyalty which we should recognize. . . . While many of those who composed these organizations, . . . are entitled to membership, many others are not.[73]

The complicated wartime dynamics of the border state made it difficult, more difficult than in other Union states, to determine the loyalty of its veterans.

The GAR did, however, extend membership to African American veterans. This no doubt helps explain the difficulty the GAR initially had in convincing Missourians that their organization was strictly nonpartisan. The presence of African American veterans within the ranks of the GAR only confirmed the suspicions of conservative white Missourians that the GAR was little more than an extension of the Republican Party. While there was internal opposition to African American membership, specifically to the integration of posts, the GAR was nevertheless one of the few societies in the late nineteenth century where white and black Americans met on terms of relative equality.[74] All told, there were at least eight all-black and four integrated posts in Missouri, but according to historian Barbara Gannon, the majority of chapters in Missouri did not report black members.[75] Nevertheless, their presence to any degree was yet a further indication of the refusal of Unionist Missourians to "forget" the importance of emancipation or of African American military service to the legacy of Union victory.[76]

Among the complications the GAR encountered while recruiting in Missouri was the omnipresence of former Confederates. As a result of Unionists' encounters with disloyal Missourians, they thought of themselves as outnumbered and, occasionally, as occupying dangerous ground. "It took courage to stand up for Old Glory in Missouri in the years of the war," A. N. Seaber reminded his GAR comrades. "With neighbors and friends going the other way; with danger of fire and sword if he stood by his colors, it took a tried and true man to stay with us."[77] Even decades after the war's end, GAR commander in chief Thomas G. Lawler acknowledged, "It costs more . . . here in Missouri, . . . to be a member of the Grand Army of the Republic than it does in . . . States differently situated."[78] The reality that not all Missourians embraced the Union, and indeed that some willingly joined Confederates in seeking to dismantle it, remained a fresh and painful memory. At a 1911 meeting of St. Louis's Ransom Post, one of the largest GAR organizations in the state, comrades gave short speeches on the fiftieth anniversary of the mustering of Missouri's first Union troops. This prompted Comrade H. W. Beermann to recall "the danger which had to be faced . . . by any one who appeared to be of German extraction, and presumably of Union sentiments" at the outbreak of the war. Two other men agreed that in the dark days of 1861, being a Unionist "wasn't a talking matter."[79]

To some degree, the GAR felt this hostility survived the war and that it posed the most serious challenge to their organization. "Grand Army men are accustomed to all sorts of sneers and abuse," Comrade John T. Clarke remarked, "but they can congratulate themselves that they suffer no greater calumny now than did loyal Missourians in 1861."[80] As Missourian and GAR commander in chief Charles Germman Burton explained,

> Ours is a peculiar Department. . . . The people of Missouri were divided. . . . Battles not a few, and lesser conflicts innumerable, were fought upon her soil. Guerilla warfare was waged, and many acts of robbery, rapine and murder were committed, . . . leaving in their wake feelings of discord and hate not to be eliminated during this or a succeeding generation. Amid such an environment was organized and has been maintained the Department of Missouri.[81]

Operating within such a divided state, the GAR was hardly unaware that not all Missourians were friendly to their efforts. Despite the GAR's promise to treat former Confederates in the spirit of fraternalism, bitterness remained. In choosing locations for their annual encampment, for example, comrades sometimes voted on the basis of how loyal that particular locale had been during the war. Some believed the GAR had a responsibility to act as missionaries of the Union Cause in less hospitable portions of the state. For example, at the 1901 departmental encampment a debate arose over whether to hold the next gathering in Jefferson City, a bastion of conservative Unionism, or in Cape Girardeau, a southeastern Mississippi River town. Cape Girardeau held one of the highest enslaved populations outside of Little Dixie before the Civil War and had a reputation for Confederate sympathies. "We may be able to reform them down there," one comrade offered optimistically.[82] Cape Girardeau carried the vote.

Because of their awareness of the persistence of Confederate feelings in Missouri, as well as the importance of reconciliation to the Union Cause, Unionists made earnest, if strained, overtures of friendship to their former enemies, who were often present to one degree or another at one another's events. Humor, even of a pointed kind, often helped to ease the tension. During a GAR encampment in Hannibal, for instance, Department Commander Louis Benecke expressed gratitude for the kind welcome shown by the city, acknowledging that Union men had not always been so well-received there. "Some thirty-four years or thirty-five years ago a regiment entered your city without any special invitation," he joked. "Today we are here without sword, but we have the olive branch of peace for all citizens; to every one, though he may have been on the opposite side to us during the time that the fierce struggle was going on."[83] In St. Louis, the Ransom Post GAR often entertained visits from their neighbors in the St. Louis Camp of United Confederate Veterans (UCV)—after first having them ceremonially arrested. Following a campfire celebrating the twenty-eighth anniversary of its post, for example, the Ransom Post circular noted the attendance of four Confederate veterans who "contributed notably to the pleasure by allowing themselves to be captured at the outpost."[84] During another meeting of the Ransom Post, a circular reported, Confederate veteran "Captain [Louis] Flat[e]au of the Confederate Camp was around the hall some place and was arrested . . . and brought before the Post and sentenced to make a speech, and you bet he made a good one, as he always does, and it was chock full of patriotism."[85] Flateau, a familiar face at gatherings of the Ransom Post, demonstrated that fraternization was easier to extend on an individual basis and along the lines of personal friendships. In 1917, the Ransom Post went so far as to pass a resolution endorsing Flateau for a federal job. It read, "We know that if the Secretary of War gives him an opportunity to serve our Country in defense of the flag, he will fight as hard and as faithfully for it now, as he once fought against it in fidelity to his principles and the Confederacy."[86] Still, there were limits to fraternization. In April 1915, the comrades of the Ransom Post planned a celebration for the fiftieth anniversary of the Confederate surrender at Appomattox. They dispatched invitations to the WRC, the Sons of Union Veterans, Spanish War veterans, the army officers at nearby Jefferson Barracks, the National Guard, and city and state government officials—in short, invitations went to virtually everyone but the ex-Confederates.[87]

There is very little evidence that Union and Confederate women fraternized even to this extent. As was true for the veterans, Union and Confederate women likely found it equally difficult to completely avoid one another. In an intriguing address before the 1903 state WRC convention, the Honorable William G. Pendleton, mayor of Boonville, suggested there were southern women within the WRC. He considered this a great testament to the success of reconciliation. "While the Woman's Relief Corps . . . perpetuate the memory of the achievements of one side only in a civil strife (rightly and necessarily so in view of the result)," Pendleton observed, "yet so complete and so sincere is the reconciliation of the people . . . that leading Southern women of this city are members of the local corps." While it is certainly conceivable that in a Little Dixie city like Boonville the ranks of the WRC contained women who had been southern-born Unionists, Pendleton seemed to believe they were actually former Confederates. While he congratulated the WRC on its inclusivity, he concluded with a plea for the organization to treat such women with kindness and sensitivity. "Permit me to gently remind you that these, your sisters of the south, had more to overcome in reaching this state of reconciliation than even you yourselves had," he said. "It is easier for the victor than for the defeated to forget and forgive. . . . You will be careful, then, I believe, not to causelessly wound their feelings."[88] Whether or not they risked wounding the feelings of some fellow members or their Confederate neighbors, the women of the Department of Missouri WRC devoted themselves to Union memory. They privileged the care of needy Union men and women, marking them as especially deserving of attention, and challenged Confederate commemoration in the process.

The reality was that in Missouri wounded feelings were impossible to avoid. Neither proximity nor fraternization bred sympathy enough to dissolve wartime allegiances. Unionists refused to yield Civil War commemoration to the Confederates. The Missourians present at the 1882 meeting of Union veterans of the Society of the Army of the Tennessee—an officers-only association—made this quite evident. Held in conjunction with the anniversary of the capture of Camp Jackson, always a significant occasion for Missouri's Unionists, it was a perfect opportunity to demonstrate the strength of Union memory in Missouri. In the course of the proceedings, former governor Thomas C. Fletcher remarked, "You know in this region of the country—I don't know that it is so everywhere else—but here there is a powerful disposition on the part of a great many people to insist that all the memories of the war ought to be buried. Now, if some of us have the same kind of memories that they have I think so too." At this, the veterans enjoyed a good laugh. "We will . . . help them to bury all the errors and mistakes committed in times gone by," Fletcher continued, "but they have no right to ask us to accompany them as chief mourners in weeping over it."[89] Again, the veterans received Fletcher's words with laughter. In a similar vein, at the 1894 encampment of the Department of Missouri GAR, WRC member Hollen E. Day begged the veterans: "As long as any loyal man lives in this country do not let him glorify the deeds and the fighting of the rebels." The men rewarded her plea with a round of applause.[90] In 1908, Thomas Dudley Kimball, department commander, expressed approval of the camaraderie between Union and Confederate veterans but warned his comrades they were "not yet relieved of duty." "As long as there are men who would dedicate public school buildings to the Commanding General of the Rebel Army, and as long as there are women who would erect monuments to the keeper of Andersonville . . . so long must we guard the picket line, halt all who approach and demand the Union countersign."[91]

Indeed, while the Department of Missouri GAR took the high road after being confronted with a Confederate flag at their 1904 encampment in Lexington, they far more consistently disavowed Confederate symbolism. The Justi Post of Cape Girardeau condemned the Confederate flag in particular, calling it "in bad taste and . . . an insult to the G.A.R."[92] In 1892, the Ransom Post submitted resolutions to the departmental encampment declaring the Confederate flag an "emblem of treason and rebellion." "To publicly display the Rebel flag," the resolutions read, "may well be regarded . . . as a public insult to every patriotic son and daughter of the Republic."[93] For those who claimed the Confederate flag served "'as a sweet memory' or 'as a sad reminder,'" the resolution insisted, "It can never be a 'sweet memory' to the survivors, nor to the friends of the non-survivors of those in Blue who beheld it floating over Libby Prison, or beheld it gloating over the horrors of Andersonville, nor to the patriotic people of this great nation that made such terrible sacrifices in blood and treasure that this 'sweet memory' might be swept from the face of the earth." Although the GAR men frequently acknowledged the bravery of Confederate soldiers and desired peaceful reconciliation, the resolution insisted that "there can be no reconciliation between the antagonistic and irreconcilable principles for which they, respectively fought—the one side triumphant and eternally right; the other defeated and eternally wrong." As a result, any resurrection of the Confederate flag was necessarily in "bad faith or bad taste."[94]

Such strong condemnations of Confederate commemoration were particularly important for Missouri's white Unionists. Between questions surrounding their wartime loyalties and the postwar resurgence of the Democratic Party, many northerners considered "Poor Old Missouri" a southern state. The Department of Missouri believed that the state's conflicted identity was chiefly responsible for this popular misconception. Missouri was, after all, as one member admitted, "a border State rent asunder by internal dissentions, brother arrayed against brother, father against son—often meeting in deadly conflict—with a traitor for Governor, and with treason rampant throughout the length and breadth of our State."[95] In light of the subsequent political history of the state, however, her loyalty had once again come under renewed scrutiny. The exploits of Missouri's outlaws, such as the James Gang, did nothing to help its tarnished reputation. Comrade David Murphy viewed it as the particular responsibility of the Department of Missouri to change people's minds. "If it becomes necessary to save the good name of our State," Murphy vowed, "the soldiers of 1861 and 1865 will come forward and stand by law and authority as firmly and unflinchingly as they did during the dark days of war." Murphy advised his comrades that Missouri's place in the Union Cause hinged on their actions. In 1882, he said, "Bringing down the memories of the war let us conduct ourselves in a manner to be worthy of the deeds of the glorious past. Let us so carry ourselves that our personal conduct may speak for us; . . . and that although Missouri, which has gone somewhat awry and strayed from the great encampment of States, may be brought into line in the forward march of progress, and her good name be once more redeemed."[96]

Leo Rassieur expressed a similar feeling at the 1890 departmental encampment. "We want to go forward and place this State as high in the estimation of citizens elsewhere as it is in our own estimation," he said. "We want to . . . dispel from the minds of our Eastern friends the idea . . . that we are merely 'bushwhackers.' I don't think they fully understand our position to-day, and when they see the kind of men we have in the Grand Army of Missouri, I think, from that time on, the grand State of Missouri will be more respected, and we will hear no more of 'poor old Missouri.'"[97]

In order to further their goal of redeeming themselves, Unionists celebrated a set of nationally renowned Union leaders who embodied Missouri's loyalty and strengthened the state's reputation within the GAR. They were especially proud of Francis P. Blair, Jr.; Nathaniel Lyon; and Ulysses S. Grant. None of these men, however, quite merited the esteem with which Unionists regarded William Tecumseh Sherman.[98] By making Missouri his adopted state, Sherman did more to legitimize Missouri's Union Cause than any other public figure. Although the general later moved to New York, he maintained his membership in the Department of Missouri and, upon his death, requested to be buried with his family in St. Louis. According to Delos R. Haynes of the Ransom Post, "General Sherman was a member of our military family. We have received no such recognition from any other source. . . . That makes our relationship stronger than existed with any other character of the whole war."[99] The Department of Missouri never failed to express its gratitude for Sherman's important association with its organization.

Indeed, it was largely due to Sherman's efforts that the Department of Missouri secured St. Louis as the site for the 1887 national GAR encampment—a critical victory in Missourians' pursuit of legitimacy within the GAR. In nominating the city, Sherman said, "St. Louis appears to be the great central city of our continent, and I assure you that from personal residence there through nearly thirty years there are no better people on the face of the globe. . . . St. Louis is now a loyal city, . . . and therefore St. Louis offers you the welcome to which you are entitled."[100] Despite Sherman's endorsement, however, the news that St. Louis would host was not met with enthusiasm in other departments of the GAR, especially when stories spread that crowds in St. Louis "hissed and hooted" at a band playing the national anthem.[101] Even the *St. Louis Post-Dispatch* seemed to suggest the city was not an obvious choice for the encampment. St. Louis, the paper reported, was "a city largely populated by men whose arms were raised against the cause for which they fought."[102] "When it was determined . . . that the next Encampment would be held at St. Louis," Department Commander Egbert E. Kimball remembered, "a feeling was freely expressed that the Grand Army would not be received with . . . hospitality. . . . It was feared that the experiment of holding our great Reunion in a city, where the ex-confederate element was so pronounced and strong, would be, at least, hazardous; that something might occur to cause the old feelings of bitterness to break out afresh."[103]

Skepticism about the suitability of St. Louis mounted when President Grover Cleveland declined an invitation to attend the encampment after "certain important members of the Grand Army of the Republic" persuaded him he "would be an unwelcome guest" in St. Louis.[104] Apparently, however, this had more to do with Cleveland's unpopularity within the GAR than with any fear that Missourians cherished particular resentment toward the federal government. During the Civil War, Cleveland had avoided conscription into the Union Army by hiring a substitute and was the first Democrat to serve as president since Reconstruction. He also appointed former Confederates to federal office, even to his cabinet, including Lucius Quintus Cincinnatus Lamar, II, author of Mississippi's secession ordinance. That same year, Cleveland vetoed the Dependent and Disability Pension Act, rousing the animosity of the GAR.[105] Still, Cleveland blamed his concern with visiting St. Louis on Missouri's checkered past. This was to be the first national encampment held "in a Southern state," and Cleveland feared "that the least discord . . . might retard the progress of the sentiment of common brotherhood which the Grand Army of the Republic has so good an opportunity to increase and foster."[106] Feeling not a little humiliated, St. Louis mayor David R. Francis assembled a committee of delegates from across the state and dispatched them to Washington, DC, to make a final appeal to Cleveland on behalf of Missouri.[107] While the president still refused to attend the encampment, he agreed to visit St. Louis as soon as it concluded as a part of a larger national tour.[108]

Not easily discouraged, the Department of Missouri still looked forward to the encampment as an opportunity to change their comrades' minds about "Poor Old Missouri." They expected eighty thousand Union veterans to attend. "Let us give our comrades form the older and larger Departments such a welcome to Missouri that it will forever set the stamp of falsehood on the malicious slanders which have been spread . . . throughout the entire country," Department Commander Nelson Cole urged.[109] Still, the Missourians evidently felt a need to explain themselves and their divisive history to their northern comrades. The event program provided a brief history of the Civil War, including a primer on Missouri history, and proclaimed, "Those who lived at the North often fail to realize the bitterness of the struggle in the border States. . . . The conflicts within the borders of Missouri were among the most sanguinary of the entire struggle." With the passage of time, the program insisted that Missouri's divisions had healed, leaving in their wake a "profound thankfulness that the Nation was preserved by the soldiers of the Union."[110] True to this promise, the encampment closed without any noteworthy clashes between Unionists and Confederates. Reflecting on the skepticism so many had voiced upon the selection of St. Louis as the site for the encampment, Egbert E. Kimball reflected, "I am glad to say that these feelings and fears were not entertained by Comrades in this Department. We had a better knowledge of the disposition and temper of the citizens of St. Louis. . . . Not a word was said nor a symbol exhibited calculated to offend any one."[111]

The Department of Missouri celebrated its strong showing at the 1887 national encampment but refused to rest on its laurels. "Our State may, in the dim past, have been properly termed 'Poor Old Missouri,'" Rassieur conceded, "but the time has come when this border slave State of *ante-bellum* days will be conceded, in the Grand Army of the Republic at least, to have fairly earned the proud designation of 'Grand Old Missouri.'"[112] In a speech before the GAR at Warrensburg in 1893, Captain George S. Grover dismantled the "Poor Old Missouri" myth point by point. Detailing the Civil War history of Missouri, Grover began by citing the state convention of 1861 and its utter disavowal of secession. With the traitorous Claiborne Fox Jackson in exile, the provisional government led by Hamilton Gamble "was as steadfastly devoted to the government of the United States as any corresponding body in the North." Missouri fulfilled her full quota of troops to the Union Army and endured far more fighting than any other Union state.[113] Grover did not fail to acknowledge the Confederate element in the state, but he made it clear that it was far more circumscribed than outsiders realized. While the Confederates enjoyed support in the Mississippi Delta counties and throughout Little Dixie, he insisted that "the great heart of her people beat as firmly for the cause of the Union as it did in similar communities in any of the northern states." He concluded by taking a decisive stand:

> any claim now made by any one, . . . that Missouri ever belonged in sentiment to the South is an unmerited slander, promulgated only by those who are . . . densely ignorant of the glorious history of our great commonwealth. "Poor Old Missouri" she is not and never was. Union Missouri she was, is and always will be. Brave Old Missouri she was in her heroic past. Great Old Missouri she is in her boundless present, and Rich Old Missouri she will be, as I fully believe, in her transcendent future.[114]

Grover's impassioned defense of the Department of Missouri spoke to its members' conviction that their northern compatriots misunderstood them and that their negative reputation was totally undeserved.

As a means of further debunking the disloyalty of their state, members of the Department of Missouri took great pride in its representation at national GAR encampments. Those meetings provided an opportunity to showcase the strength and vitality of Missouri's local societies on the national stage. "Such public demonstrations," one departmental order read, "tend to remove all improper and unfounded unfavorable impressions regarding the people of this State."[115] The WRC expressed a similar opinion and often measured its success by the standards set by other organizations. At the 1896 National WRC Convention in St. Paul, Minnesota, member Julia E. Dockery observed, "I may say without boasting, Missouri's representation was equal to the average." She went on to note with pride that a Missourian received a nomination for the national president of the WRC. In her report back to the Department of Missouri, Dockery reflected with satisfaction over how far the border state had come from the "dark days" of the war.[116] Mattie E. Rich, attending the national WRC convention in 1903, reported to her department: "How does Missouri compare with other States? . . . It was a *grand* assembly of women from all *over* the United States, and Mrs. President, I felt that your heart must swell with pride when you realized that your delegation from Missouri, a border state, compared so favorably with other States."[117] Missouri did enjoy strong representation in the national organizations of the GAR and the WRC—particularly among the border states—and yet suspicion quite unfairly dogged the department. Acutely aware of this problem, Missouri's Union men and women directed pointed efforts at confronting it. Still, they could never entirely dislodge the stigma of their imperfect loyalty.

The efforts of Missouri's white Unionists to commemorate the Civil War expose persistent misunderstandings about the Union Cause in general and Missouri's Union Cause in particular. Missouri's Unionists were consistently active and maintained the Union Cause in the face of local opposition and national skepticism. While other northerners dismissed "Poor Old Missouri," Missouri's Unionists never accepted that narrative. They celebrated the preservation of the Union and worked hard to commemorate the war in a way that reflected their experiences. In so doing, Union veterans in particular favored a conservative approach, allowing them to bridge wartime hostilities and partisan divides. They looked forward to reconciliation and even permitted fraternization with Confederates—in part because it was impossible to avoid. At no point, however, did Missouri's Unionists relinquish their particular memories of the war. While they called attention to Missouri's difficult position as a border state and mourned its accession to Democratic rule, they accentuated its contributions to Union victory and sought the approbation of their northern comrades. Although they never seemed satisfied that their work was complete, they nevertheless distinguished Missouri's place not only as the most loyal of the border states but as a Union state in its own right.

THREE

"No Longer Cowed"

African American Missourians and the Emancipation Cause

> **We are no longer cowed beneath the name of chattels and of brutes, but we own ourselves, our families and our homes, and as men demand that this freedom shall bear the spirit as well as the form . . . that the skeleton of liberty may be clothed with flesh and blood.**
>
> —"An Address by the Colored People of Missouri to the Friends of Equal Rights," St. Louis, October 12, 1865

DECIDING ON THE LOCATION FOR the annual encampment of the Department of Missouri Grand Army of the Republic (GAR) often produced good-natured debate among the men. Local pride and the prospect of stimulating business all meant comrades hoped their own home towns would be picked. The ease of rail access, availability of lodgings, and quality of the cuisine and beer were important points of contention. In Missouri, the perceived loyalty of the area was also a significant consideration. During the 1898 encampment of the Department of Missouri, a debate typical of the border state arose. One white delegate suggested the next encampment be held in Carthage, in the southwestern corner of the state. Another proposed Hannibal, in the northeast. The ensuing debate revealed the complex political and racial dynamics that plagued Civil War commemoration in Missouri.

Initially, African American comrade George W. Edwards, representing the all-black Robert Gould Shaw Post of St. Louis, listened quietly as the debate unfolded.[1] Hannibal, a quintessential Mississippi River town made famous by its association with author Mark Twain, would have made a good choice. It had hosted the state encampment in 1896 to great success. It was also an easy train ride from St. Louis, home of the largest and most active GAR posts—including Edwards's own Shaw Post. Hannibal boasted a sizable and prosperous African American community, supporting several black businesses, two black schools, and numerous black societies, including the Colonel Brooks Post, GAR, and Corps No. 21 of the Woman's Relief

Corps (WRC).[2] In light of the recent U.S. Supreme Court ruling in *Plessy v. Ferguson*, which sanctioned racial segregation, this must have appealed to Edwards. In Hannibal, Edwards and his black comrades could be assured that even with segregation in force, there were locals who would accommodate them.

Carthage, on the other hand, had seemingly little to commend it to Union men in general and even less to African American men. Jasper County, of which Carthage is the seat, lies along Missouri's western border with Kansas. It was known for its wartime Confederate sympathies and active guerrilla bands. It was also the site of the 1861 Battle of Carthage, where federal troops commanded by General Franz Sigel, despite superior numbers, were routed by the Missouri State Guard under the leadership of Missouri's Confederate triumvirate: Claiborne Fox Jackson, Sterling Price, and Jo Shelby. In short, as far as Unionists were concerned, Carthage was Confederate country. As the GAR continued its debate over the location for the encampment, a white delegate from southwestern Missouri reassured his comrades that an infusion of "Yankee pluck" had transformed Carthage in the aftermath of the war and that his comrades would find the city friendly and convenient.[3]

The local amenities, however, did little to persuade Edwards. He doubted whether he and other African American members of the Department of Missouri would find Carthage welcoming. "I must say that in Hannibal I was better taken care of than at any other place," he interjected. "I had money in my pocket to pay for what I got, but the people made me keep it. We colored comrades take money enough to pay for everything we eat, and I don't want to go down into the Southern country and starve to death with money in my pocket." For Edwards, any hostility he might encounter as a Union veteran in the divisive atmosphere of postwar Missouri was compounded by the very real prospect of racial discrimination and violence. Speaking in defense of Carthage, white comrade George C. Howenstein promised Edwards, "We are as patriotic, and have as much love for the old colored soldiers as they have in any other section of the State. . . . I can assure the colored comrades that they will be treated just as well as though they were white."[4] Carthage won the vote. Ultimately, Edwards and at least five other African American comrades attended the encampment, but if they met with any ill-treatment, the Department of Missouri kept no record of it.[5]

In the full scope of the published proceedings of the Department of Missouri, the fleeting exchange between Edwards and Howenstein was one of only a few places where the participation of black comrades in the GAR is documented. This illuminates the difficult position black Missourians found themselves in within the realm of Civil War commemoration. While they shared in the remembrance of the Union Cause, African American veterans encountered marginalization and discrimination from white Missourians, Unionists and former Confederates alike. Nevertheless, African American veterans worked together and in cooperation with Missouri's black communities to articulate what the Civil War meant to them. Rather than becoming mired in an effort to contextualize Missouri's complicated relationship to the Civil War, as white Unionists did, African American Missourians employed Civil War commemoration in the service of mutual aid and racial uplift. In the process, they inaugurated the long struggle for civil rights in Missouri, fighting for political equality, access to education, and race pride—as manifested through Emancipation Day celebrations. Sometimes these goals could be served through cooperation with the GAR and with other white Missourians, but more often they were accomplished through the efforts of all-black organizations and black communities as they drew on their Civil War history to lay claim to a better future.

African American Missourians viewed their efforts on behalf of racial uplift as the fulfillment of the Emancipation Cause, a memory of the Civil War that placed the institution of slavery at the heart of the conflict. While emancipation featured in the Union Cause as well, resulting in some overlap in the memories of white and black Unionists, the Emancipation Cause reflected a particular perspective. African Americans certainly celebrated the preservation of the Union and embraced its founding principles of freedom and equality, but they primarily remembered the Civil War as a war of liberation. As a result, the Emancipation Cause foregrounded the experiences of African Americans. Commemoration of the Emancipation Cause emphasized the brutality and oppression of slavery, belying the popular perception among many white Americans of a benevolent, paternalistic institution. It also stressed the resiliency of African American people as well as their potential for citizenship. Finally, it triumphed in the patriotism and service of black soldiers, who not only achieved the emancipation of more than four million enslaved individuals but also forged a path for the entrance of African Americans into the rights and privileges of a free society.[6]

Historians have persuasively demonstrated that Civil War commemoration privileged the memories of white Americans.[7] In Missouri, this problem was particularly pronounced, in part because of the small number of African American veterans in the state but also because of the overall complications posed by its geography and politics, the same complications that sometimes hampered the efforts of white Missourians to celebrate the Union Cause. As a border state, slaveholding was vital to the culture, economy, and politics of antebellum Missouri. In the aftermath of the Civil War, historians claim, Missouri's deeply seated white supremacy led white Unionists to embrace the pro-Confederate, Lost Cause memory of the war.[8] While the Lost Cause certainly exerted influence over Missouri, rival Unionist commemorations flourished in the state throughout the late nineteenth century, and African American Missourians contributed. Unlike their white comrades, however, African Americans tied Civil War commemoration more to the unique concerns of their racial, as opposed to regional, identity. While the loyalty of white Missourians often proved difficult to disentangle, the color line clearly distinguished African Americans as Unionist. This was a superficial distinction, one that failed to take into account the diverse motivations of African Americans for supporting the Union war effort, but a pervasive one nonetheless. As a result, African American Missourians expressed little interest in defending their loyalty to outsiders but focused instead on their pursuit of equal rights.

Still, black Missourians encountered particular challenges in Civil War commemoration that stemmed not only from Missouri's uneasy relationship to both the Union and the Emancipation Cause but also from their own complicated history with those causes. While most white Missourians were unequivocally Unionist, they generally considered the Union and slavery to be perfectly compatible. They only reluctantly endorsed African American military service and gradually embraced emancipation. For example, in 1861, when John C. Frémont, federal commander of the Department of the West, proposed emancipating the slaves of disloyal Missourians, he met with a firestorm of disapproval that ultimately cost him his job. Indeed, Missouri's status as a loyal, slaveholding state required Union officials to tread with caution. As a loyal state, Missouri was exempt from the Emancipation Proclamation and slavery in Missouri remained intact in 1863, though significantly undermined by the Second Confiscation Act. The Emancipation Proclamation did, however, authorize the recruitment of black Missourians into the Union Army. Because of the provisional government's concern over how this measure would impact the property rights of loyal slaveholders, General John Schofield, commanding the Department of Missouri, initially banned those men enslaved to loyal Missourians from enlisting. Schofield reversed this policy a few months later and opened enlistment without exception to all African American men, free and enslaved. He further promised freedom to all enslaved recruits, although he planned to compensate loyal slaveholders for their loss.[9]

Despite such bureaucratic obstacles, not to mention slaveholders' persistent and sometimes violent attempts to block their enlistment, Missouri fielded 8,344 African American troops—perhaps 39 percent of eligible African American males in the state.[10] These Missourians eventually formed seven regiments of the famed United States Colored Troops (USCT). The military service of African Americans proved incredibly symbolic, demonstrating that the war for the Union had become a war to end slavery and to usher in a new era for the American republic. Nevertheless, enlistment was a calculation that black men made based less on ideology than on their own circumstances and those of their families. As historian Miller W. Boyd, III, demonstrates, enslaved Missourians were far more likely to enlist in the regular army than free men. Even so, the decision to fight was a highly individualized and fraught proposition, particularly considering the persistence of slavery in Missouri. Enslaved men not only faced the likelihood of violent opposition to their enlistment but also worried about the fate of the enslaved family members they left behind. Vindictive slaveholders retaliated against the relatives of recruits through violence, increased workloads, sales, and out-of-state evictions.[11] Faced with such serious threats to themselves and their loved ones, enslaved Missourians did not volunteer lightly. African American men, Boyd argues, "did not have the luxury to be guided by aspiration, ideology, or altruism." He further contends that "the lofty goals of destroying slavery in America and securing black citizenship did not push most African-American soldiers in Missouri to enlist."[12] Those men who would benefit from enlistment did; those—typically free men—who enjoyed sufficient income and security at home did not. In short, like white Missourians, African American Missourians did not share a universal experience or perspective on the war.

Regardless of the extent of their ideological commitment to the cause, African American Missourians faced discrimination in pay and duty as soldiers. Like all black troops they were forced to serve in segregated units, under white officers, and often relegated to the most menial and dangerous duties. They endured some of the worst conditions and highest mortality rates of the war. Their service, however, transformed both themselves and their white comrades. Over the course of the war, the conduct of black soldiers earned them the respect and admiration of many of their white comrades, who increasingly supported emancipation as a Union war aim. Military service also had a profound effect on African American men. It presented them with an opportunity to demonstrate not only their patriotism and manhood but, more importantly, their humanity.[13]

Considering the hesitancy with which the provisional government undertook the recruitment of black soldiers, it is unsurprising that officials delayed emancipation until it posed the least damage to loyal, white Missourians.

Even as support for emancipation grew, African Americans often found themselves at the mercy of their enslavers, who sought to retain their property by any means necessary. In Missouri, as Union general Clinton B. Fisk famously observed, "slavery dies hard."[14] Mattie Jackson, an enslaved woman from St. Louis, discovered this for herself. To avoid losing his property through emancipation, Jackson's enslaver smuggled her and her family into Kentucky where they were sold and separated. Illegal sales of this nature were such a persistent problem that General William Rosecrans, commanding the Department of Missouri, "banned the exportation of negroes from Missouri" in 1864.[15] Jackson eventually escaped, reuniting with a portion of her family and returning to St. Louis at the end of the war. There, the aftermath of emancipation and Union victory left the racial dynamic uncertain. On one occasion, Jackson nearly bumped into her former enslaver on the street. According to Jackson, "He was so surprised that before he was aware of it he dropped a bow." On still another occasion, she recalled with satisfaction, "My mother met . . . her old mistress, with a large basket on her arm, trudging to market. It appeared she had lived to see the day when her children had to wait upon themselves, and she likewise. The Yankees had taken possession, and her posterity were on an equality with the black man."[16]

It is compelling that the Missouri General Assembly abolished slavery on January 11, 1865, before the ratification of the Thirteenth Amendment. But while emancipation and Union victory certainly unsettled white hegemony in Missouri, they did not unseat it. True equality of the kind Jackson anticipated followed emancipation haltingly. While the 1865 Drake Constitution endowed African American Missourians with greater legal equality, property rights, freedom of worship, and access to education, it failed to provide for black suffrage and prohibited black officeholding.[17] White Missourians, including the Radicals, broadly opposed African American suffrage, fearing it would draw a mass of freed people from the South into Missouri—migrants who would pose competition with poor whites for land and jobs. In pursuit of better opportunities, many African American Missourians left the state. As they had throughout the war, African Americans moved to Kansas, Iowa, and Illinois; a quarter of those who remained relocated to the St. Louis area. By 1870, African Americans made up only 6.9 percent of Missouri's population, the smallest percentage of any of the formerly slaveholding states besides Delaware.[18]

The relatively small African American population in Missouri, in addition to the state's exemption from Reconstruction, has led some to overlook the importance of black political power in post–Civil War Missouri.[19] Yet, "Like their counterparts elsewhere in the former slave South," historian John W. McKerley argues, "black Missourians engaged in a wave of popular political organizing in the wake of emancipation. . . . They framed their demands within a nonracial vision of republican manhood, but they also expressed grave doubts about the influence of 'traitors' and 'rebels' at the ballot box, calling for a biracial loyalist alliance."[20] Black Missourians began to organize a challenge to the Drake Constitution's racialized restriction on voting, and veterans led the effort.

African American Missourians, particularly Union veterans, understood that the conclusion of the war was only an interlude in their fight. Like white Unionists, these individuals organized into societies to promote their agenda. In this case, they established the Missouri Equal Rights League on October 3, 1865. The league was founded in part by distinguished African American leaders James Milton Turner and Moses Dickson.[21] Born to a family of enslaved Missourians, Turner's father eventually purchased freedom for himself, his wife, and his then four-year-old son. In his teenage years, James Turner attended Oberlin College in Ohio—the first interracial and coeducational college in the United States. He returned to Missouri in 1856 or 1857. Both his education and his exposure to the activist culture of Oberlin primed him for a leadership role in Missouri's black community.[22] Unlike Turner, Moses Dickson was born free in Ohio. He moved to St. Louis as a young man, where he and a group of friends founded the Knights of Liberty. The Knights of Liberty acted as a secret abolitionist society that conspired to arm enslaved people and coordinate a massive rebellion. By 1857, Dickson claimed, the Knights had built a network of tens of thousands of fellow conspirators and enslaved people across the South. Recognizing that the Civil War was imminent, however, Dickson decided to forestall the insurrection. At the outbreak of the war, both Turner and Dickson joined the fight. Turner acted as a servant to a Union officer, Colonel Madison Miller, commander of the Eighteenth Missouri Volunteer Infantry. In the thick of the fighting at Shiloh, Turner apparently suffered a wound that left him with a permanent limp.[23] Meanwhile, Dickson served, in McKerley's words, "as an 'independent fighter.'"[24]

Although Turner and Dickson both claimed military service, the Missouri Equal Rights League was not exclusively a veterans' society. Its members also included free-born civilians, the formerly enslaved, and members of the black professional class. Still, the Equal Rights League invoked the Emancipation Cause in its fight for suffrage. On October 12, 1865, the league drafted "An

Address by the Colored People of Missouri to the Friends of Equal Rights," calling on the memory of slavery, the Civil War, and black military service to demand political equality for African American men. In the address, the league asserted that the Civil War had been a war for emancipation. "Out of the fierce conflict which has just closed," it declared, "we at length have been released from chains, lashes, bloodhounds and slave marts, and to us has a 'freedom at large' been ordained." Only access to the vote, the group argued, could secure that freedom. Its members demanded suffrage as their birthright as Americans, as recompense for the forced labor of the enslaved, their loyalty to the Union, and their sacrifices on behalf of the Union war effort. "We demand this in the honored name of the nine thousand colored troops," the address continued, "who with the first opportunity enlisted under the banner of Missouri, and bared their breasts to the remorseless storm of treason, and by hundreds went down to death in the conflict." Despite their sacrifices, these African Americans knew their fight was far from over. "We are no longer cowed beneath the name of chattels and of brutes," they wrote, "but we own ourselves, our families and our homes, and as men demand that this freedom shall bear the spirit as well as the form . . . that the skeleton of liberty may be clothed with flesh and blood." As far as the league was concerned, extending suffrage to African American men, especially to veterans, was only justice. "He who can be trusted with an army musket," the men observed, "which makes victory and protects the nation, shall also be entrusted with the right to express a preference for his rulers and his laws." The idea that former Confederates would return to political power and enjoy privileges still denied to loyal veterans was too much to bear. The league insisted "that colored loyalty, industry and intelligence shall receive as full rights, guarantees and privileges as those accorded to white treason, arrogance and indolence."[25]

In order to disseminate its message as widely as possible, the Equal Rights League distributed copies of the address to Missouri newspapers. Turner and John Mercer Langston, president of the National Equal Rights League, also embarked on statewide speaking tours advocating black suffrage.[26] On January 9, 1866, Langston made the league's case before the General Assembly.[27] Such appeals, however, failed to attract the support of a sufficient number of Radical allies. Although multiple measures for black suffrage appeared before the General Assembly, and even though Radical Republicans remained in power, none of the society's efforts were successful. The fear that the expansion of voting rights would encourage black migration, plus the reluctance of whites to support black suffrage while the Iron Clad Oath remained in effect, proved too difficult to overcome.[28] In the November 1, 1868, *St. Louis Daily Missouri Democrat*, Dickson vented his frustration with the Radicals:

> We stood shoulder to shoulder with the loyal white man and aided to put down the great rebellion. . . . For this we have incurred the lasting enmity of the rebel Democracy. They will not forget us, but oppose us in everything that tends to elevate and enlighten. Will the loyal white men come to our aid now, and give us the ballot to protect us against this same rebel Democracy? We promise to use the ballot as we did the bayonet, to uphold the honor and dignity of our common country.[29]

Dickson's impassioned appeal to Civil War memory fell on deaf ears in the statehouse. Ultimately, African American men in Missouri would not obtain the vote until the passage of the Fifteenth Amendment in 1870. Still, the presence of black voters at Missouri's polling places was an incredibly symbolic expression of emancipationist memory. It indicated a fundamental change in American life brought about through Union victory and emancipation: black men were citizens. Whether they endorsed black suffrage or not, white Missourians had to recognize the political order of the state would never be the same.[30]

While the Radical administration proved unsympathetic to black Missourians' pursuit of suffrage, it was more willing to act in support of public education. In the antebellum period, most African American Missourians found their educational opportunities severely limited. Missouri's 1847 Constitution prohibited enslaved people from receiving instruction in reading or writing. Some free African Americans, primarily in St. Louis, had access to private schooling, and during the Civil War, the American Missionary Association and the Western Sanitary Commission opened new schools.[31] Following the war, the Freedmen's Bureau continued these efforts. By 1869, they had established 114 schools enrolling 6,240 black students.[32] While they held political power, the Radicals endorsed educational reform. The 1865 Drake Constitution provided for the creation of the first publicly funded school system in Missouri and committed to establishing both white and black schools.[33] These accomplishments were due in no small part to the advocacy of black Missourians like James Milton Turner and Moses Dickson. Many considered education an essential basis for citizenship and the elective franchise. The schools established by and on behalf of African

Americans explicitly linked the pursuit of education to the legacy of the Emancipation Cause.[34]

Without question, however, the most significant and long-lasting African American school founded in Missouri was the Lincoln Institute, now Lincoln University, in Jefferson City. The creation of the Lincoln Institute was the most profound achievement undertaken by African American veterans in Missouri in the aftermath of the Civil War. As the only institution of higher education in the country founded by Civil War veterans and by black veterans in particular, this school represented Missouri's Emancipation Cause more than any oration, parade, or monument. Even its very name—the *Lincoln* Institute—connected this school to what the Union Army accomplished through the abolition of slavery and the service of black soldiers.[35]

The Lincoln Institute was the vision of the men in the 62nd USCT. During the war, and with the assistance of their white officers, these African American soldiers learned to read and write.[36] While serving in Texas at the conclusion of the war, Richard Baxter Foster, a former teacher and white officer in the 62nd, worried about what the future held for the education of his black comrades. "It was a pity these men should find no schools when they returned to Missouri," he opined, "and that the education so happily commenced should cease." Foster continued,

> I had thought much, during the months that followed [Robert E.] Lee's surrender, of the prospect of the country. I felt that the past was dead and must soon be buried; that an era had commenced in which all things should become new. "The war" I said to myself, "has given us opportunity. It has been a grand iconoclast, breaking down idols and clearing away rubbish. . . . No more shall the auction block be mounted by human chattels. No more shall education be forbidden and virtue be impossible for any part of our population. The fugitive slave law is behind us. Universal suffrage is before us."[37]

Foster and his men fully understood that for freed people, access to education was the essential first step in achieving all the things the destruction of slavery and Union victory promised African Americans.

As a result, Foster and the veterans of the 62nd conceived a plan to establish a school for newly emancipated slaves in Missouri. It was to be called the Lincoln Institute in honor of the "Great Emancipator" himself. Indeed, Lincoln figured prominently in black Missourians' recollections of the Civil War. For example, Mattie Jackson, the formerly enslaved woman who had so surprised her old master in the streets of St. Louis, wrote that she hoped the publication of her narrative would pay for her education, an effort she felt she owed "our beloved martyr President Lincoln." In the volume, Jackson also recounted an incident in which her enslaver discovered a picture of Lincoln her mother had cut from a newspaper and hung on her wall. According to Jackson, "he asked her what she was doing with old Lincoln's picture. She replied it was there because she liked it. He then knocked her down three times, and sent her to the trader's yard for a month as punishment."[38] Decades later, the *Professional World*, an African American newspaper from Columbia, Missouri, said of Lincoln: "What he has done will stand as a monument under the sun, and his name, reaching down thro' the ages of time, will still through the years of eternity shine."[39]

To make their tribute to Lincoln a reality, the veterans began collecting funds on behalf of the school. The officers raised $1,034.60 and the enlisted men an additional $3,966.50, while the 65th, another Missouri USCT unit, contributed a further $1,379.50. They also received support from the Western Sanitary Commission and the Freedmen's Bureau.[40] In fact, donations came in from a wide variety of Missourians; legend has it that notorious outlaw Jesse James even donated to the cause.[41] "But two conditions were made to the gifts," Foster explained: "that the school should be established in Missouri, and that it should be open to colored people. The fundamental idea was indeed that it should be for their special benefit; but special does not necessarily mean exclusive. . . . It is not for the benefit of the colored people to encourage the spirit of caste that would make one school white and another black; that would mark the race inferior. . . . The caste spirit is the legitimate child of slavery."[42] By insisting that the Lincoln Institute would be open to all men, white or black, Foster and his colleagues signaled their belief that the trappings of slavery—illiteracy and racial segregation—should be abolished forever.[43]

Funding, however, was only one of the obstacles facing the veterans and the Lincoln Institute. The enterprise also encountered reticence on the part of black Missourians and racist opposition from white Missourians. Some black Missourians worried about the influence of white administrators and teachers at Lincoln. They felt an important need, historian Miller W. Boyd, III, argues, "to demonstrate to both blacks and whites that they could play a leading, if not the principal, role in their own uplift."[44] On the other hand, many white Democrats believed public education was an unnecessary expenditure and that black Missourians were particularly unworthy of the expense.[45] From as far afield as Maryland, the Democratic press criticized the idea. "One of those dubious institutions, called the Freedmen's Bureau," the *Maryland Free Press* reported, "has donated $2,000 to a Lincoln Institute . . . for the benefit of worthless negroes. The right of these bureau officials to give away the people's money, in making their boasted charities, is without law or profit, and is nothing short of down-right stealing."[46] The Lexington, Missouri, *Weekly Caucasian*—a notoriously vitriolic and racist Democrat newspaper—called the Lincoln Institute "a gorilla school." "It is a sweet-scented African college," the paper continued, "named after the late lamented."[47]

White Missourians often manifested ambivalence, if not outright hostility, to the efforts of African Americans to attain education. While the Drake Constitution called for the creation of segregated, though equally funded, schools for African Americans, the state did little to enforce the law.[48] In 1869, fifty-five Missouri counties still had not complied, although some districts simply did not have large enough African American populations to justify the construction of a school.[49] "But few schools have thus far been established," one newspaper admitted. "The landholders, who were once slaveholders, are still Democrats, and will only allow schools to be established in their midst when they are compelled to do so by law."[50] In addition to the failure of the state government to adequately support black education, some white Missourians also mounted violent resistance. Throughout the late 1860s, a number of black schools were attacked and burned. In 1869, one veteran of the 62nd was lynched.[51]

In seeking to establish the Lincoln Institute, the veterans of the 62nd and 65th set themselves no easy task. Still, in spite of many and persistent challenges, they found success. In 1866, Foster acquired a two-room schoolhouse in Jefferson City. He described the building as "a shell, a wreck, a ruin," but it was soon crowded with students. Fundraising challenges, however, threatened the veterans' accomplishments. Foster, Turner, and Dickson hoped to secure government funding for the school, but while there was no legal obstacle to such a plan, their initial attempts failed. Foster insisted that was "not by hostility to the measure."[52] In 1870, Turner petitioned the Radical-controlled General Assembly to create an endowment for the Lincoln Institute, promising the gratitude—and the votes—of black Missourians in return.[53] Finally, on February 14, 1870, the legislature signed a law providing an annual appropriation to support the Lincoln Institute, with the provision that it would principally serve as a training school for black teachers.[54] These funds, supplemented by another donation of six thousand dollars from the Freedmen's Bureau, enabled the Lincoln Institute to construct a much larger three-story masonry building to house the school.[55] This was a remarkable triumph not only for the veterans of the 62nd and 65th but for every black

Missourian who would benefit from the training the Lincoln Institute provided to educators.

At the formal dedication of the new building on the Fourth of July 1871, there was every reason to be proud of the Lincoln Institute. In his address, Colonel David Branson, a former white officer in the 62nd, related to the crowd the progress the school had made. Since its humble beginnings in that ramshackle old schoolhouse, Branson reported, enrollment had reached 150 students and there were more applications coming in than there was space for boarding.[56] Although there was still plenty of work ahead, Branson envisioned the Lincoln Institute as the embodiment of the Emancipation Cause. "Looking in the faces of my old comrades . . . here to-day," Branson said, "memory goes back to the past . . . and emotions fill me that no language can express. . . . Our enemies predicted, that upon the disbanding of our volunteer army—particularly the colored portion of it—it would turn to band of marauding murderers and idle vagabonds, and this Institute was our answer."[57] The Lincoln Institute became a site of memory that symbolized the hard-won fulfillment of emancipation and the promise of equality for all African Americans.

Even with meaningful strides made toward educational equality in Missouri, the Radical government did not fully support African Americans in their attempts to translate the memory of the war into a movement for

Figure 2. Lincoln Institute, Jefferson City, c. 1910. Courtesy of Missouri Post Card Collection (P0032). 024274. The State Historical Society of Missouri, Photograph Collection

further rights. The Radicals failed to endorse black suffrage, and despite Turner's promises, their support for the Lincoln Institute did not secure the unqualified allegiance of black voters. When black Missourians reached the polls in 1870, they supported Radicals, Liberals, and even Democrats.[58] For his part, Turner remained committed to the Radicals. They continued to be supportive of initiatives in education and employed him as a school inspector. A number of Missouri's leading Radicals also recommended Turner's appointment as the U.S. minister to Liberia.[59] Other black Missourians, however, felt the Radicals had largely failed them. They feared that the Radical's adherence to the Iron Clad Oath made white moderates less willing to countenance civil rights measures for African Americans and might even increase the likelihood that former Confederates would target black voters for reprisals.[60] S. V. Casey, a black Liberal Republican from Marshall, voiced this very sentiment in a letter printed in the *Weekly Caucasian*. Casey insisted the disenfranchisement of former Confederates no longer served a purpose and might actually harm black Missourians. He wrote,

> Now that the fruits of the victory have been carefully gathered and preserved, that the smoke of battle has long since cleared away, that peace everywhere reigns in our land, I can see no reason why the colored men of the State should wish this state of affairs longer to continue. . . . Leaving out of mind the manifest wrong and injustice of this course, it cannot be to the interest of our race to place ourselves in a position of unauthorized hostility to this powerful and controlling class. Politically and financially our interest and theirs are identical. The best interest of the State is the common good of all.

Casey went on to accuse the Radicals of abandoning black voters. "There is not one particle of patriotism or friendship for our race in them. . . . Our votes have been used to elect; *but we are not elected*. . . . We do the voting; they receive the benefits."[61] It is worth noting that, according to the 1870 census, Casey was born in Ohio and reported his occupation as a barber.[62] His free birth and class status set him apart from the majority of black Missourians, who had been enslaved. Still, it is compelling that the frustration of black voters like Casey with the failings of Radical rule led some to sympathize with the moderate, reconciliationist approach of the Liberals.[63]

While the diminishing power of the Republican Party in Missouri might be read as a retreat from the Emancipation Cause, the reality was more complex. The return of the Democrats in 1872 was not a wholesale redemption of the Confederacy or a triumph for white supremacy. Black voters helped oust the Radicals and, in some instances supported the Democrats in response to the changing dynamics of their state. The relocation of black Missourians to urban areas, which began in the aftermath of the Civil War, had only increased in the following decades. By 1890, 47 percent of African American Missourians resided in cities.[64] This trend was precipitated in part by a rise in African American migration from the Deep South during the Exoduster movement. These migrants were drawn to Missouri's cities for work and for greater equality of opportunity. Missouri law mandated segregated schools and banned interracial marriage, but the color line remained more flexible than in the South.[65]

This is not to suggest that Democrats in Missouri were any less invested in racism than their southern fellows. Rather, as was often the case in the border state, practical concerns intervened. In Missouri's growing urban centers in particular, black votes could carry weight. According to historian John W. McKerley, appeals to black voters "did not necessarily blunt the influence of white supremacy in the party, but it did continue to open new avenues for black Missourians to craft limited alliances across the color line," which they used "to advance their individual and collective interests."[66] Chiefly, the importance of the black vote prevented Democrats from implementing more widespread acts of legalized segregation and disenfranchisement.[67] By using their vote to secure more equal conditions of life, black Missourians enacted the emancipationist legacy of the Civil War in a profound and transformative way.

Even under Democratic oversight, neither white nor African American Missourians abandoned the Emancipation Cause. African American veterans and their white officers cooperated in the foundation of the Lincoln Institute, indicating a camaraderie that developed through the shared experience of military service. To a degree, that camaraderie was also reflected within the ranks of the Department of Missouri GAR. From its inception, the GAR opened its membership to African American veterans, making it one of the largest integrated societies in post-Civil War America. Across the nation, the GAR included both all-black and integrated posts. According to historian Barbara Gannon, the presence of integrated posts in particular makes the GAR a truly remarkable organization. Comrades voted on whether or not to admit prospective members to their posts. This simple fact meant that white veterans willingly integrated. "Given this voting system and the dismal state of race relations in this era," Gannon writes, "the existence of any integrated posts, let alone the existence of hundreds, is astonishing."[68] As fellow veterans, many white comrades acknowledged the political equality of African American men as well as their right to veterans' benefits. Just because some white veterans espoused tolerance within the ranks of the GAR, however, does not mean that such tolerance extended to life outside of the post or to black civilians.[69]

Interestingly, however, Gannon argues that GAR posts in the Midwest had the best record of inclusivity. This, she maintains, reflected the different wartime experiences of the eastern and western armies. In the first place, more African Americans served in the West than in the East. In addition, western soldiers' more frequent encounters with enslaved people in their campaigns across the Deep South made them increasingly supportive of emancipation and political equality.[70] In the Department of Missouri, there were eight all-black and four integrated posts. In 1891, at the peak of GAR membership, there were at least 223 African American comrades in the Department of Missouri.[71] This does not account for black veterans within integrated posts, although Gannon insists their numbers only amounted to "a handful."[72] It is also likely there were many eligible African American Missourians who could not gain GAR membership due to a variety of factors. First, the comparatively low African American population outside of the cities meant it was difficult to gather enough members to form posts. In addition, the costs associated with membership including dues, regalia, and travel expenses may have been prohibitive for many veterans. Finally, racism presented a major obstacle to black enrollment in the Department of Missouri. Some posts deliberately excluded black veterans. The Kansas *Leavenworth Advocate* reported that the Lincoln Post in Moberly, Missouri, "refuses to receive the Negro soldier, that walked side by side with them in battle."[73] According to James Milton Turner, St. Louis's Frank Blair Post also refused to admit black veterans.[74]

Such blatant racial discrimination, in direct contravention of GAR policy, was a problem shared by African American veterans across the country. This issue came to a head at the 1887 national encampment in St. Louis, after a group of black veterans in New Orleans protested that the GAR Department of the Gulf, composed of a few posts in Mississippi and Louisiana, refused to admit them because of their race. They claimed the white comrades in the Department of the Gulf "prefer to fraternize with the ex-Confederate organizations . . . rather than with their colored ex-comrades, and they fear that the admission of the colored ex-soldiers to the G. A. R. would result in a rupture of the relations existing between the ex-Federal and ex-Confederate organizations . . . that are now so pleasant a feature of the social side of the respective associations."[75] White comrades in the Department of the Gulf justified their actions by insisting black veterans were incapable of managing the business of their posts and that they "were not soldiers in the same sense" as white volunteers.[76] According to the *St. Louis Post-Dispatch*, one man "admitted that there were a few colored people who would be entitled to membership, but the number were like angels' visits, few and far between."[77]

The black community of St. Louis formulated a plan to resist the racial discrimination practiced not only in the Department of the Gulf but throughout the GAR. Although not himself a veteran, Professor Arthur Dessalines Langston, son of founding Missouri Equal Rights League member John Mercer Langston, took the lead in coordinating the protest. As the principal of the Dumas Elementary School, one of the first schools for African American children established in St. Louis, Arthur Langston had an important leadership role in the community. He envisioned inviting delegations of African American leaders and veterans from across the country to attend the 1887 national encampment. He particularly wanted every African American GAR post to be represented.[78] To gather support for the protest, Langston traveled to New York and planned to visit Philadelphia, Baltimore, Washington, DC, and Virginia. In anticipation of Langston's visit, the Washington *Evening Star* impressed on its readers the symbolic importance of attending the national encampment in St. Louis, the first "to be held in a Southern city."[79] While the Department of Missouri as a whole would not have agreed with that assessment, it was a subtle indication that Missouri perhaps felt more like the South to African American veterans than it did to their white comrades.

Langston's demonstration promised to be a full expression of the Emancipation Cause. While partaking in the general commemoration of the Union Cause occasioned by the GAR encampment, Langston understood that African American veterans could not rest on remembrance. This was an opportunity to press for change. He put together a program designed both to confront racism in the GAR and to highlight black achievement. There would be speeches by celebrated black leaders, a chorus of hundreds of African American school children, and a parade. "It will be a jubilee of the colored people," the *Evening Star* proclaimed. "While paying their respects to the Grand Army of the Republic," it continued, "the colored people are actuated by another motive in coming together—that is to consider how best to improve themselves and promote their interests."[80]

It is hard to say to what extent Langston's plans actually came to fruition. While African American veterans did attend the national encampment, none of the Department of Missouri's black posts joined the parade.[81] Integrated posts Dix and Custer participated, but it is difficult to tell whether any African American members were in attendance. There is some evidence, however, that Langston fulfilled his promise to host important black leaders. On the first day of the encampment, James Milton Turner gave a provocative speech calling for "absolute social equality" within the GAR. In a fierce and damning tone, Turner condemned the hypocrisy of white veterans who allowed black soldiers to serve as the vanguard in the deadliest engagements of the Civil War but now refused to treat them like comrades. "We were the breastwork for the cowards in battle who shirked their duty and placed the negro in advance," Turner said. "No negro soldier can join the [St. Louis] Frank Blair post or any other post of the G. A. R., but during the war, in case of emergency, he was a welcome reinforcement." In its account of the speech, the *Iron County Register* acknowledged that by virtue of its association with the Republican Party, Turner had reason to expect equal treatment from the GAR. Still, the paper maintained that as a purely social organization, no one could compel the GAR to admit anyone its members saw fit to exclude. "Mr. Turner . . . has no civil right to social equality with any man in the G. A. R.," the *Register* concluded. "He cannot force those veterans to eat at the same mess, to drink from the same cup and to assemble around the same campfire with him."[82]

Nevertheless, the 1887 national encampment did tackle the issue of racial discrimination within the GAR. The delegates debated a proposed amendment to the GAR rules and regulations that would allow any African American post that was rejected by a department on the basis of color to appeal to the national commander in chief. The commander could then grant the post special permission to join under the oversight of the national organization instead of the local department. In the course of the debate, Edgar Allan, a white member from the Department of Virginia, admitted the question of accepting black comrades was a frequent point of contention among GAR posts in the South. "I can readily understand how some of my comrades there might dread the effect upon their social relations with the people amongst whom they live, of having within this organization, in their limits, the black men who fought side by side with them during the war." Given the conservative political and social atmosphere of their own state, white members of the Department of Missouri may well have sympathized with this perspective. Still, Allan said, he would much rather socialize with African American veterans than with former Confederates.[83] Despite the determined opposition of the Department of the Gulf, the amendment passed.

African American veterans were not insensitive to the potential for conflict posed by the GAR's frequent interactions with former Confederates. They shared the fears of their white comrades who felt that commemorating the Union Cause in Missouri might actually be dangerous. For black comrades, however, the likelihood of violence was far more real. As a consequence, black veterans did not fraternize with former Confederates in the way their white comrades did. Indeed, Langston's and Turner's impassioned criticisms of the GAR indicate that veterans and members of the black community more generally disapproved of fraternization. They recognized it for what it was—a means of excluding African Americans from participating in the commemoration of the Civil War.

Despite the challenges that limited African American involvement in the GAR, the presence of black comrades in the Department of Missouri was a tribute to the Emancipation Cause. The creation of African American posts was especially indicative of the needs of black communities. These posts existed not merely as a consequence of segregation within the GAR but were organized by black veterans themselves to shape Civil War memory to their own ends. According to Gannon, their existence "reminded their community, black and white, of the centrality of slavery to the Civil War's causes and consequences" and served as a means to "memorialize African American military achievements."[84] But this was about more than martial glory. As the Missouri Equal Rights League made very evident, the memory of military service was essential to African Americans' claims to civil rights. African American GAR posts also served the Emancipation Cause by providing mutual aid for black communities. Indeed, the charitable nature of the GAR was extremely important. In an era before the proliferation of welfare programs, the GAR raised money for sick and needy comrades and their families. It also lobbied for pensions and provided a source of collective knowledge to help black veterans and their families access those funds.

Participation in the GAR was not limited to men either. Its auxiliaries allowed women to engage in the Emancipation Cause as well. The Department of Missouri included at least four African American WRC organizations, including A. Hightower Corps in Kansas City, Albert Chandler Corps in Macon, Corps No. 21 in Hannibal, and Col. Robert Gould Shaw Corps in St. Louis. Although the white leadership of the Department of Missouri WRC seemingly welcomed the organization of black corps, it is unlikely black women joined because they sought sisterhood with white women—and even less likely because they sought to engage with formerly Confederate women. African American women joined the WRC to commemorate the Civil War and, more particularly, to carry out the work of the Emancipation Cause. Membership provided them with an opportunity to recall the suffering of the enslaved, honor black military service, and support black veterans in their work on behalf of racial uplift, particularly through education.

The narrative of Lucy A. Delaney, an African American Missourian, provides some insight into what WRC membership meant to black women. Born enslaved, Delaney successfully sued for her freedom in the St. Louis courts in 1844 on the grounds that she lived with her enslaver for a time in the free state of Illinois. After the Civil War, she became an active congregant in the African Methodist Episcopal Church and joined several benevolent societies, including an auxiliary to the Freemasons, the Daughters of Zion, and the Daughters of the Tabernacle. She also became an officer in the Col. Robert Gould Shaw Corps WRC.[85] Such a high degree of community engagement was typical of black clubwomen in the late nineteenth century. While African Americans organized to address many of the same issues white clubwomen did, especially related to social activism, black clubs also served as vehicles for racial uplift.[86] In the case of the WRC, membership linked racial uplift and activism to the participation of African American soldiers in the Civil War and the memory of emancipation. Delaney's 1890s memoir, *From the Darkness Cometh the Light; or, Struggles for Freedom*, explicitly commemorated the experiences of the enslaved. Although she appreciated the memory of slavery "cannot recur with any happiness," she hoped her book would resonate with formerly enslaved people and that "those . . . who have never suffered as we have, perhaps may . . . accept with interest and sympathy the passages of life and character here portrayed and the lessons which should follow from them." Pointedly, she dedicated the volume to the GAR. The dedication reads,

> To those who by their valor have made their name immortal, from whom we are daily learning the lessons of patriotism, in whom we respect the virtues of charity, patience and friendship as displayed towards the colored race and to those "Whose deeds crowd History's pages / And Time's great volume make," is this little volume reverently dedicated—THE GRAND ARMY OF THE REPUBLIC.[87]

Delaney's memoir made her a living tribute to Missouri's Emancipation Cause. She testified to the inhumanity of slavery, recognized the role of the Union Army in its destruction, and embodied the opportunities emancipation created for African Americans. By preserving her story and by virtue of her association with the respectable world of WRC clubwomen and the

Union soldiers and nurses they honored, Delaney asserted her identity as a woman, a free person, and a patriot.[88]

African American Missourians also organized outside of the ranks of the GAR and its auxiliaries. Their desire to commemorate the Emancipation Cause and to work in support of mutual aid resulted in the formation of local African American veterans' associations. True to the Emancipation Cause, these groups mobilized the legacy of the Civil War into gains for African American Missourians. In 1883, for example, the "state reunion of colored veteran soldiers" gathered for a three-day meeting in Sedalia. According to the *Iron County Register*, "The principal object sought was the enrollment of all colored veterans in the State in order that those who had claims against the Government might be able to more intelligently and systematically present them."[89] This kind of service was crucial for veterans and widows, especially in preparing pension applications.

While the extension of equal pensions to black veterans served as an important recognition of their service, the process was convoluted and many applicants were rejected. Applicants had to first complete a form demonstrating honorable service and claiming a legitimate disability. That form had to be supplemented by proof, usually in the form of witness statements from fellow veterans and reports from medical examiners. The application could be such an onerous task that many veterans relied on the assistance of dedicated pension attorneys. Racism placed the pension applications of black veterans under additional layers of scrutiny. Prevalent assumptions that African Americans were lazy and dishonest cast doubt on the worthiness of their claims. By providing guidance for pension applications, these black veterans offered mutual aid and demonstrated their conviction that the federal government owed them a measure of support for the part they had played in saving it. Furthermore, in an era when needy African American Missourians faced discrimination in access to work and medical care, pensions could provide essential relief. Thus, the "colored veteran soldiers" operated not only as a vehicle for Civil War commemoration but for community service as well.

Still another African American veteran's society, the Negro Soldiers of the Civil War of the State of Missouri, served a similar function. Founded in 1907, the Negro Soldiers hosted at least two annual reunions, but it is unclear how long-lived the society was or how many members it boasted. Even on the basis of such scant evidence, however, the Negro Soldiers clearly embodied the Emancipation Cause. In addition to celebrating black military service, the society considered itself vitally important to the project of racial uplift. It primarily celebrated the virtues of black soldiers in the hope that their reflective glory would lend distinction to the African American community as a whole. The Negro Soldiers also believed its members represented aspirational role models for the rising generation of black Missourians. In a promotion for its annual reunion, the Negro Soldiers emphasized the "encouragement and moral weight that it gives to the Negro race in various occupations of life." "Among those who have help[ed] to preserve the Union," it continued, "few have stamped themselves the more clearly upon the nation's memory than the Negro soldiers of the Civil War." As veterans, the members insisted they were owed a debt not only by the nation they helped to save but by African American civilians. Their Civil War service inaugurated the struggle for racial equality and opened the door for unprecedented opportunities. "The Negro race robs itself of . . . those opportunities when it neglects to attend the annual reunion," they argued.[90]

Perhaps as a commentary on the pervasive discrimination within the GAR, the Negro Soldiers insisted its reunion would welcome all comers on terms of complete equality. "The spirit of the Republic reigns in this annual reunion rather [than] Racial Distinction or Social Status," the organization proclaimed. "There is neither Black, Yellow, White, Red, nor Brown, but all are American citizens, and all are welcome." At the same time, however, the Negro Soldiers intended its reunion to serve as a forum for racial uplift. During the 1908 gathering, for instance, the Negro Soldiers joined forces with local community leaders to host an agricultural and industrial fair to showcase African American potential.[91] The Negro Soldiers also advertised its reunion as fertile ground for establishing and recruiting members into new black societies, including one called the Old Negro Settlers of Central Missouri and the Great West.[92]

African American clubs and societies, whether explicitly tied to Civil War commemoration or not, were vital to community life in the late nineteenth and early twentieth centuries. In Missouri and across the country, black organizations reflected the burgeoning of "race pride" and stimulated racial uplift. Membership in clubs and societies offered a stamp of respectability not readily granted in the social, economic, and political life of the state—a stamp many early civil rights advocates felt was essential to legitimizing their fight for equality. African American societies also served as a school for civic participation. With their formal rituals, rules, regulations, elected offices, and bureaucratic structures, these organizations helped prepare African Americans for public service.[93] Finally, they played a vital role in challenging racial discrimination and violence. In Missouri, for example, African American chapters of the Freemasons, Knights of Pythias, and Odd Fellows organized community events, raised funds for schools, provided insurance, and distributed charitable relief. On one occasion, they also participated in a national "Lamentation Day" to protest the epidemic of lynching.[94] Held in St. Louis on May 31, 1892, the participants heard a series of sermons and speeches, including an address by famed African American abolitionist Peter Humphries Clark. In one particularly moving moment, all 1,500 attendees stood and sang "The Battle Hymn of the Republic."[95] With the choice of that song on that date—the day after Memorial Day, a day reserved for the remembrance of the Civil War dead—black Missourians exalted victims of racial violence and linked their deaths to the legacy of the war.

The relative scarcity of African American Missourians within the GAR points to the likelihood that veterans found camaraderie and support within all-black societies. Some joined a society called the International Order of Twelve Knights of Tabor, which nurtured a direct connection to the memory of slavery and the Civil War. Founded in Missouri on August 12, 1872, the Knights of Tabor was the creation of Moses Dickson, the African American veteran who helped found the Missouri Equal Rights League. Dickson conceived of the Knights of Tabor as a tribute to the Knights of Liberty, Dickson's secret antebellum abolitionist society.[96] Although it eventually became a national society, the Knights of Tabor established local lodges all across the state. By 1896, the group claimed an estimated ten thousand members in Missouri alone.[97] The Knights of Tabor also included an auxiliary organization for black women called the Daughters of the Tabernacle or Daughters of Tabor. Much like the GAR, the Knights of Tabor was a patriotic and benevolent mutual aid society, dedicated to providing relief to the needy, especially widows and orphans.[98]

More than any other African American association, however, the Knights of Tabor embodied the Emancipation Cause. Founded on the memory of slavery, resistance, and black military service, its objective was racial uplift. It was "a race institution," in the words of the *Kansas City Sun*. "Every phase of its government, its ritualism, its literature and all its manifold paraphernalia is the work of Negro mind, Negro brains, Negro ingenuity."[99] The Knights sought to provide African Americans with the tools and support they needed to capitalize on the gains achieved through the Civil War.

Thus, for African American Missourians, Civil War commemoration centered on the black community. The importance of community involvement was particularly evident during Emancipation Day celebrations. African American Missourians observed Emancipation Day on a variety of dates, including January 1, the date of the Emancipation Proclamation; January

11, the date of the Missouri Emancipation Ordinance in 1865; April 16, the end of the Civil War; and—most often—August 1, the date of the abolition of slavery in the British Empire in 1834.[100] By linking the end of slavery in Britain to its end in the United States, African American Missourians highlighted the connection between the Civil War, the destruction of slavery, and the determination of people of African descent to confront the racist legacy of colonialism and press for racial equality—not just in Missouri, but around the world.

Although Emancipation Day festivities had tremendous symbolic importance, to some degree they also provided an excuse for fun. As the *Holt County Sentinel* explained, "The celebration by the colored people of an event which is, in many respects, to them what the Fourth of July is to their white friends, is attended with a corresponding amount of enthusiasm and rejoicing."[101] Emancipation Day events in Missouri were often quite large, sometimes with several thousand attendees.[102] Celebrations often featured speeches, parades, barbecues, music, drilling, and athletic events, usually baseball games. During an emancipation celebration in Oregon, Missouri, on July 30, 1897, aeronaut M. E. Baldwin delighted the crowds by parachuting from a hot air balloon at 2,500 feet.[103]

Among the throngs gathered on Emancipation Day, white Missourians were omnipresent. Not only did white Missourians attend emancipation commemorations, they also contributed funds and actively participated both in the solemnities and in the fun.[104] In August 1914, for example, the *Kansas City Sun* noted that "more than 5,000 white people" attended Emancipation Day in Marysville. "The Colored people were actually lost in the crowd," the paper remarked. At other times, white athletes challenged African Americans to baseball games and white dignitaries delivered speeches, including, on one occasion, Governor Thomas Fletcher.[105]

Promotions for Emancipation Day events made a point of promising that all participants, regardless of color, would enjoy equal treatment. A poster advertising an 1895 celebration in Clinton, Missouri, stated, "We guarantee equal rights to all and exclusive privileges to none."[106] This was a compelling, meaningful gesture, reminiscent of the determination of the USCT veterans that the Lincoln Institute would admit any student, regardless of race. It was perhaps meant more as an effort at racial reconciliation than reconciliation between Unionists and former Confederates. Still, it evinced the determination of African American Missourians to channel Civil War memory into a movement for greater equality.

The motives that prompted the attendance of white Missourians at Emancipation Day observances were varied. Some expressed sympathy for the struggles of black Missourians for equality. At a celebration in 1868, a white speaker named Major A. J. Williams used the occasion to press for black suffrage, which he insisted had been more than merited by the contributions of African Americans to the Union Cause:

> We went in to the war not to liberate the slaves, but the slaves came to our aid and helped us to save the government. Who were the thousands that flocked to the standard of Sherman, and moved with that grand army to the sea? They were the blacks. Who were the friends of Union soldiers, giving them aid and succor—furnishing them information—and doing every thing in their power to make their cause a success? The black people. . . . I shall vote next fall for the black man to have the elective franchise, but not the rebel. Let him show works of repentance first. It will be time enough then.[107]

The tone of other white speakers, however, could be patronizing. In 1905, according to the *Holt County Sentinel*, "Harry M. Dungan delivered a splendid address, expressing the good will of the whites toward the colored people in their efforts to better their condition; to be respected they must respect themselves and live an upright respectable life."[108] Reflecting their awareness of the importance of the politics of respectability to the early civil rights movement, both African American and white newspapers consistently noted whether any disruptive or criminal activity occurred during emancipation celebrations.

White Missourians likely had their own reasons for participating in Emancipation Day, not always stemming from support for black equality. For example, in the *Holt County Sentinel* of July 15, 1892, Cummins & Hershberger's clothing store placed an advertisement for a forthcoming celebration with a racist caricature of a grinning black man offering the following invitation in dialect: "We stends a codial invitation to all yo whites to come an celebrate wid us. Wes a goin to hav one o' granest ole fash'nd plantation times." Not only did the ad trade on racist stereotypes but it also undercut the essential meaning of Emancipation Day. The ad depicted this event as a remembrance of "plantation times" as opposed to a remembrance of their demise. Cummins & Hershberger's lack of sensitivity reveals they viewed Emancipation Day as a business opportunity rather than as a powerfully symbolic act of Civil War commemoration. And they were not alone. In an adjacent column, the paper noted, "Our colored citizens . . . are receiving liberal subscriptions from all our business men to aid them in observing Emancipation Day in this city."[109] Evidently, white Missourians regarded Emancipation Day not only as fun but as something of a spectacle and an opportunity to promote their own financial interests.

Despite the holiday-like atmosphere of Emancipation Day and despite the fact that white Missourians often coopted the festivities in some measure, it remained an important occasion for African American communities. These celebrations were organized by African Americans on behalf of African Americans. Even if they shared the stage with their white neighbors, Emancipation Day foregrounded the experiences of black Missourians. Former slaves in attendance at these events sometimes received special recognition. During an Emancipation Day observance in 1905, for instance, Ananias Tahl was made the "president of the day." Tahl, the *Holt County Sentinel* reported, "was an ex-slave, full blood and full of wit" who had been enslaved to a Confederate officer.[110] Tahl's presence was a reminder of what the day was all about—recognizing black history. While African American speakers credited white leaders like Abraham Lincoln for enacting emancipation, they reified Frederick Douglass and the African American soldier. In a speech in 1904, for example, a black college student evoked "the sacred memory of the invincible Negro soldier" who fought not only for the Union but for the liberty of "oppressed people."[111]

Although Emancipation Day was nominally about the end of slavery, it typically addressed the long history of racial oppression in the United States. Speechmakers included emancipation as only one part of the great sweep of African American history from the trans-Atlantic slave trade, through the Civil War and Reconstruction, to the present day. At a celebration in August 1897, for example, the Honorable J. Silas Harris of Kansas City gave an address on the "Past, Present and Future, of the Negro Race," "showing their progress in all the elements of citizenship; their advance in the arts and sciences, and predicted a glorious future [for] them."[112] Such accounts buoyed race pride by shifting the focus from the trauma of slavery and the Civil War to black achievement in the face of adversity. During Emancipation Day, as the *Sedalia Weekly Conservator* observed, "the spirit of intelligent patriotism and race love prevailed."[113] African American Missourians, however, were far from naive. They knew that emancipation could not erase the suffering of slavery nor did they believe it had opened an unobstructed path to equality.

At an event in Fulton on January 1, 1902, Reverend J. M. Harris declared, "We have not met here to heal the wounds of slavery—that we cannot do. Neither can we add to or take from the mighty monster his crown of thorns that once pressed down upon four million slaves. But we have a right to celebrate the day on which that crown of thorns was broken in pieces, never to be mended again."[114]

African American Emancipation Day speakers made it clear that while they were commemorating the end of one ordeal, they still anticipated a difficult future. Remembering slavery served as a clarion call for the continuing struggle against oppression, but Emancipation Day speakers stressed the importance of combating that oppression through respectability. At an 1868 observance in Macon, Reverend S. R. Rosboro encouraged African Americans to "teach your children the value of the liberty thus secured to them, and instruct them to become educated, wise, good and true citizens. The colored people are now free, and it is your duty to make the best possible use of your time. Be diligent, prudent, honest. Study to make yourselves familiar with your duties and your rights."[115] Similarly, at an emancipation celebration hosted at Missouri's all-black George R. Smith College in January 1904, Jessie M. Jackson used the occasion to comment on the challenges facing the "leading men" of the African American community. Jackson insisted it was their responsibility to uplift their people by instilling "broad principles of devotion to duty, of a business like integrity, and by fostering the very purest type of womanhood and manhood." Only these attributes, Jackson argued, would help them "withstand the censure and criticism of the tide of coming years."[116]

Just because African American Missourians understood the utility of the politics of respectability, however, does not mean they failed to take white supremacy to task. At the same 1905 Emancipation Day celebration where Harry M. Dungan told his black audience they must earn the respect of whites, African American speaker Dr. Matthew Othello Ricketts issued a powerful condemnation of white hypocrisy and racism. Ricketts was a distinguished African American leader whose career embodied the aspirations of the Emancipation Cause. Although born into slavery, Ricketts obtained an education, graduated from the Lincoln Institute, and became a physician. He went on to serve as the first African American in the Nebraska House of Representatives.[117] Still a child at the end of the Civil War, Ricketts told the crowd, "neither he nor any white man" was equipped to convey the meaning of emancipation for formerly enslaved people. In his speech, he related the history of American slavery, chronicled the remarkable progress of literacy among African Americans, and then defiantly challenged white Americans:

> If the civilization of the white man is worth a boast, if his law has any worth, if his religion any substance, his liberty any nobility, if his intelligence yields any light or guidance, if he values his conception of justice, if his free government is worth the first place in the systems of government, if he prizes that the American should stand foremost in the files of time, let him show it and prove it by doing justice to the colored people whose lots and lives are cast alongside of his.

In its account of Rickett's address, the *Holt County Sentinel* concluded, it "was . . . calculated to do the colored people much good."[118]

While African American Missourians faced persistent discrimination and lived in the shadow of racial violence, they nevertheless partook in the commemoration of the Civil War and emancipation. While they shared many of the same sympathies and concerns as white Unionists, they faced the additional obstacle of racial discrimination. Through the perpetuation of the Emancipation Cause, however, African Americans pursued suffrage, education, mutual aid, and racial uplift. Their efforts ensured that the Lost Cause did not go unchallenged in Missouri. Black Missourians advanced the Emancipation Cause in highly political, sometimes militant ways. While they often encountered resistance and did not always meet with success, they created a platform from which they called attention to persistent racism at the local and national levels.

FOUR

"Glory Enough for Us All"

Missouri's Lost Cause

Who can portray the deep disgust
Missourians feel when they are told
To lay their banners in the dust,
Lay down their arms and be paroled? . . .
March backward through this land of flowers, . . .
Again to seek our Western bowers
And tell our mothers we are slaves.

—Captain James Porter (CSA),
"A Missourian's Feelings on the Surrender," c. April 1865

ON MONDAY, DECEMBER 26, 1887, Governor John Sappington Marmaduke took to his bed in the executive mansion in Jefferson City. Seemingly healthy the week before, he caught a chill on a weekend visit to St. Louis. Shortly after his return home, Marmaduke was diagnosed with pneumonia. Summoned by an emergency telegram, R. E. Young, the governor's close personal friend and physician, arrived by train from southwestern Missouri on Tuesday. He confirmed the diagnosis and offered his patient a glass of milk. Marmaduke drank it and muttered his final words: "It is all over." By Wednesday morning, doctors pronounced the governor's case hopeless. With his two brothers, numerous friends, state officers, and several physicians gathered around him, Marmaduke slipped into unconsciousness and passed away. Young made note of the time. It was December 28, 1887, at 9:37 p.m.[1]

With the death of Marmaduke, Confederate Missourians mourned the loss of one of their most celebrated heroes. The son of an established Missouri political family, Marmaduke's father, Meredith, and his uncle Claiborne Fox Jackson both served as Missouri governors. John Marmaduke, however, initially pursued a military career. He graduated from West Point in 1857 and became an officer in the U.S. Army. At the outbreak of the Civil War,

Marmaduke resigned his commission and joined his secessionist uncle in the Missouri State Guard. He soon obtained a commission in the regular Confederate Army and quickly received promotion to brigadier general. In the Confederate Army, Marmaduke earned a reputation for bravery as well as for violence. In 1863, Marmaduke killed his superior officer, Brigadier General Lucius Marshall Walker, in a duel. Later, Marmaduke permitted the massacre of nearly two hundred African American soldiers at the Battle of Poison Spring in Arkansas. He ended the Civil War as a prisoner at Johnson's Island in Ohio, having been captured during Price's Raid. After the war, he returned to Missouri and took up politics. Following in his father's footsteps, John Sappington Marmaduke served as governor from 1885 until his death.[2]

The suddenness of Marmaduke's passing prompted an outpouring of grief in Jefferson City. The *Butler Weekly Times* noted a "feeling of sorrow and gloom hanging over the city."[3] In the generally somber atmosphere of the capital, however, Confederate veteran and state adjutant general John C. Jamison could not fail to note one glaring exception. In the national cemetery, barely twenty-five yards from Marmaduke's gravesite in the adjoining city cemetery, the flag had not yet been lowered to half-mast as was customary following the death of a dignitary. Tasked with arranging the governor's funeral, Jamison could not let the matter go and fired off an angry message to Senator George Graham Vest in Washington, DC. "For some reason, easily to be surmised," Jamison fumed, "the superintendent of the National Cemetery here has ignored any respect usual under such sad circumstances as have befallen our state, and neglected or refused to place the national flag at half-mast." Jamison accused the superintendent, Union veteran and member of the Grand Army of the Republic (GAR) John S. Ferguson, of a deliberate insult. "He has been opposed to the Governor and the Governor's friends on account of the part he took in the late war," Jamison claimed, "and now declines to bury his malice."[4]

For his part, Ferguson swore he enjoyed a friendly relationship with Marmaduke. If indeed Ferguson "declined to bury his malice," however, it would have been little wonder. He fought against Marmaduke in the 1864 Red River Campaign, during which Ferguson suffered thirteen separate wounds before being taken as a prisoner of war. As far as the flag was concerned, Ferguson insisted that he had never received orders to lower it and blamed the whole misunderstanding on bad weather. He claimed the pulley on the flag pole had frozen and did not thaw until the morning of the governor's burial, at which time he said "it was raised at half-mast, draped in mourning."[5] Ferguson did not offer it as an excuse, but the frozen pulley may have presented him with an additional difficulty. Ferguson lost his right arm at the 1864 Battle of Sabine Crossroads.[6] Whether Ferguson intended to insult Marmaduke's memory or not, the incident illustrated that wartime tensions still ran high in Missouri, particularly among former Confederates, who felt their memory of the war was under assault.

It was in this contentious atmosphere that Confederate Missourians struggled to come to terms with their defeat. The Lost Cause, the predominant memory of the Civil War among white southerners, did not readily fit the experiences of most Missourians. In the first place, many Missourians did not feel they had "lost" the war at all. In their efforts at Civil War commemoration, Missouri's former Confederates therefore faced a twofold dilemma: redeeming the defeated Confederacy as a whole and redeeming Missouri's place in its memory. This was no easy task. Missouri's Confederates vied against significant forces that undercut the relevance of the Lost Cause in their state, including the marginalization of the West in Civil War history, disinterestedness on the part of local Confederate veterans, an unwelcome association with guerrillas, a complicated political landscape, and competing Union commemoration. To counteract these challenges, Missourians took great pains to stress why the peculiar circumstances of their border state made them *more* deserving of an honorable place in Confederate commemoration, not less. They articulated two main arguments in their defense: First, Missouri was southern by virtue of its strong antebellum ties to the South. Second, Missouri suffered occupation and martyrdom on behalf of the Confederate war effort. Despite their determination, however, they never succeeded in establishing the Lost Cause as Missouri's uncontested Civil War memory.

Many former Confederates sought solace and redemption through the commemoration of the Lost Cause. That narrative depicted the Civil War as an honorable if ultimately hopeless fight, which exemplified the skill of Confederate commanders, the courage of Confederate soldiers, the fortitude of southern women, and the alleged loyalty of enslaved African Americans. It insisted that secession was not treason but a justifiable action inspired by the American Revolution and in keeping with the principles of the Constitution. The Lost Cause further maintained secession was not motivated by a desire to protect slavery but rather to defend a state's right to self-government. The ensuing Civil War had not been a "rebellion" but a war between rival nations. Finally, the Lost Cause perpetuated the belief that although white southerners devoted their unqualified support to the Confederacy and fought at least as bravely as their foes, they succumbed to the superior resources of the Union.

For a variety of reasons, Missouri's unusual wartime history presented a challenge to this conventional Lost Cause narrative. Despite longstanding demographic, cultural, political, and economic ties to the slaveholding South, Missourians unequivocally repudiated secession at their state convention in 1861. Due to the extralegal machinations of Governor Claiborne Fox Jackson, Missouri did get a star on the Confederate flag, but it kept its place on the Star-Spangled Banner as well. As a result, it could not categorically claim to be a part of the Confederacy. Furthermore, Missouri's complicated relationship with slavery set the state apart from the Deep South. Although many white Missourians defended the institution, there was an active antislavery movement in the state and the General Assembly enacted emancipation before the ratification of the Thirteenth Amendment.

Missouri's political history also proved an obstacle to the Lost Cause. If Confederate Missourians expected to follow the trajectory of their sister border state Kentucky in "becoming Confederate," they were disappointed.[7] In the case of Kentucky, historian Anne Marshall argues, Confederate commemoration gained enough traction to obliterate the memory of the state's wartime Unionism. Marshall acknowledges, however, that her study does not necessarily apply to other border states—especially Missouri. "While Maryland, Delaware, and Missouri each had strong proslavery, antifederal factions," she writes, "they all, for various reasons, came under Republican control by the end of the war."[8] Not so in Kentucky, where the Democratic Party quickly reasserted itself and white supremacist extralegal violence derailed efforts by local Republicans to affect Reconstruction in their state. In Missouri, on the other hand, Radical Republicans imposed their own form of Reconstruction. The 1865 Drake Constitution and its infamous Iron Clad Oath disenfranchised former Confederates and discouraged southern migration. Even when the Democrats regained power in 1872, their record was largely pro-Union and moderate. The political power exercised by Missouri's black communities also prevented white Democrats from imposing widespread, legalized discrimination. As a result, Missouri did not prove fertile ground for the Lost Cause. The state was simply too entrenched in Unionism and moderation to follow Kentucky's path toward embracing a Confederate identity.

Still, Confederate Missourians turned to the Lost Cause as a means of coming to terms with defeat and, in the process, sharing in the suffering of their southern compatriots. They felt the sting of surrender every bit as keenly. At least Captain James Porter of the Tenth Missouri Cavalry certainly did. Shortly after learning of the end of the Civil War, Porter scribbled down a song written to the tune of "Maryland, My Maryland," venting his despair and voicing his certainty that the vanquished Confederates would be made "slaves." Porter's lyrics also spoke of his family's ties to Virginia and expressed his determination to die for "Dixie's land." "We yet would die . . . for thee," he wrote, "If this last bloody act of ours / Could only set thy people free."[9] Porter employed the metaphor of slavery and freedom without a hint of irony and, while he may have justly feared disenfranchisement or even arrest under Missouri's Radical regime, no one proposed stripping former Confederates of their personhood. While Porter grieved for the fate of Dixie, however, he also identified himself as a westerner. For disaffected Missourians like Porter, their identity as westerners existed alongside a deep emotional connection to the southern Confederacy. They mourned its defeat and celebrated the Lost Cause in aid of its vindication.

One of the ways in which Missourians sought to commemorate the Lost Cause was by promoting pro-Confederate histories of the Civil War. Missourians were not alone in this undertaking. Fearing history—particularly if left to northern authors—would cast them as traitors dedicated to an immoral cause, former Confederates took up their pens in defense of secession, slavery, and their military prowess. In Missouri, however, Confederate histories took on an extra duty: vindicating not only the Lost Cause but Missouri's place in it too. Confederate Missourians believed history would bear out their devotion to the Lost Cause if they could only regain control of the narrative.

No one worked harder than John Newman Edwards to craft a Confederate history for Missouri. Both in his work as a journalist and as the author of two books, *Shelby and His Men; or, The War in the West* (1867) and *Noted Guerrillas; or, The Warfare of the Border* (1877), Edwards became one of the chief architects of Missouri's Lost Cause.[10] Himself a veteran of Jo Shelby's Iron Brigade, Edwards sought to enshrine a pantheon of western Confederate heroes, including Shelby and William Clarke Quantrill, to stand alongside Robert E. Lee and Stonewall Jackson. He also stressed Missouri's strong ties to the South and its sacrifices on behalf of the Confederate war effort. According to historian Matthew C. Hulbert, Edwards believed his work would build a "bond" of "shared experience of federal oppression and postwar discontent," tying together the experiences of Missourians under martial law and southerners under Reconstruction.[11] Confederate Missourians, for their part, venerated Edwards. At a Confederate reunion in 1890, for example, Edwards rated as highly as any Confederate hero of the war. According to one account, "Every time Shelby's or Price's or Marmaduke's names were mentioned . . . the assembly broke into tumultuous cheers, and when reference was made to the late John N. Edwards the very rafters trembled under the thunders of applause."[12]

In order to further propagate the mythology of the Lost Cause, Missouri's former Confederates organized into societies. The first statewide organization for Confederate veterans was the Ex-Confederate Association of Missouri. Founded in 1881, the Ex-Confederates were a social and benevolent society not wholly unlike the GAR. The group insisted it had no desire to perpetuate wartime hostilities but dedicated itself to the preservation of Confederate history and to the public commemoration of the Lost Cause.[13] Such efforts, the Ex-Confederates observed, "serve a double purpose" of both honoring Confederates and impressing a sense of their virtue onto future generations.[14] Another of the primary motivations for the organization was to raise funds for a Confederate veterans' home in the state.

Any veteran of the Confederate military was eligible for membership in the association, even if they served in another state. The Ex-Confederates, however, never extended membership to guerrillas. Although former guerrillas could certainly be found within the roster of the Ex-Confederate Association, they joined only with proof of service in the regular army. Captain William H. Gregg, for instance, rode with infamous guerrilla chieftain William Clarke Quantrill but joined the Ex-Confederates by claiming his service in Shelby's Brigade.

Even with its liberal eligibility requirements, the Ex-Confederate Association struggled to fill its ranks. In December 1887, the organization claimed 2,400 members but lagged far behind the enrollment of the Department of Missouri GAR, which stood at 15,392.[15] It is worth remembering, however, that more than twice as many Missourians served in the Union Army, that the numbers of Union veterans in the state had swollen through migration from the North, and that Missouri hosted the national GAR encampment in 1887—a special occasion that surely boosted the GAR's numbers. Still, the officers of the Ex-Confederate Association expressed frustration at their society's lack of growth, pointing out that its membership composed "less than a tenth of the Ex-Confederates of the State."[16]

The legacy of guerrilla warfare represented another source of irritation for the Ex-Confederate Association. On the whole, the Ex-Confederates and the guerrillas had a distinctly uncomfortable relationship with one another, which speaks volumes about Missouri's complicated place in Confederate memory. For their part, many guerrillas sought recognition as legitimate

Confederates. According to historian Jeremy Neely, they worked to incorporate themselves into the Lost Cause and to "rescue" their reputation from what they perceived to be "the undeserved fates of historical obscurity and villainy."[17] With the help of John Newman Edwards, guerrillas cultivated depictions of themselves as Robin Hood–like heroes.[18] This mythology contained several key themes. Former guerrillas emphasized their honor by claiming they had never harmed women, and they justified their brutality as retaliation for outrages committed by Union soldiers in general and Kansans in particular. Their war, they claimed, was one of self-defense. Guerrillas further asserted that they were, at heart, peaceful men. William J. Courtney, a veteran of Shelby's Brigade, insisted that since the end of the war, "no charge of crime or violation of the law has ever been laid at their doors. They have been law-abiding, industrious citizens since the close of hostilities."[19] In most cases, he insisted, the guerrillas blended into society, their outlaw ways forgotten. They "exhibited 'no evidence of the old spirit' and had 'successfully lived down the bad repute of years ago.'"[20] The guerrillas' perception of themselves as peace-loving members of society, however, was directly at odds with the conduct of former guerrillas like Jesse James and his gang, who became notorious outlaws in the aftermath of the Civil War and tainted Missouri's Confederates by association.

The exploits of Missouri's guerrillas attracted much popular interest, especially as these rough-and-tumble characters merged with the mythic appeal of the West. Indeed, the guerrilla was an overtly western character—individualistic, antiestablishment, hostile to government intrusion, resourceful, flamboyant, romantic, and deadly. Their brutality and their association with postwar banditry deepened Missouri's identification with the "Wild West," further distinguishing Missouri's Civil War experience from the rest of the country.[21] While the guerrillas themselves sought to adapt their unique wartime experience to the broader themes of the Lost Cause, they far better embodied its distinctiveness.

Whatever popular appeal the guerrillas enjoyed was lost on the Ex-Confederate Association. Its members expressed annoyance, if not outright contempt, for guerrillas. In the Ex-Confederates' efforts to legitimize the western theater of the war, the guerrillas represented a stumbling block. After all, guerrillas were not regular soldiers and operated outside of the Confederate government. They delegitimized Missouri's war as a "side-show," a campaign run by murderous bushwhackers motivated by self-interest, not honorable soldiers serving a noble cause. In 1882, a few short months after the death of Jesse James, the Ex-Confederate Association made it quite plain such outlaws had no affiliation with legitimate Confederates. Thomas Caute

Reynolds, who succeeded Claiborne Fox Jackson as Missouri's Confederate governor-in-exile, insisted, "It so happens that people who are not and never were Confederates, but are simply criminals, have committed train robberies and other outrages in sections of the country where Confederates happen to be in numbers. . . . It becomes our special duty, then, to be foremost in sustaining law and order and in aiding authorities in putting down those wrong-doers." According to the *Iron County Register*, Reynolds's remarks were met with "loud applause."[22] Later, the Ex-Confederates took an even more damning tone, voicing "especial detestation" for the likes of the James Gang. "We will be content with nothing less than the extermination of this class of enemies of society," the Ex-Confederates vowed.[23]

While Missouri's Confederate veterans struggled to organize and define themselves in the shadow of the eastern Confederacy and in opposition to the guerrillas, their wives and daughters were becoming a force to be reckoned with. In 1890, a group of women in St. Louis organized as an auxiliary to the Ex-Confederate Association, calling themselves the Daughters of the Confederacy. Their primary objective was to assist the association in its effort to establish a Confederate veterans' home in Missouri, but they became instrumental to the proliferation of the Lost Cause on the national level.[24] As the first society of Confederate women to christen themselves "Daughters," they helped inspire the organization of the national United Daughters of the Confederacy (UDC) in 1895. The UDC consolidated various state and local organizations, like the Missouri Daughters, under a central organization, and it often credited the Missouri Daughters as instrumental to its origins.

As the driving force behind the commemoration of the Lost Cause all across the United States, the UDC adopted a multifaceted mission: historical, benevolent, educational, memorial, and patriotic. Like the Woman's Relief Corps (WRC), the UDC was a characteristic woman's club of the late nineteenth century, providing a forum for women to take an active role in civic life. Women's interest in charitable works and education played into the pervasive stereotype that they were more nurturing than men and especially suited to such work. According to historian Karen L. Cox, the UDC provided women "a venue, thinly veiled by tradition, in which to express themselves politically." As much as these women sought to provide aid and support to Confederate veterans, they also acted in overtly political ways to control the narrative of Civil War history in order to redeem the honor of defeated white southerners.[25]

Following the creation of the UDC, the Missouri Daughters of the Confederacy renamed themselves the Missouri Division UDC in 1898.

Not only had this group helped found the UDC but the Missouri Division also became the first UDC organization in the West.[26] Any woman who could demonstrate a familial relationship to a Confederate veteran was eligible to join. It was a descendant society, which ensured its survival even after the passing of the Civil War generation. In the meantime, however, its following in Missouri remained relatively small, especially compared to the other border states. In 1902, the Missouri Division UDC reported 698 members.[27] In Maryland, the Baltimore chapter alone had 714 members, while the Kentucky Division boasted a membership of 1,263.[28] Meanwhile the UDC's local rivals—the Department of Missouri WRC—held an enrollment of 1,769 women.[29] Still, its sparse roster did not damper the initiative of the Missouri Division UDC. As President Matilda Weidemeyer Gantt reflected with pride: "The Missouri Division may not be the largest of the State Divisions in point of numbers . . . and as for the readiness in every good work, her eagerness in attempting, is only excelled by her capacity for finishing."[30] The Missouri Division UDC took the lead from the veterans in establishing the Missouri Confederate Home, erecting the state's most notable Confederate monument at Forest Park in St. Louis, and sponsoring Confederate histories of the Civil War. Indeed, what claim Missourians could stake to the Lost Cause was due largely to these women's efforts.[31]

Just as the Missouri Daughters became part of a national Confederate society, the Ex-Confederate Association evolved into the Missouri Division of the United Confederate Veterans (UCV) in 1895. The UCV, a national organization founded in 1889, characterized itself as a social and benevolent society. The UCV primarily functioned as a fraternal association, providing a forum for veterans to meet, hold reunions, and revive the camaraderie of military life. Membership required proof of service in the Confederate Army or Navy and evidence of an honorable discharge, though, as with the Ex-Confederate Association, veterans were not required to have served in a Missouri unit. The UCV charged itself with caring for the Confederate dead and providing charity for disabled and needy veterans, as well as Confederate widows and orphans. Beyond this, it determined to write Confederate histories and construct monuments.[32] These would ensure that Missouri's contributions to the Confederacy would not be overlooked. At the same time, the UCV professed a desire to heal the breach between Union and Confederate veterans. As he assumed command of the Missouri Division in 1895, Jo Shelby proclaimed, "Let the country know that our inclination and desire as well as duty demands at our hands whenever we find the Union veteran in distress or need of aid to extend to him the same relief that we would tender to one who may become a member of this organization."[33]

Figure 3. Reunion of Missouri Division United Confederate Veterans, Warrensburg, 1913. Courtesy of Liljenquist Family Collection of Civil War Photographs, Library of Congress, Washington, DC

Despite their reconciliationist avowals, Missouri's Confederate societies were not bashful in their propagation of the Lost Cause. At a reunion of the Ex-Confederate Association in Higginsville, for instance, former Confederate senator George Graham gave an impassioned paean to the Lost Cause. He spoke of the "glory" of Confederate soldiers "who fought for the cause they knew to be right, but which . . . became a lost cause." Encouraged by the increasing enthusiasm of the audience, he continued, "There is no stain on our honor. [Cheers and interruption]. There is no blemish on our manhood [renewed cheers]; we have no apologies to make, and we don't intend to make any." At this last, the crowd went out of control. According to the published proceedings of the reunion, "The Senator had to pause quite a minute while the badge-wearers yelled, sprang to their feet and waved their hats."[34] Like other former Confederates, these Missourians insisted on the legitimacy of the Confederate nation and mourned its demise. Justifying the Civil War and mitigating their own responsibility for it became an important refrain in Confederate commemoration. For example, the minutes of the Campbell Camp UCV noted that on one occasion, "Dr. H. B. Bonde . . . delivered an eloquent and thrilling address on 'was the South wrong, if so in what respect.'" Bonde so thoroughly defended the defeated Confederacy that he "aroused the old veterans to a high pitch of enthusiasm and on motion . . . a vote of thanks was given."[35]

Missouri's Confederate associations also endorsed partisan politics. They were associated with the Democratic Party just as their rivals in the GAR were linked to the Republicans. Again, it was no accident that the Democratic Party returned to power in Missouri after the state restored the franchise to former Confederates. One-time guerrilla William H. Gregg brashly encapsulated the Confederates' unswerving fealty to the Democrats, giving insight into their racial politics as well. Frustrated by a Kansas City politician who declined to meet with the Ex-Confederate Association for fear of being branded a "rebel," Gregg demanded, "What could the Democratic party of this state do without the ex-Confederate influence?" And, employing unapologetically racist language, he answered, "The fact is we ex-Confederates stand in the same relation to the Democratic party that the niggers do to the Republican party. . . . There is just this difference. The niggers have to be bought sometimes and we don't."[36] Wartime allegiances continued to inform state politics, dividing Missourians along partisan and racial lines. On more than one occasion the UCV petitioned the state government to appoint former Confederates and Democrats to political positions, particularly where veterans' affairs were concerned.

Although Missouri Democrats, even with the support of former Confederates, were never able to institute Jim Crow laws resembling those in the South, white supremacy was no less militant or dangerous in the border state. Often, former Confederates espoused racism masked as pride in their Anglo-Saxon heritage or in paternalistic reminiscences about supposedly "loyal" slaves. On occasion, however, the veneer of benevolence cracked and exposed the deep-seated racism many former Confederates endorsed. In her 1905 presidential address to the Missouri Division UDC, Mrs. J. H. Campbell evoked the mythology of the enslaved mammy and spoke "with unspeakable appreciation of all the devotion, the fidelity, and the heroic abnegation exhibited by negro servants towards the families of their masters." Practitioners of the Lost Cause employed this trope to illustrate the supposedly harmonious, nearly familial relationships between slaveholders and enslaved. "Forgetting none of this," Campbell continued, "yet . . . I would most earnestly solicit this body . . . to put itself on record as being forever and forever opposed to any crossing of the color line toward the possible final outcome of social equality, and as being just as solemnly sworn to maintain to the end of the world the integrity of the white race."[37] Campbell's sentiments were not only racist but dangerous. Her insistence that segregation was necessary for the preservation of the white race evoked the defense most often used to justify racial violence and lynching—miscegenation.

Indeed, some of Missouri's Confederates explicitly sanctioned the white supremacist violence so characteristic of the era. Although lynching did not reach the same epidemic proportions in Missouri that it attained in the Deep South, sixty African American Missourians were lynched between 1877 and 1950.[38] Lynchings were therefore part of the context of Civil War commemoration, and local members of the UCV approved of them as a means of racial control. In 1909, for example, the Campbell Camp UCV of Springfield, Missouri, lent its support to a national movement asking President William Howard Taft to pardon Joseph F. Shipp, a prominent Confederate veteran and sheriff of Hamilton County, Tennessee. Shipp was tasked with holding Ed Johnson, an African American man, in custody while Johnson awaited an appeal to the U.S. Supreme Court on his conviction for the rape of a white woman. When news reached Tennessee that Johnson had received his appeal, a white mob broke Johnson out of jail and lynched him. The extent of Shipp's involvement was not entirely clear. At worst, he voiced approval for the lynching; at best, he did nothing to prevent it. The Supreme Court ultimately convicted Shipp of contempt of court for failing to protect Johnson and sentenced him to ninety days in prison. The case drew national attention as "the first time the federal government has placed men behind the bars as an outcome of the lynching of a negro."[39] The Campbell Camp sought Taft's pardon on the basis of Shipp's "long and honorable service in public life and his splendid military record as well as his spotless private character," but they evidently sympathized with Shipp's acceptance of this highly racialized mode of vigilante justice.[40] Nevertheless, the camp's appeal failed to move the president. Shipp never received his pardon.

The prevalence of racist attitudes among white Missourians, however, cannot be taken as proof that a majority of them sympathized with the Lost Cause. Even while Democrats filled Missouri's political offices, the Missouri Division UCV struggled to recruit and retain members. Membership steadily declined after 1895, and camps reported poor attendance. Although this was due in part to the advancing age and death rate of veterans, some former Confederates accused their fellow Missourians of apathy, perhaps borne of a more general lack of interest in the trans-Mississippi theater of the Civil War. "Am sorry to see so few items from this side the Father of Waters," W. L. Morrison opined in an 1895 issue of the *Confederate Veteran*. "From reading the VETERAN," he continued, "one would almost conclude we had no war west of the Mississippi." After recounting a wartime incident when three of his comrades saved him from certain capture, Morrison concluded, "As a Missouri ex-Confederate, I appeal to my old comrades to support and write for the Veteran. Wake up, old boys in gray!"[41] In 1901, former Confederate

Leroy B. Valliant swore to the Missouri Division UCV that "Missouri is not lacking in appreciation of the Confederate soldiers," but he admitted there was precious little evidence to support his claim.[42] The following year, John C. Landis, adjutant general of the Missouri Division, lamented "the very serious lack of organization there is with the Confederate Veterans of the state of Missouri, and which lack is fast burying a great mass of Missouri Confederate Soldiers beneath the waves of forgetfulness and oblivion."[43]

It is easy to understand why these men felt like they were fighting a losing battle in their efforts to distinguish Missouri's Confederates. After all, they were contending with serious opposition. The memory of Missouri's staunch Unionism was not easily dismissed. However hard they tried, Missouri's Confederate veterans could not compete with the GAR. In 1890, for example, there were nearly twice as many members of the Department of Missouri GAR as the total number of Confederate veterans residing in the state.[44] Furthermore, shortfalls in membership diminished the influence and prestige of Missouri's Confederate societies at the national level. As a consequence of the low enrollment in the Missouri Division UCV, for example, it never earned the distinction of hosting a national UCV reunion. Even though the border cities of Louisville, Kentucky, and Washington, DC, each hosted twice, the UCV never came to Missouri.

The difficulty the Missouri Division UCV experienced in maintaining its membership was certainly compounded by the state's complicated wartime history. Many Confederate sympathizers in Missouri served as irregulars, either in the State Guard or as guerrillas, and were therefore ineligible for UCV membership. This did not prevent guerrillas from organizing themselves. Surviving members of Quantrill's band gathered for the first time on September 11, 1898. The timing was relatively late compared to the formation of other memorial organizations, but guerillas had reason to lay low. Some, like the infamous Cole Younger, may have been serving prison sentences. Younger became a regular presence at guerrilla reunions only after his release from a Minnesota prison in 1901. By 1905, the ex-guerrillas organized a society known as the Quantrill Men and began hosting regular events.[45] To outward appearances, guerrilla reunions were much like those held by regular veterans. "These comrades are hale specimens of Confederate veterans," the *Confederate Veteran* observed, "ever rea[d]y to reminisce and tell anecdotes, as are all comrades when they meet after long separation."[46] Guerrillas often encouraged regular Confederate veterans to join them and, on a couple of occasions, invited Union veterans as well. There is little evidence, however, that the UCV ever returned the courtesy. While former Confederates certainly attended guerrilla reunions, the Missouri Division

UCV does not appear to have offered them any recognition as equal members of the Confederate services.[47]

The organization of the guerrillas certainly accentuated Missouri's awkward position in relation to the southern Confederacy and to the Lost Cause. Indeed, Missourians' sense of marginalization from the rest of the Confederacy—in terms of both geography and experience—became fundamental to how they constructed the Lost Cause in their state. They stressed the complicated context of the border state, which presented Missourians with distressing practical and emotional realities few southerners had to face. "The geographical situation of the State made it in the beginning one of the most important places for military occupation in the Confederacy," Confederate veteran Leroy B. Valliant elaborated, "while at the same time the inclination of the people was such as would have given it easily into the possession of Confederate forces. But, unfortunately, our people hesitated."[48] As James B. Gantt, a distinguished judge and prominent member of the Missouri Division UCV, explained,

> Hard as was the experience of all the Southern States . . . the situation of Missouri, surrounded on three sides by free States, all of which were bound to adhere to the North, was such as to cause the most fearful apprehensions. Her people prayed that war might be averted. They had no desire to imbrue their hands with the blood of their countrymen, North or South. These conditions produced a division of sentiment. . . . At the beginning they fondly hoped they might be allowed to observe a policy of neutrality. They refused to see the situation as their Southern kindred saw it—that war was inevitable—and that they must side either with the North or the South. Indecision and vacillation seemed to have ruled the hour.[49]

While they continued to work toward a peaceful solution, war caught them unprepared. "Before the people of the State realized that there was to be a war," Valliant said, "they were in the hands of a Federal garrison."[50] Once the Union Army won control of the state in the summer of 1861, the Confederate cause in Missouri was well and truly lost.

In a way, Confederate Missourians insisted, their state's failure to secede was an even greater testament to their loyalty. They took pride in emphasizing the sacrifice they made of the defense of their state in order to serve where the Confederacy needed them most. Despite anxieties about the fate of loved ones at home and behind enemy lines, Missourians proved as dedicated and brave soldiers as any in the Confederate armies. As the *Missouri Republican* insisted, Missourians "were not backward when the crisis came. . . . No braver or truer men followed the fortunes of the lost cause to its ultimate issue."[51] President James Bannerman of the Ex-Confederate Association reassured his comrades: "Missouri Confederates, you may well be proud of your record as soldiers. The Confederacy was proud of you and your opponents held you in the respect that bravery always commands at the hands of brave men."[52] In the pages of the *Confederate Veteran*, James Gantt asked Confederates everywhere to remember the "men who left their homes here in Missouri without arms or ammunition . . . and made the name of Missourians forever glorious."[53] Confederate veteran Maecenas E. Benton explored a similar theme at a UCV reunion in Mexico, Missouri. "After the first few months of war the Missouri Confederate was put to the front to fight for Arkansas, Texas and the other states," he said, "while Missouri, his home, with his family exposed, was left for the most part without any protection." Drawing a colorful metaphor, he continued, "The game cock fights better on his own dung hill, but the Missouri Confederate, forgetting self, sacrificed his state and family in his loyalty to the general cause."[54]

In their attempts to earn recognition of their own service to the Confederacy, however, Confederates of the trans-Mississippi theater were careful never to slight the juggernaut of the Lost Cause—the Army of Northern Virginia. One of the most prominent apologists of the western Confederacy was Kentuckian Bennett H. Young. Speaking at the 1901 national UCV reunion in Memphis, Tennessee, Young insisted, "Western soldiers make no claim of being better than the men who fought in the East. . . . All these men . . . ask is to have it known that they exhibited the same heroism, the same gallantry, the same readiness to suffer and die, the same unselfish patriotism."[55] Young admitted that the western Confederacy was far removed from the active eastern theater and lacked its distinguished commanders, but took pride that western soldiers fought with unrivaled bravery and won the admiration of their comrades in Virginia. Indeed, some of the most prominent members of the Missouri Division UCV, including James Gantt, served in that revered legion. At one reunion Gantt testified, "Let one who followed that 'Son of Thunder,' Stonewall Jackson, on the sanguinary plains of the Old Dominion, bear witness to his brethren of the western and transmississippi armies that the Virginia soldier recognized in his western comrade the same indomitable spirit, the same unconquerable courage which distinguished the Confederate soldier in the East." Speaking as a postwar migrant to Missouri, Gantt admitted that easterners like himself "occupied a more favored position in that we fought with the consciousness nearly all the time that our loved ones were largely shielded from the scenes of desolation that swept over Missouri. . . . It seemed to me then, and it does now, that it took yet stouter hearts than ours to remain faithful as the Star of Hope grew dim and final success seemed impossible, and yet such was the record of the Missourians." "No, my countrymen," Gantt concluded, "there is glory enough for us all, and there is no place for invidious comparisons."[56] Nevertheless, Missourians felt overlooked in the pantheon of the Lost Cause. "No man in the West envies them a single laurel," Young observed, "or would take from them one ray in that luminous glory which gathers round their heads; but the Western Confederate soldier . . . says: 'We too bear the Confederate name.'"[57]

If Confederate Missourians felt misunderstood and underappreciated as westerners, Missouri's status as a loyal border state presented an even greater challenge to their attempts to commemorate the Lost Cause. A significant part of the struggle for Confederate memory in Missouri stemmed from the fact that Missouri was, after all, a Union state. Even more problematic, Missouri was also a state with a large and active organization of the GAR and its auxiliaries. It was inevitable that Union and Confederate Missourians would cross paths on their separate missions of commemoration. As a result, former Confederates maintained a cordial, if strained, relationship with white Unionists. In Springfield, for example, the Campbell Camp UCV often fraternized with their neighboring GAR organizations, the McCroskey and Matthews Posts. The UCV and GAR men entertained one another at periodic banquets and sometimes joined in Memorial Day services.[58] Upon the death of John B. Gordon, the revered national commander in chief of the UCV, the Matthews Post quartet attended the Campbell Camp's meeting and "rendered in pathetic style" a ballad called "'The Blue and the Gray.'"[59]

Although there is less evidence of fraternization between Union and Confederate women in Missouri, GAR members often contributed to the charitable causes of the Missouri Division UDC, particularly on behalf of the state Confederate Home. On one occasion, however, the Stonewall Jackson Chapter UDC in Kansas City was moved by a visit from Father Thomas Ewing Sherman, son of Union general William Tecumseh Sherman. It would be hard to think of a man more widely reviled by former Confederates than Sherman, yet the Daughters greeted his son with a song. Father Sherman made a "graceful, tactful talk" and gave one young woman his rosary as a parting gift. In all, the chapter minutes noted, it was "a pleasing incident, illustrating how the whirligig of time brings changes."[60]

Such fraternization did not always come easily in the border state. In September 1889, the GAR posts of southwestern Missouri hosted a reunion in Cassville. As was not uncommon, the Union veterans made a goodwill gesture and invited former Confederates to participate. At first glance, the invitation might be taken as evidence that Missourians had put wartime differences behind them—that time and fraternalism had eroded the bitter memories of the Civil War—but the goodwill did not last long. According to an account in the *Cassville Democrat*, the high spirits of the occasion got the better of the Union men and they began to sing a rendition of "John Brown's Body." As the song went on, the Confederates must have grown increasingly uncomfortable, but unknowing or uncaring, the Union veterans plowed gleefully into the provocative verse: "Hang Jeff Davis from a sour apple tree." Realizing their faux pas, the GAR officers made a hasty apology and insisted they had not intended offense, but the Confederates were not appeased. "It was in exceeding bad taste," the paper fumed. "If you invite a man to your house it is your duty to treat him courteously as long as he behaves himself, and no one has intimated that the confederates misbehaved."[61]

Another serious contretemps occurred in 1897. In observation of the thirty-sixth anniversary of the Confederate victory at the 1861 Battle of Wilson's Creek, the Campbell Camp UCV joined in an effort by local veterans to organize a "National Reunion of the Blue and the Gray."[62] A similar reunion took place on the battlefield in 1883, so there was likely little apprehension about its success. The Missouri Division UCV promoted the event at the national encampment and expected hundreds of veterans to attend. While the Confederates initially evinced genuine enthusiasm at the prospect of a joint reunion, attitudes soon soured. According to H. B. Bonde, the Campbell Camp's representative on the reunion committee, "There had been some friction between members of the committee on account of the proposed carrying of the Confederate flag in procession during the reunion."[63] At a meeting of the Campbell Camp, Bonde reassured those present that "it was the intention of said committee to accord full recognition and place Confederates on equal footing with Union soldiers." In at least one case, however, his assurances fell on deaf ears. An unnamed comrade interjected "that he had attended one so-called reunion of Blue and Gray and that it satisfied him; that he had been persuaded to march by the side of an ex-Union soldier and that he had been grossly insulted and did not purpose to take another such risk."[64]

The final damper on the Campbell Camp's enthusiasm came when the reunion committee ruled that Confederate veterans could not carry the Confederate flag in the planned parade. The news prompted "a lengthy and animated discussion" at the next meeting of the camp.[65] Frustrated, Bonde placed some of the blame for this turn of events onto his own comrades. He complained "that ex-Confederate or Southern members . . . failed to take the interest that the importance of the enterprise demanded and that he had many times been forced to act almost alone as a Confederate member of the committee which fact accounted for certain changes made in the program," specifically the ban on the Confederate flag.[66]

Unionist opposition also proved a serious obstacle to the completion of one of the most significant symbols of Confederate commemoration in the state: the Confederate monument at Forest Park in St. Louis. The St. Louis Confederate Monument Association, its members largely drawn from the Missouri Division UDC, began work on the project in 1905.[67] It was intended to commemorate the soldiers and sailors of the entire Confederacy, not only Missourians, but it would still stand as a testament to St. Louis's devotion to the Lost Cause. The association soon decided on Forest Park as the best location for the monument. After serving as the site of the 1904 World's Fair, Forest Park had become increasingly important in the cultural life of the city.

The monument association certainly envisioned its work as an act of Civil War commemoration, but its members also considered the monument a form of beautification. Public art, so characteristic of European cities, would lend St. Louis an air of distinction. The association therefore began its efforts with optimism, even expecting the cooperation of Union veterans. "In the past St. Louis has drawn no party line in giving," the *St. Louis Post-Dispatch* observed. "The blue and the gray have opened their purses, without regard to buried differences."[68] Just a few months later, however, the opening round in a nearly decade-long controversy over the monument was underway. In December 1906, St. Louis's Harry P. Harding Post GAR passed a resolution condemning the proposed monument, deeming it totally inappropriate "in the loyal union city of St. Louis." The Harding Post's members insisted it was their duty as Union veterans, as well as their obligation to the Union dead, to oppose the monument. "If their living representative[s] did not protest against the erection of a Confederate statue on the public property of the city of St. Louis during their lifetime," the post's resolution concluded, "they would not be worthy American citizens."[69]

The Harding Post's statement angered the Confederate Monument Association, but it also spurred the organization to renewed action. Mrs. P. G. Robert, president of the Margaret E. A. McClure Chapter UDC, "said that she was too mad to talk about the protest, and feared that if she said anything she might say too much." Mrs. W. G. Moore, president of the monument association, said, "It would not be a dignified and proper course for the women to fight back," but noted with satisfaction that the resolutions precipitated a spike in ticket sales for a fundraising ball on behalf of the monument. Despite its indignation, the monument association felt compelled to defend its efforts. Members insisted the monument would pose no reasonable grounds for offense. First and foremost, it was to be a monument to the valor of *American* soldiers who *happened* to fight for the Confederacy. This dissembling was learned and quite deliberate—white Unionists were often willing to recognize the bravery of enemy soldiers but unwilling to do anything that would legitimize the cause they served. In the *St. Louis Post-Dispatch*, Commander James B. Dobyne of the Ransom Post GAR clarified his society's position on the proposed monument. "If it is to be a monument to the brave deeds of the Confederate soldiers I can see no objection to it," he said. If it "is to be erected as a monument to the 'Lost Cause' I can see no reason for it. I have traveled all of the world, and I don't remember to have ever seen a monument erected to causes that have been lost."[70]

In addition to the reluctance of Union veterans to glorify the Lost Cause, the idea of a substantial Confederate monument in St. Louis struck some Missourians as incongruous. Katherine E. Mann, president of the Department of Missouri Ladies of the Grand Army of the Republic (LGAR), sided with the Harding Post. The proposed monument, she felt, would be totally out of place in St. Louis. With the apprehensions that had dogged the 1887 national GAR encampment in St. Louis apparently long forgotten, Mann argued that the city ranked among the most loyal in the country. "If the [Daughters] wish to put up such a monument," she wrote the *St. Louis Post-Dispatch*, "let it be in the South, where it belongs. . . . Why should such a monument be erected here? St. Louis is not a Southern city, and never was. Do you think New York, Boston or Chicago, or any city north, east or west, would listen to such an idea?"[71]

Even the monument's proponents had to admit that St. Louis was not renowned for its southern sympathies. "History," one newspaper observed, has "taken away from St. Louis much of the sentiment that linked it with the cause of the South." The author felt St. Louis's reputation for Unionism was an exaggeration, despite the fact that both Ulysses S. Grant and William Tecumseh Sherman had once called the city home and that it had quickly succumbed to Union occupation in 1861. "But because Grant once lived here and the Government liked the St. Louis climate," the author joked, "is no indication that there was no sympathizers with the Confederacy." After all, the writer added, the women of St. Louis helped found the UDC.[72]

Nevertheless, prevailing sentiment in the city was not generally friendly to the Lost Cause. On one occasion, UCV official James Gantt noted with chagrin that it was impossible to "purchase a single Confederate flag in St. Louis."[73] "It is a recognized fact," another UCV member complained in the *Confederate Veteran*, "that the large foreign and Northern population in St. Louis is an opposing element that retards the raising of funds to erect in St. Louis a suitable monument to the soldiers and sailors of the Confederacy, some having carried it to the point of making a public protest against our being allowed to do so. No Chapter in the South has this obstacle to contend with."[74] In the face of such hostility, work on the monument proved frustrating. Roma J. Wornall, president of the Missouri Division UDC, attributed these tribulations to Missouri's removal from the Confederacy proper. "In the Border States it is more difficult to keep up enthusiasm in our work than in Southern States," she explained.[75]

The challenges local Unionists raised against the Lost Cause, if vexing, were at least predictable. With Union and Confederate Missourians both actively working to control the narrative of Civil War commemoration, such clashes were unavoidable. More surprising was the dismissal Confederate Missourians met with from their southern comrades. Despite the ongoing efforts of Missourians to memorialize their service to the Confederacy, some southerners evidently questioned whether Missouri was truly a Confederate state. The strength of Missouri's wartime Unionism, its postwar Republican politics, and the omnipresence of the GAR all served to dim Missouri's star in the eyes of other Confederates. This realization came as something of a shock to Missouri Confederates during the planning for the UDC monument to Confederate president Jefferson Davis in Richmond, Virginia. The monument would feature a bronze statue of Davis surrounded by thirteen columns—one representing each state of the Confederacy, including Missouri. This resulted in a controversy when the border state of Maryland felt excluded.[76] As a solution, some suggested the border states should not receive columns on the Davis monument at all because they were only "step-sisters to the Confederacy." Sallie R. McCutchen, a member of the Missouri Division UDC, responded angrily in the *Confederate Veteran*: "Only eleven columns! No! no! a thousand times no!" "None were braver or more loyal to the Southern cause than grand old Missouri's sons and daughters," McCutchen insisted. "The spirit that would oppose the 'thirteen columns,'" she concluded, was "a spirit that is too narrow for a generous people to comprehend."[77] Ultimately, Missouri was recognized with a column on the Davis monument, but its quest for "Confederate credibility" was far from complete.[78]

The ongoing fight to build a Confederate monument in Forest Park would not do much to redeem the border state. In a futile attempt to allay the controversy surrounding the monument, the association revised its plans. The group promised the monument would not depict a Confederate soldier nor any battle scenes. This, its members hoped, would "avoid any possibility of arousing antagonism."[79] Sculptor George Julian Zolnay tried to craft a compromise. In his design, selected through a competition, the monument featured the "Spirit of the Confederacy" hovering over a young volunteer on the verge of parting with his family for the service. To appease Unionist Missourians, Zolnay insisted his volunteer would not appear in uniform but as a civilian.

Far from abating, however, opposition to the monument only escalated. When Zolnay revealed the young boy in his family group would be sculpted holding a Confederate flag, Union veterans raised more resistance.[80] In November 1912, the city council refused to grant the association permission to erect the monument in Forest Park.[81] The Ransom Post GAR applauded the council's decision. "I am opposed to Confederate monuments anywhere," member Francis P. Becker told the *Post-Dispatch*, "but if they insist on having them I am opposed to having them in public parks. If there is to be one in St. Louis it should be at Jefferson Barracks, where Confederate soldiers are buried."[82]

The public debate over the monument continued to revolve around whether or not St. Louis was a southern city. The monument's supporters, for example, warned that the council's refusal would not sit well with Southerners. Did the council wish to convey, the *St. Louis Post-Dispatch* asked, that St. Louis "which, through [*sic*] containing thousands of people of Southern blood, shows no tenderness, but only bitterness of memory, towards the vanquished?" Mrs. Robert Funkhouser, a member of the monument association, bristled at the news. She wrote the *Post-Dispatch*: "It ill becomes a few men in St. Louis to say that this Southern city should not honor its sons who took part in the great struggle."[83] The Sterling Price Camp UCV passed a resolution asking the council to reconsider its decision.[84] By mid-December, the city council had relented and gave the monument association permission to continue with its plans.[85]

In spite of the serious delays caused by the protests, the Confederate monument was unveiled in Forest Park on December 5, 1914. Hundreds attended the event, and the national president of the UCV, Bennett H. Young, spoke at the ceremonies. Its completion was a testament, so association president H. N. Spencer said, to the strong southern feeling in Missouri.

She hoped the city would "guard it as a sacred trust."[86] Zolnay also delivered an address, reflecting on the care he took with his design, understanding that "a monument remains forever."[87]

The monument, however, continued to draw the ire of the GAR, especially after the unveiling revealed the monument's inscription. On the back of the thirty-two-foot-high monument was a lengthy dedication honoring the soldiers and sailors of the Confederacy. The inscription claimed Confederates demonstrated "sublime self-sacrifice," and that "actuated by the purest patriotism," they fought to preserve the republic and the Constitution established by the founders. It maintained that Confederates exhibited unparalleled courage in battle but were finally "overwhelmed" and "forced to yield."[88] After all the concern and controversy surrounding Zolnay's sculpture, the monument's inscription, far more than its iconography, reified the Lost Cause.

Figure 4. Confederate monument in Forest Park, St. Louis, 1937. The flower bed in the foreground indicates the resentment many St. Louisans felt toward the monument. Courtesy of St. Louis Division of Parks and Recreation Photographs (P0814). 027016. The State Historical Society of Missouri, Photograph Collection.

At a meeting of the Ransom Post held on February 27, 1915, Union veteran George W. Bailey lambasted the monument. Bailey accused the inscription of perpetuating "Monumental Misrepresentations." He called the purported facts recorded therein "supremely ridiculous" and "a joke." Bailey went on to accuse the association of deliberately withholding the inscription because they knew its content was incendiary. "Why," he mused, "is it that in all the numerous publications descriptive of the design, the erection, and dedication and presentation of this monument, we have seen no reference whatever to these inscriptions? . . . Why have they apparently been so studiously withheld from public notice?" All things considered, Bailey argued, the monument was far less a testimony to Missouri's southern sympathies than it was "a worthy monument to the patience and forbearance of a patriotic people." Bailey felt the monument association had abused the goodwill of St. Louis's Unionists. He regretted that "this beautiful and imposing structure was erected in a public park, in a patriotic city of a Union State by permission of a patriotic people." Rather than serving as a unifying symbol, it was "perverted into a mere shrine where only a select coterie of mourners for the Lost Cause may appropriately pay tribute." One can imagine Bailey shaking his head with irony and disgust as he added, "A secession monument in a Union state and city!" The Confederates could manipulate the facts however they saw fit, Bailey concluded, but no such monument could ever redeem "the inhuman Cause of the Slave Holders' Rebellion."[89] As a testament to the Ransom Post's endorsement of Bailey's speech, they had his remarks printed and distributed.

Not content to leave the preservation of the Lost Cause to a few scattered monuments, former Confederates remained committed to promoting histories of the Civil War in Missouri. The UDC, in particular, considered this work of paramount importance and dedicated significant energy to the campaign throughout the first two decades of the twentieth century.[90] No other act of commemoration, UDC historian Matilda Weidemeyer Gantt proclaimed, could "measure up to the far-reaching effects of true and impartial Confederate history, as we are now endeavoring to gather." More so than any monument, they felt, this history would enshrine the "bravery, heroism and self-sacrifice of the women of our State during that dreadful time."[91] Published in 1913, *Reminiscences of the Women of Missouri during the Sixties* was a collection of accounts of the wartime experiences of Confederate Missourians, most of them women, including eyewitness testimonies of raids and battles. More than anything, however, *Reminiscences* was a chronicle of the sacrifices endured by women on the home front, recounting tales of robbery, destruction, and exile borne for the sake of their loyalty to the Lost Cause.[92]

Reminiscences and the other histories produced by the Missouri Division UDC echoed the tenets of Missouri's Lost Cause established by John Newman Edwards. Confederate Missourians continued to emphasize their state's close affiliation to the antebellum South and the dedication of her people to the Confederate war effort. Virginia Creel, an officer in the Kansas City Confederate Dames Chapter UDC, offered a particularly cogent defense of Missouri's southerness in an essay called "Missouri, Dixie's Affinity." Originally prepared as a speech for her chapter, it proved so popular that her fellow Daughters encouraged her to submit it not only to the state historical society but also to the *Confederate Veteran*, which she did.[93] "By blood and culture and tradition, by similar customs, ideas, ideals, and aspirations," Creel avowed, "Missouri has always been as close to the heart of the South as any State below the Mason and Dixon line." "As long as Missouri is Missouri," she concluded, "it is the South that will command her spiritual allegiance and devotion."[94] Taking up a similar refrain, Mrs. George D. Baxter, an officer in the Springfield Chapter UDC, wrote in the *Confederate Veteran,* "Missouri, owes her very existence to the South." Baxter acknowledged, however, that not all Missourians shared this sense of obligation. "When the dark hours of the War between the States came and these great Southerners had to make a choice," she confessed, "not all of them (the pity of it) chose to go with the State of their nativity."[95]

By stressing Missouri's ties to the South, former Confederates attributed the state's failure to secede not to a lack of sympathy but rather to an accident of geography that left Missouri isolated from the South and vulnerable to enemy occupation. "With the outbreak of the War between the States," Creel observed, "Missouri's position became painful in the extreme."[96] In a letter published by the Sterling Price Chapter UDC in the *Confederate Veteran*, B. F. Murdock wrote that "the Missouri boys who went out to battle for the South knew that even if the South was successful, Missouri, owing to her peculiar surroundings, would never be on the south side of the Mason and Dixon Line." Even so, their commitment never wavered. "Wherever fighting was done," Murdock continued, "Missouri blood flowed like water."[97]

Even the task of writing Civil War histories, however, could draw Confederate Missourians into conflict. In 1922, for example, a national controversy over one particularly contentious history boiled over in Missouri. The offending text, written by Colonel Huger W. Johnstone, *Truth of the*

War Conspiracy, 1861, blamed Abraham Lincoln for inciting the Civil War.[98] The national UCV passed a resolution supporting Johnstone's history, which prompted various GAR posts to condemn the UCV for "disloyalty and treason."[99] While the national UCV prepared its response to the GAR, the Missouri Division UCV disagreed over the best position to adopt. Opposing resolutions circulated, with one endorsing Johnstone's tract, another condemning it. Missouri Division UCV commander Archibald A. Pearson subverted the issue by refusing to recognize the competing resolutions and ensuring his own moved forward. Invoking Missouri's compromise tradition, Pearson's resolutions declared,

> That we can see no good results to be attained by crimination and language calculated to offend and irritate the people of one part of the United States by the people of another section. . . . We do not believe any one man responsible for the war between the North and the South. We wish to foster and encourage friendly and pleasant relations between the different sections of our beloved country. We wish to work in harmony with all good American citizens for pease [*sic*], prosperity, social and moral development of our United Country.

In defense of his resolution, Pearson added, "I wish to urge the imperative necesity [*sic*] and harmony of action not only by the wearers of the blue and the wearers of the gray but by all who are 100% American to stand together."[100] In a statement to the press on behalf of the Missouri Division UCV, Pearson said, "We want the world to know, . . . that the majority of the Confederate veterans believe that Lincoln was one of the greatest and noblest Americans that ever lived. We think that recent criticism of Lincoln is unfounded and foolish."[101]

While Pearson's action might be read as a disavowal of the Lost Cause and a turn toward reconciliation, he had another motivation. In a letter to the *Confederate Veteran*, he explained that in retaliation for the UCV's endorsement of Johnstone, the GAR was preparing resolutions at its national encampment in Des Moines, Iowa, to block the return of captured Confederate flags to their respective states. Catching wind of the rumor, Pearson sent a telegram to Des Moines insisting that the Missouri Division UCV esteemed the memory of Abraham Lincoln and hoped the fraternization between their two societies would continue. A local GAR member reported back to Pearson that his telegram "received more applause than anything that occurred during their session" and certainly prevented the GAR from withholding Confederate flags.[102] As often proved to be the case in Missouri, reconciliationist sentimentality masked more practical considerations.

At least one Confederate Missourian, however, was not appeased. Mrs. W. Dolan, a member of the Missouri Division UDC, wrote to a friend condemning Pearson's actions. "I am almost beside myself," she fumed. Outraged, Dolan accused Pearson of siding with the "the G.A.R.(obbers)," betraying the Lost Cause, and deifying Abraham Lincoln. "If I were Major Pearson I would hang my head in shame and *never* look a *real* Daughter of the Confederacy in the face again," she concluded.[103] Dolan's anger no doubt stemmed from the long and determined work the UDC invested in aligning Missouri more firmly with Confederate memory, particularly through the creation of pro-southern histories. By denouncing Johnstone's book and making a reconciliationist appeal to the GAR, Pearson broke ranks with the national UCV and took Missouri's Confederate associations right along with him.

Despite the concerted efforts of Missouri's Confederates, Missouri remained on the periphery of the Lost Cause. While certain legacies of the Confederacy had long been evident in the state—namely, a disposition to overlook the importance of slavery to the conflict and a willingness to perpetuate its legacies of racial discrimination—Missouri's Confederates never succeeded in establishing the Lost Cause as Missouri's uncontested Civil War memory. They struggled to organize, meeting with resistance on the part of Unionists and marginalization from their southern comrades. Although they endorsed the primary tenets of the Lost Cause, Confederate Missourians added additional dimensions in the hope of fully adapting their wartime experience to the broader southern narrative of defeat. Still, Missouri's Civil War history was ill-suited to the parameters of the Lost Cause and made Confederate commemoration a challenging endeavor.

FIVE

"The Recuperative Powers of Missouri"

Reconciliation in a Border State

The animosities of the past should be forgiven and its conflicts remembered only that they may serve to guide us in the future. . . . The recuperative powers of Missouri do not need to be demonstrated to her citizens. Sister and surrounding States were unacquainted with the ravages of war. Here, in this commonwealth of compromise, our fields were laid waste, our homes were pillaged, and arrayed in hostile strife were father against son, and brother against brother.

—Governor David R. Francis, Jefferson City, April 10, 1890

AS CIVIL WAR VETERAN THOMAS Dudley Kimball strode onto the historic French and Indian War battleground of the Plains of Abraham near Quebec, the Missourian ruminated on the divisive legacy of warfare and on the challenge of reconciliation. The Plains were the site of a decisive 1759 battle that claimed the lives of both the opposing British and French commanders, James Wolfe and Louis-Joseph, Marquis de Montcalm. British victory in the battle precipitated the end of a long and bloody conflict. As a consequence, the French relinquished their vast North American colony and Canada fell under the sway of the British Empire. The French and Indian War in Canada had not been a civil war, but it raised questions of identity and loyalty as formerly French Canadians became British. In 1827, their bifurcated identity was memorialized by the erection of a joint monument to Wolfe and Montcalm in Quebec—in the words of the monument itself, as a "common memorial" to their "common death" and "common fame." Standing before the monument, Kimball found himself "thrilled with emotions." Moved by this tribute to reconciliation, he wondered if such a monument would ever be constructed to commemorate the Civil War in his own country.[1]

As a longtime resident of St. Louis, Kimball would have had daily proof of the ability of Unionists and former Confederates to productively cooperate and peacefully socialize in everyday life. A Massachusetts native and Union veteran, Kimball relocated to Missouri on December 20, 1865.[2] He became an active member of the Grand Army of the Republic (GAR) in the Ransom Post and, in 1907, was elected commander of the Department of Missouri. At the turn of the twentieth century, St. Louis was enjoying tremendous prosperity and national prominence—much of it made possible by the work of Civil War veterans like Kimball. Indeed, St. Louis was home to the Veterans of the Blue and Gray, a short-lived fraternal society open to veterans of both the Union and Confederate militaries. Tellingly, Kimball was not a member. In his mind, the bitter wartime divisions that once wracked the city had not been entirely obliterated. Indeed, it was Kimball's own Ransom Post GAR that so stringently opposed the Confederate monument in Forest Park. Kimball himself was a passionate advocate of the Union Cause. As commander of the Department of Missouri, he warned his comrades to be vigilant against public celebrations of the defeated Confederacy.

For that brief moment in 1908, however, as Kimball remembered the Wolfe-Montcalm monument in Quebec, the prospect of reconciliation between Union and Confederate Americans stirred his heart. If reconciliation was too difficult a proposition for Kimball to embrace himself, he cherished hope that future generations might make it a reality. "It is yet too soon," he reasoned,

> but an hundred years hence, when those who wore the Blue and those who wore the Gray, their children and their children's children shall have passed beyond the vale, when all the trials and sufferings, the losses and the bereavements of that awful time shall have become vague traditions, and all troublesome and vexatious questions, the outgrowth of sectional differences, shall have long been settled, then, somewhere in the great Republic there shall be reared a noble structure of suitable design, to commemorate the American soldiers and sailors who, in the War of 1861 to 1865, gave the finest example of dauntless courage and intrepid valor the world has ever seen.[3]

Kimball could not have known that within ten short years—not the hundred he anticipated—Missourians would have constructed just such a monument on the Civil War battlefield at Vicksburg.

The spirit of reconciliation held tremendous influence over Civil War commemoration in Missouri at the turn of the twentieth century, particularly among white veterans. Considering the importance of compromise to the state's political tradition, it is unsurprising that an earnest and effective movement toward reconciliation took root there. It is easy, however, to overstate the pervasiveness of reconciliation. Certainly not all Missourians remembered the war in a cohesive or harmonious fashion. Missourians walked a fine line between tolerant accommodation and overt hostility. Oftentimes, when white Missourians extended the olive branch, it was as much an act of pragmatism—spurred by financial necessity or in a bid for commercial or political patronage—as it was a meaningful gesture of reconciliation. And, as African Americans made clear at the 1887 national GAR encampment in St. Louis, white veterans were far more willing to reach across the "bloody chasm," in the words of newspaper magnate Horace Greeley, than across the color line.[4] Sectional reconciliation and racial reconciliation remained distinct efforts. On the whole, reconciliation in Missouri was not all-encompassing and was sometimes contested, but it prompted at least three remarkable initiatives: the incorporation of Confederate burials into the Springfield National Cemetery, the organization of several blue and gray veterans' societies, and the construction of a monument to both Union and Confederate Missourians at Vicksburg National Military Park.

Reconciliationist feeling was a national trend at the turn of the century but subject to myriad individual and local interpretations. For members of the Civil War generation, the meaning of reconciliation ranged from simply the cessation of hostilities to true and heartfelt forgiveness.[5] In Missouri, as elsewhere, reconciliation between white Civil War veterans was most often forged over a particular set of shared prejudices including racism, nationalism, and gender biases. Reconciliation also appealed to veterans' mutual economic and political interests—interests that transcended section and had important implications for the preeminence of the United States on the world stage.[6] Reconciliation was not only practical, however, but also profoundly sentimental.[7] Across the country, white Unionists and former Confederates elegized the common heroism, honor, and sacrifice of their one-time foes.

The high tide of reconciliationist sentiment also coincided with the rise of Jim Crow laws. In the deeply segregated environment of turn-of-the-century America, reconciliation remained overwhelmingly a white proposition. This held true in Missouri. Although African American Missourians explicitly offered open invitations to their Emancipation Day celebrations, white veterans did not return the favor in any of the initiatives described here. That does not mean, however, that white Unionists forgot the origins of the Confederacy lay in slavery and secession. Nor does it mean that they entirely abandoned their black comrades in their pursuit of equality.[8] There were, after all, white veterans who supported the movement for education and suffrage among black Missourians. Still, the fact that white Missourians undertook Civil War commemoration as a segregated endeavor comes as no surprise. While many white Unionists gradually accepted emancipation as a war aim and even came to respect the contributions of black soldiers to Union victory, those realizations did not translate to advocacy for full racial equality, particularly not in the conservative stronghold of Missouri.[9]

Whiteness, however, was no guarantee of reconciliation. Historians have rightly doubted the extent of reconciliation between Unionists and former Confederates, particularly in Missouri. They have pointed out that reconciliationist sentimentality could not transcend longstanding political and sectional divisions. In particular, it could not overcome the irreconcilable ideological and moral issue at the heart of secession and the Civil War—the perpetuation of chattel slavery. Reconciliation could not bring back the war dead. Nor could it expunge the profound grief over the war's extensive death toll. Neither could it fully persuade either side to abandon their own particular recollections of the war and its legacy.[10] If these realities proved obstacles to reconciliation on the broader national level, they were that much more imposing in Missouri, where local wartime fractures remained deep and intensely personal. Historian Jeremy Neely, for instance, argues that along the Missouri and Kansas border in particular, "Reunion came more slowly and unevenly . . . than elsewhere in America."[11] Although social ties as well as mutual political and economic prerogatives eased tensions, the legacy of guerrilla violence kept resentments alive.[12] Historian Aaron Astor also doubts the efficacy of reconciliation in Missouri. "For true reconciliationism to make sense in a border context," he insists, "there would have to have been an equal number of Unionist reunions, memorials, and celebrations as there were Confederate—perhaps more so."[13] In the Little Dixie counties Astor studied, he found little evidence of reconciliation before the end of Reconstruction. It is certainly true that in Missouri, as elsewhere, veterans generally preferred the company of their own comrades over that of their former enemies. But as active as white Union and Confederate Missourians were independently of one another, they were also accustomed to cooperation.

Among the tenets of reconciliation that resonated particularly strongly within Missouri's veterans' organizations were nationalism and imperialism.[14] In the 1890s, many Americans shared a desire to see the influence of the United States expand across the continent, the hemisphere, and even the world. Such ambition mitigated Civil War–era grudges, which became even easier to overlook in the face of new threats to national security. The Spanish-American War seemed to represent just that. Portrayed as a defensive war with the objectives of extending political and economic freedom to oppressed peoples, the United States declared war on Spain and liberated its colonial possessions in Latin America and the Pacific. Fueled by jingoism and yellow journalism, however, the war became an avenue for the United States to supplant the Spanish Empire with one of its own. The Spanish-American War also had important ramifications for how Americans reflected on the legacy of the Civil War. The general enthusiasm for this war filled Americans with confidence that the Civil War had not weakened their unity and that all former differences had been resolved.[15] Furthermore, the racial justification behind America's overseas expansion, that it was the particular responsibility of Anglo-Saxons to introduce democratic ideals to "uncivilized" people of color, reinforced the idea that the reunified American nation was a white man's republic.

The specter of international conflict provided former Confederates in particular with the opportunity to redeem their patriotism. They long denied that they had committed an illegal or treacherous act by taking up arms against the government. In their minds, they had been and remained patriots the country could depend on in times of crisis. Confederate veterans often asserted that they would be the first to defend the United States from a foreign foe. As Colonel George P. Gross told his comrades in the Missouri Division United Confederate Veterans (UCV): "We must never forget that this is our country, and we stand ready to defend our flag—on land or sea—because we are AMERICANS."[16] The idea that ex-Confederates and their children joined the ranks and fought against Spain reassured Americans that reconciliation had been completed. "It took but the nation's call to arms to face a foreign foe, to completely reunite our people into one harmonious whole," Boonville mayor William G. Pendleton remarked before the Department of Missouri GAR. "Since 1898, since Manila and Santiago," he continued, "Mason and Dixon's line can no longer be traced in the hearts of the people of this land, and to-day, as never before within this generation, our dear country is united, one and inseparable."[17] Union veterans often proved willing to accept this narrative. It was important for the commemoration of the Union Cause to imagine that the defeat of the Confederacy had well and truly reunified the country—that there were no longer any rebels, only loyal Americans. When former Confederates seemed to have accepted that outcome, white Unionists felt proud.

For late nineteenth-century Americans, nationalism was also a highly racialized and gendered concept, as historian Nina Silber has demonstrated.

According to Silber, concerns about the impact of industrialization and immigration on national character at the turn of the century became centered in a new understanding of masculinity. According to this formulation, true men possessed a number of qualities, including patriotism, nobility, strength, courage, selflessness, and independence.[18] White Americans believed that only Anglo-Saxon men, and more particularly western men, embodied these characteristics. They imagined the West as a crucible that broke down provincialism and believed westerners exhibited a more national, as opposed to sectional, identity.[19]

White Missourians had long considered this characteristic to be one of the virtues of their region, but the idea gained new relevance through Frederick Jackson Turner's influential though often-criticized 1893 "frontier thesis." Turner described the West as instrumental to the evolution of American identity. "American history has been in a large degree the history of the colonization of the Great West," Turner famously argued. "The existence of an area of free land, its continuous recession, and the advance of American settlement westward, explain American development." One of the most important functions of the western frontier, in Turner's estimation, was its "nationalizing tendency."[20] In a later essay he wrote that the West broke down sectional divisions and remolded individuals into Americans. According to Turner, "The West . . . received the great streams from the North and from the South, and . . . compelled these currents to intermingle." As a result, the region imparted Americans with certain shared and defining traits, including self-confidence, industriousness, fair-mindedness, egalitarianism, pragmatism, and rebelliousness.[21] Thus, ideas about race, region, and nation coalesced into a new vision of American manhood that, in Silber's words, "blurred the reality of class, ethnic, and sectional division."[22]

White Missourians also expressed a sensibility, much as they had during the secession crisis, that the geographic position of their state gave them both an additional imperative and a special responsibility to restore sectional harmony.[23] They felt not only that their Civil War had been different but also that their way of coming to terms with it was different. They realized that in spite of their competing interpretations of the war, they shared a conviction that the contributions of westerners were underappreciated. This notion provided a sense of commonality that facilitated reconciliation. Former Confederate Robert McCulloch told an assembly of Union and Confederate veterans at an 1889 reunion in Higginsville that no matter what side they served on, their identity as Missourians was more important. "To you who wore the blue, and you who wore the gray," he commented, "these men were your brethren, blood of your blood and bone of your bone." Addressing the same crowd, Confederate general Jo Shelby echoed McCulloch: "There were only two sets of people on earth that understood civil war—those from Kansas and those from Missouri." According to published proceedings of the reunion, the crowd "greeted his remark with the most deafening applause."[24] At the 1895 GAR encampment in Macon, Union major general Benjamin M. Prentiss espoused a similar sentiment. "We are different up here from most of the people," he said. "We had a different warfare in Missouri from what they had down there."[25] Their unique wartime experiences and mutual identification as Missourians had established a bond. "Here in Missouri," Confederate veteran James Gantt observed in 1902, "where we have lived together, we understand each other."[26]

Missouri's geography also made reconciliation a more immediate necessity than in other places. The conflicted allegiances of Missourians persisted into postwar life, and as both Union and Confederate veterans often discovered, it was impossible to avoid any and all interactions with former enemies in this deeply divided state. To adjust to this postbellum reality, white Missourians evoked their antebellum tradition of compromise to forge common ground.[27] In an address welcoming the GAR to Jefferson City for its state encampment in 1890, Governor David R. Francis spoke of "the recuperative powers of Missouri." "Here," he explained, "in this commonwealth of compromise, our fields were laid waste, our homes were pillaged, and arrayed in hostile strife were father against son, and brother against brother."[28] The following year, speaking before the Ex-Confederate Association, Francis marveled at the successful cooperation of Union and Confederate Missourians. Drawing on the reconciliationist potential of the West, as well as appealing to masculinity and nationalism, he observed, "Northern and Southern push and pluck have become associated in advancing the Western frontier toward the setting sun, and here the ingenuity of the puritan and the chivalry of the cavalier, harmoniously blended and inspired with the liberal and progressive spirit of the growing West, constitute a representative type of American manhood."[29] Governor Joseph Folk took up the refrain from his gubernatorial predecessor in a 1906 address to the GAR. Missourians may have fought on different sides of the Civil War, he acknowledged: "Some are ex-Federals now, some are ex-Confederates—all are Americans. There is now but one heart in all, North, East, South, West—and that is the heart of America."[30] Such reconciliationist rhetoric transformed Missouri from the epicenter of sectional division into the heartland of the reunited republic as it grew both in territory and in prosperity.

This made it possible for white men in Missouri to dismiss their wartime opposition to one another as mere differences of opinion that clouded an underlying and essentially shared American masculinity. A gendered esteem for military service further strengthened the bonds of masculinity. Many turn-of-the-century Americans believed soldiers, especially *volunteer* soldiers, represented the peak of true manhood. This attitude became the basis on which white Union and Confederate veterans interacted. Fraternization had roots in the Civil War itself, as soldiers crossed picket lines to barter, share news, and commiserate.[31] Civil War veterans' associations particularly nurtured recollections of such acts.[32] Having shared, as Oliver Wendell Holmes, Jr., famously put it, "the incommunicable experience of war," Missouri's Civil War veterans identified as fellow Americans, as westerners, as survivors of a monumental struggle, and as embodiments of militaristic masculinity.[33] Confederate veteran James Gantt, for example, attributed the reconciliation of the blue and gray in Missouri to "racial affinity" and to the necessities of commerce but added, "at the bottom of it all, and more lasting than all, is that mutual respect which each side *pounded* into the other on 'the firing line' for four years." Gantt concluded, "Brave men love brave men the world over."[34] During the 1903 Department of Missouri GAR encampment in Boonville, Mayor W. G. Pendleton also expounded on the bonds of militaristic masculinity:

> It has always been noticed that the prejudices engendered by the war affected the soldiers on either side less than it did their friends who had no actual participation in the conflict. And while this, if true, may at first thought seem strange, upon reflection I believe it can be readily explained. Hardships, dangers and privations endured by the soldier on the march and battlefield, in camp, hospital and prison, softened his heart toward the soldier on the other side who suffered the same hardships, dangers and privations. Hence each had a ready sympathy for the other, a sympathy that has ever drawn the old veterans upon either side closer and more closely together, until to-day they meet and mingle everywhere more as old friends than as foes.[35]

While white Union and Confederate veterans in Missouri never relinquished their distinctive memories of the Civil War, fraternization nevertheless held significant appeal.

One of the places where white Union and Confederate veterans occasionally "mingled" was in the headquarters of the GAR's Ransom Post in St. Louis. At a meeting in June 1912, for example, thirteen Confederate veterans visited the post and one "live Johnnie," Robert McCulloch, delivered an address. In the course of the evening, McCulloch joked with his former enemies. He teased one Union veteran "for having been on the wrong side of the great conflict" and gave a lighthearted account of wounds he suffered at the Battle of Gettysburg. Then—quite suddenly—McCulloch's speech took a somber turn. He made an erroneous but widely accepted claim that the number of Union soldiers killed in the war dwarfed the enrollment of the "entire Confederate army." The effect of McCulloch's statement was profound. According to the post circular, "a sudden chill" fell over the men, "which soon, however, gave way to thankfulness that we were not all annihilated." The account went on to say that "the lengthy duration of the war was a testimonial to the bravery and valor of the men on both sides, and the respect engendered by the knowledge that each had a foe worthy of his steel, made the brave men of both armies the better friends after the close of the war." As a testament to that fact, as the meeting ended, McCulloch joined hands with the comrades of the Ransom Post as they sang together "Auld Lang Syne."[36] By acknowledging the manhood of their enemies, the members of the Ransom Post enhanced their own by extension.

Such reconciliationist avowals, rooted in sentimentality, racism, nationalism, and masculinity, were common across the United States at the turn of the century.[37] For Missouri's white Civil War veterans, however, reconciliation also took on local peculiarities and served practical ends. They undertook a series of collaborative efforts that reflected the unique atmosphere of Civil War commemoration in Missouri: the incorporation of the Springfield Confederate Cemetery into the national cemetery system, the formation of a number of blue and gray veterans' societies, and the creation of a monument to both Union and Confederate Missourians at Vicksburg National Military Park. Although these efforts should not be divorced from their larger context—as bitter contestations over Civil War memory continued within the state—taken together, they speak to the effectiveness of reconciliationist rhetoric among white veterans in Missouri.

Springfield Confederate Cemetery

One of the most serious impediments to reconciliation, on both the national and local levels, was the terrible death toll of the Civil War. As Americans grieved over the war's approximately 851,000 combatant deaths, they could not help recalling the profound divisions over slavery that compelled Unionists and Confederates to offer up their lives.[38] The prevalence of death complicated the meaning and legacy of the Civil War. Memorialization of the dead put the memory of the war at the forefront of the national consciousness and thus kept hostilities alive. To some veterans, reconciliation felt like a betrayal of the dead. In one instance, however, white Missourians sidelined their bitterness to take part in an unprecedented act of reconciliation by incorporating the Springfield Confederate and National Cemeteries. Three practical considerations enabled this act of reconciliation. First, a number of Civil War battles in the area left Springfield with the pressing necessity of arranging burials for roughly two thousand fallen soldiers. Second, the close proximity of the Confederate and national cemeteries forced interactions between veterans of both sides. Finally, financial necessity drove Confederate veterans to solicit cooperation from their Union neighbors in order to ensure long-term care for their dead.

One of the earliest commemorative efforts on the part of Missouri's Confederate veterans was to establish a cemetery near Springfield for the Confederate dead who were hastily buried on the battlefields of southwestern Missouri, especially after the 1861 Battle of Wilson's Creek. In 1867, the U.S. government established a national cemetery in Springfield where they ultimately reinterred the remains of 1,521 white Union soldiers but not a single Confederate.[39] While the War Department dedicated resources to locating, identifying, and interring the Union dead, it was up to private groups and local governments to undertake such efforts on behalf of fallen Confederates.[40] This was a matter of federal policy, even though former Confederates sometimes felt victimized by the practice.[41]

It was more than frustration at Union prejudice, however, that prompted the call for a Confederate cemetery in Springfield. There were also pressing public health and humanitarian concerns. The passage of time proved the hasty wartime burials of Confederate soldiers insufficient. By 1869, according to one newspaper report, human remains could be seen "exposed and bleaching" on the battlefield at Wilson's Creek and around hospital sites in the city, including the courthouse square.[42] In the spring of 1870, one disturbed Confederate veteran wrote to the *Springfield Leader* voicing his concern that many graves were "so very shallow that the coffins are now almost visible, and the water of the least rain is washing them out."[43] Sometimes, according to another report, erosion revealed an "arm, foot, hand or skull."[44] During a road improvement project in Springfield, grading equipment unsurfaced a number of human bones.[45]

To provide a more dignified final resting place for these neglected dead, former Confederates in Springfield established the Confederate Cemetery Association on November 23, 1869. Although the group's stated intention was to reinter the Confederates in an appropriate setting where they could rest undisturbed, some in the community evidently felt the creation of a

Confederate cemetery amounted to the glorification of those dead and their Lost Cause. As a result, some locals regarded the association with suspicion and even hostility. According to one newspaper report, "This date being so close to the closing of the war few Southern people could be found in Springfield that would allow their names to be used in the movement." Indeed, opposition threatened to derail the first meeting of the association. After securing permission to meet at the courthouse one evening, the members arrived to find the building locked and they were refused admittance. Not to be deterred, the association complained to Judge W. F. Geiger the following morning. Geiger, though himself a Union veteran, reassured the association it had his permission to use the courthouse and, in a show of support, agreed to attend the meeting.[46] While the incident of the previous evening may have been due to a simple misunderstanding or scheduling conflict, Geiger's decision to attend suggests there was more to the story. His presence both as a local judge and as a Union veteran would have likely defrayed concerns about whether or not the association intended to celebrate the Lost Cause.

Now free to meet, the association undertook a variety of fundraising efforts to help make the cemetery a reality. One woman even wrote to Robert E. Lee, asking for a lock of his hair to raffle off on behalf of the cemetery. The general obliged, sending back a "few hairs" that were fashioned into a ring. Raffle tickets sold for only one dollar each, but the ring netted the association three hundred dollars.[47] Gradually, the Confederate Cemetery Association gathered enough funds to purchase six acres of land in Springfield near the national cemetery. In fact, the two cemeteries would be separated only by a small, two-acre tract. The association then began the grim and difficult task of locating, disinterring, identifying, and relocating remains to the cemetery.

The results of their efforts were modest, particularly in comparison to the neighboring national cemetery. By 1871, 505 men were interred in the Springfield Confederate Cemetery.[48] In the following decade, the grounds were enclosed with a simple wooden fence and each soldier received a painted wooden headboard marked with an identifying number—although most of the dead were unknown.[49] Ultimately, however, the work proved too costly for the Confederate Cemetery Association to continue on its own. In 1882, it transferred the property to the Ex-Confederate Association of Missouri—later the Missouri Division United Confederate Veterans—who designated it the State Cemetery for Ex-Confederates. Even with this distinction and the backing of a statewide organization, funds continued to be insufficient to their aspirations.

The inevitability of comparisons to the national cemetery put pressure on former Confederates to ensure their cemetery made a good impression. They feared an appearance of neglect might cast doubt on the sincerity of their sympathies and reflect badly on Missouri's legitimacy within the Lost Cause. As Captain Leroy B. Valliant put it, "If we wish our children . . . to revere our memories as soldiers, we must leave behind us evidences to them that we ourselves revered our cause."[50] Such "evidences," he suggested, included improvements to the cemetery so that it would more closely resemble the national cemetery, such as the addition of a stone fence, stone grave markers, and a keeper's lodge.[51] While the Ex-Confederates eventually constructed a stone wall and acquired marble headstones, they struggled to afford simple maintenance.

Beyond drawing attention to the Ex-Confederates' lack of resources, the proximity of the Confederate and national cemeteries made them an ideal setting for reconciliationist overtures. The Ex-Confederates recognized this and hoped to capitalize on reconciliationist feeling to alleviate their financial problems. For example, John Sappington Marmaduke, then president of the Ex-Confederate Association, launched an effort he hoped would raise $20,000 for the cemetery. He admitted former Confederates bore the chief responsibility for its maintenance and insisted they neither expected nor sought government funds. Still, he also understood that Missouri's Confederates were too few and perhaps too apathetic to foot the burden alone. As a result, Marmaduke directed his appeal to all of his fellow Missourians. "These dead belong to Missouri," he wrote, regardless of their wartime allegiances, and "every consideration of humanity admonishes that they be taken care of by the people of the entire state." He envisioned the cemetery as a memorial to the bravery and devotion of Missourians irrespective of loyalty. "With twenty thousand dollars," Marmaduke insisted, "the Confederate cemetery can be so improved and beautified that no Confederate soldier or his descendants, in contemplating it hereafter, will need to blush when he steps a few feet north to look upon the monuments which have been erected to the memory of the gallant Federal dead."[52] Marmaduke found his audience receptive. The association soon received donations from the GAR for cemetery improvements, including from the McCook Post in nearby Lamar.[53]

Although some GAR members had offered aid to the Confederate cemetery, each side generally tended to its own. This became increasingly difficult after the 1880s when the national cemetery acquired the two-acre tract separating the two burial grounds. Now the cemeteries actually adjoined one another, though divided by a stone wall. Following the acquisition of that land, there was periodic talk about opening a gateway in the wall to allow easier access between the graveyards. But in 1887, the Department of Missouri GAR expressed its reluctance to support such a measure. The GAR insisted that "the desire and wishes of ex-Union soldiers of Missouri, and the surviving comrades, relatives and friends of the Union dead would be best subserved by maintaining and preserving intact said National Cemetery and its surroundings as at present existing."[54] The preservation of the wall, however, did not prevent continual interaction between white Union and Confederate Missourians at the two cemeteries. In 1891, the *Sedalia Weekly Bazoo* observed that Memorial Day ceremonies in the Confederate cemetery were well attended, including "quite a number of whom had no partisan sympathy with the 'lost cause.'" On such occasions, the *Bazoo* noted, "the spirit of peace and reconciliation seemed to hover over the graves of both cemeteries."[55] Indeed, the frequent fraternization between Springfield's Campbell Camp UCV and the Matthews Post GAR was facilitated by joint Memorial Day exercises at the cemeteries.[56]

While they sometimes enjoyed the company of Union veterans and occasionally benefited from their generosity, Missouri's Confederates still wished to commemorate the Lost Cause. They felt the placement of a monument in the cemetery would go a long way to legitimizing their efforts. At the turn of the century, there were no significant Confederate monuments in the state—the Forest Park monument was still years in the future. The proponents of the Springfield monument therefore insisted it would be "a credit to the state," and pointedly noted that "in nearly all the southern states where any considerable number of confederate soldiers are buried, monuments were built long ago."[57] If Missouri's former Confederates wished to lay claim to the Lost Cause, they could not neglect this important mode of commemoration.

Their long-cherished dream became a reality on August 10, 1901, the fortieth anniversary of the nearby Battle of Wilson's Creek, when a monument to the Confederate dead was dedicated at the cemetery.[58] Completed at an expense of $12,000, raised mostly by the United Daughters of the Confederacy (UDC), it was a meaningful tribute to Missouri's Lost Cause.[59] At the dedication, Confederate flags flew and a band played "Dixie."[60] In his dedicatory address, Confederate veteran and Chief Justice of the Missouri Supreme Court Leroy B. Valliant emphasized its importance as the state's first Confederate monument. "Missouri is not lacking in appreciation of the Confederate soldiers . . . but without this there would not be in all the land for posterity to see, one visible token that Missouri honored and loved the memory of her own sons who bore her banner in those perilous times."

Valliant explained that this lone monument had to stand in not only for the Confederates buried in Springfield but for all of Missouri's Confederates. As a result, he insisted, it might have merited a prominent place in any of the state's major cities, "but it was the wish of our people that it should be placed here in a spot somewhat secluded, but to us most sacred." The monument was a "portraiture of a memory," Valiant said, and a testament to the manhood and bravery of Missouri's Confederates.[61]

It is entirely likely, however, that the successful completion of the monument was principally due to its location in the cemetery. In the contested commemorative atmosphere of Missouri, Union veterans demonstrated more tolerance for the war dead. The stringent opposition later mounted by GAR members against the Confederate monument in Forest Park, for example, indicates that they drew a line between venerating the dead and honoring the Confederate cause more broadly. Unlike the Forest Park monument, Union veterans helped fund the Springfield monument. Indeed, according to one former Confederate, its construction would not have been possible without what he described as the "substantial assistance" of Union veterans.[62] In 1900, Confederate veteran Harvey W. Salmon, a member of the monument committee, reported receiving three checks for fifty dollars each donated by Union veterans. Salmon noted they were "Missourians, by adoption" and called their gesture "too beautiful for words." He reflected, "Such an incident could occur in no country other than this great American republic."[63] In the case of the Springfield Confederate monument, financial necessity, sentimentality, shared notions of masculinity, nationalism, and regional feeling prompted reconciliationist overtures. Both as fellow Missourians and as fellow soldiers, white Union veterans sympathized with the desire of former Confederates to honor their fallen comrades.

Perhaps because of this goodwill, as early as 1903 Missourians debated transferring control of the Confederate cemetery to the federal government. As the number of American veterans seeking burial in the national cemeteries grew following the Spanish-American War, the Springfield National Cemetery became increasingly crowded while much of the Confederate cemetery remained vacant. The War Department thus sought to acquire the Confederate cemetery as a means of expanding its own limited space and relieving the Missouri Division UCV of a significant expense. Reactions to the proposal were mixed, as neither Union nor Confederate Missourians universally supported this plan. UCV officer William H. Kennan said, "I am in favor of turning it over to the United States and tearing out the division wall between the two cemeteries, for the reason I believe it will be better cared for, and as long as the United States Government stands, which I pray may be to the end of time. We have a union of states and should have a union of hearts and hands."[64] The *Confederate Veteran* reported that in other quarters of the UCV, however, "the resolution brought forth the most violent discussion, and was opposed . . . bitterly."[65]

Although the Missouri Division adopted a resolution in 1904 endorsing the incorporation of the cemeteries, local Confederate organizations remained divided.[66] In Springfield, for example, several members of the Campbell Camp UCV and the Springfield Chapter of the UDC petitioned the Campbell Camp to rescind its support for the resolution. Ultimately, they were voted down.[67] Even after the Missouri Division formally voted to cede the cemetery in 1907, the Springfield Chapter UDC continued to resist the plan. Minnie B. Roberts, recording secretary of the Springfield Chapter, asked the Missouri Division UDC to join in her opposition. "This is the very first instance where Southern people have wanted to give away their cemetery," Roberts lamented. She begged her fellow Daughters to consider the implications for Confederate commemoration should they relinquish control. She doubted the federal government would care for the monument and worried they might restrict former Confederates from holding exercises in the cemetery on Confederate Decoration Day. She insisted the UDC had a responsibility to tend to this "sacred ground" for as long "as the Pyramids stand and the Nile winds its course through a sandy desert."[68] Despite Roberts's impassioned plea, the Missouri Division UDC took no action to block the transfer. The partisan sentimentality of the Springfield Chapter UDC could not outweigh the practical concerns that necessitated the action. The need for space in the national cemetery and the lack of funds for the Confederate cemetery made incorporation a logical solution.

On March 3, 1911, by an act of Congress signed by President William Howard Taft, the federal government assumed responsibility for the Springfield Confederate Cemetery.[69] Nothing like it had ever been done before. While Confederates may be found interred in other national cemeteries across the country, those men died in federal custody—in hospitals or as prisoners of war. The Springfield National Cemetery was the first to accommodate Confederates who died in arms against the government. And the amity extended even further. As a condition of the transfer, the Confederates received a guarantee that they could continue to hold Decoration Day services on the grounds. In return, the vacant land surrounding the cemetery enclosure was opened to new burials. In the meantime, calls circulated to demolish the stone wall between the two cemeteries. "United as all sections of the country now are in sentiment," one Missouri newspaper observed, "the heavy stone wall that separates the two spots at Springfield serves no useful purpose and should be taken down."[70] Others suggested constructing a commemorative archway in the wall topped with a marble dove, as "a fitting and strikingly beautiful emblem of endless peace and good will between the North and South and of a more perfect union."[71] Although the wall was opened, allowing free access between the two cemeteries, the proposed archway never materialized.

The adoption of the Springfield Confederate Cemetery into the national cemetery system was an unprecedented act of reconciliation. Radical as it was, this measure was not uncontested nor was it entirely indicative of forgiveness or forgetfulness. Although couched in reconciliationist sentimentality, the assumption of the Confederate cemetery was ultimately made possible by more practical realities. The lack of adequate provisions for the hundreds of Confederate soldiers killed in nearby battles, the proximity of the national cemetery, and the inability of Confederate veterans to fund maintenance ultimately made the incorporation of the Springfield Confederate and National Cemeteries a reasonable and mutually beneficial act of reconciliation among white veterans.

Blue and Gray Societies

At the close of the nineteenth century, blue and gray veterans' reunions became a highly publicized, if infrequent, expression of reconciliation. Such reunions were few and far between, especially considering the much greater numbers of independent Union and Confederate reunions. Blue and gray reunions, therefore, can hardly be said to indicate unqualified reconciliation between Unionists and Confederates. They are, however, a marker of the reconciliationist sentimentality that flourished in that era. This sentiment reached its apotheosis at the famed 1913 reunion celebrating the fiftieth anniversary of the Battle of Gettysburg. On that occasion, tens of thousands of aged Union and Confederate veterans gathered on the battlefield to remember their service and celebrate reunification. They revisited important sites and shook hands for the cameras, the hostilities of those terrible three days in July 1863 seemingly forgotten. A telling silence covered both African American contributions to the war as well as their presence at the reunion. This was a celebration of white manhood and nationalism, which obfuscated racial tension and overrode—if only fleetingly—lingering sectional bitterness.

The creation of blue and gray veterans' societies was a related phenomenon. Interestingly, Missouri was home to several, including the Henry County Veterans' Association, the Johnson County Veteran Association of the Blue and Gray, the Taney County Veterans' Association, the Old Soldiers and Old Settlers' Reunion Association, and Kansas City's Veteran Company A.[72]

The two most active of these local societies were the St. Louis Veterans of the Blue and Gray and the Kansas City Old Soldiers' Association of the Blue and Gray.[73] Organized in the same spirit of fraternalism and militaristic masculinity that inspired the formation of the GAR and UCV, these blue and gray societies served to cultivate economic and political patronage among the veterans of the opposing armies. By enabling white Missourians to forge mutually beneficial alliances in spite of their wartime divisions, the Veterans of the Blue and Gray and the Old Soldiers' Association further illustrate the pragmatic nature of reconciliation in Missouri.

As a formerly slaveholding Union state, the challenge of reconciliation was particularly fraught in Missouri and St. Louis in particular. Rent by political, social, and racial divisions, the wartime inhabitants of St. Louis necessarily crafted what historian Adam Arenson calls "a flexible neutrality." Because St. Louis was spared much of the fighting during the war and suffered no significant destruction, the political and economic business of the city proceeded with little interruption. To facilitate cooperation, the city's divided population practiced impartiality. Whether that impartiality stemmed from courtesy, practicality, or coercion by federal authorities was another matter.[74]

This mentality persisted into the postwar period, as Missourians continued to live and work alongside their former foes. Rather than allow wartime divisions to stifle cooperation and paralyze the development of their city and state, the elite of St. Louis championed reconciliation as vital to business. They envisioned their city as the economic heart of the reunified nation and the forefront of expansion across the continent and the world.[75] Some local boosters even proposed relocating the nation's capital to St. Louis. They had reason to be optimistic about the city's future. Although lagging somewhat behind Chicago, St. Louis emerged from the Civil War as a center of regional and national economic life.[76] St. Louis ranked third in the nation in manufacturing, and the value of goods produced in the city grew from $27 million in 1870 to $229 million in 1890.[77] The number of industries in St. Louis also grew from 2,924 in 1880 to 6,148 in 1890. Vital to this success was the increasing prevalence of railroads in Missouri. Between 1870 and 1890, thousands of miles of new track connected Missouri to national markets, and St. Louis served as a terminal for twenty-four rail lines. This prosperity brought new conveniences to the city's growing number of residents. Members of the business and professional classes retreated to comfortable homes on tree-lined streets, made accessible by street cars in 1889.[78] All of this progress depended on the continued cooperation of the people of St. Louis and on harmonious commerce among the North, South, and West.[79]

Although the restoration of trade between the North and South was an important national priority in the aftermath of the Civil War, it was particularly vital to Missourians. In business, they simply could not afford to give offense over wartime allegiances. Recognizing that overcoming their prejudices was essential to the prosperity of their state, white Missourians encouraged reconciliation.[80] "When the soldiers of Missouri met each other in battle," Confederate veteran and congressman William H. Hatch noted, "there was a desperate fight. But now the animosities are buried and the Northern and Southern soldiers are partners together in every avocation of life."[81] J. F. Liddle, a Union veteran from Warrensburg, remarked, "We do not stop to inquire in business whether a man belonged to the Union or Confederate army and ought not to do so in any connection."[82] At the first reunion of the Department of Missouri GAR, Kansas City mayor Thomas B. Bullene acknowledged a time, not long distant, "when here, upon our border land, men looked into each other's faces with the suspicion and distrust born of extreme antagonism." But, he assured his listeners, "the generation of these deeds has passed away, and whatever of bitterness dwelt in after years in our memories is soothed by the great healer, time, and by the splendid advance of our common country in the building up of her material industries."[83]

This economic imperative was critical in the creation of an unusual organization known as the Veterans of the Blue and Gray. The organization formed in St. Louis in 1896 after "a party of six old soldiers who had fought on opposite sides in the Civil War met at the Planters [Hotel] one evening. The fact of the warm friendships that had sprung up among them, both in a business and social way," the *St. Louis Republic* reported, "led to the suggestion being made that some sort of a fraternal society should be formed."[84] They envisioned the creation of "a Military Corps, composed of those, who during the War of the States, wore the 'Blue and the Gray.'"[85]

On October 19, 1896, the six charter members invited other prosperous and influential Civil War veterans to join them in an organizational meeting at the Planter's House Hotel. The fifty men in attendance, with both Confederate and Union veterans fairly represented, "were . . . business men of St. Louis," the *St. Louis Republic* reported, "who have seen battle lines fade away among the memories of the past to be replaced by the commercial and social intercourse of the present." As friends, neighbors, and business associates, they reminisced about the war—all enmity apparently forgotten. According to the newspaper, "Peace, good fellowship, fraternity and cigar smoke permeated the assembly. . . . Everybody agreed to everything anybody else proposed, and antagonism, even of the most amiable kind, for once found itself out of a job."[86] The men vowed "to cultivate feelings of friendship and fraternity between those who were once opposed in arms; to extinguish all animosities which were engendered by the late Civil War; to eradicate sectional jealousies; to prevent civil convulsions and future conflicts between the various sections of our common country; and finally to unite the surviving soldiers and sailors of the Union and Confederate Armies and Navies more closely in support of good government, and in defense of the Constitution and Laws of the United States."[87] The Veterans of the Blue and Gray strongly echoed the prevailing sentiments of many antebellum Missourians, who evinced a self-imposed responsibility for mediating sectional divisions and facilitating peace.

The primary avenue for reconciliation within this organization was through the cooperation of the elite of St. Louis. The membership included bank directors, manufacturers, judges, and politicians. Its founding members included Charles G. Warner (vice president of the Missouri Pacific Railroad), George T. Cram (president of an insurance company and former bank director), Samuel M. Kennard (president of J. Kennard & Sons carpet manufacturing and another former bank director, who "helped build" the Planter's Hotel), and finally Seth W. Cobb (four-term congressman, former president of the St. Louis Merchant Exchange, and founder of S. W. Cobb & Co., an agricultural company).[88] Several members of the Veterans of the Blue and Gray were neighbors in St. Louis's fashionable central west end, an enclave of private, gated streets near Forest Park dotted with newly built mansions now regarded as some of the finest examples of Gilded Age architecture in the country.[89] The central west end was also home to the "Big Cinch," a coterie of elite industrialists, financiers, and politicians who dominated St. Louis economic life at the turn of the century. Introduced, in some cases, during their Civil War service or through an overlapping network of social and business associations, the "Big Cinch" hoped to make St. Louis a national commercial center.[90]

For men of their class, political and economic pillars of their community, reconciliation meant mutual prosperity. "We do not flatter ourselves when we say that our organization is comprised on the best citizens of the City of St. Louis," the Veterans of the Blue and Gray reported with pride.[91] In a letter of invitation to other prominent veterans in the city, founding members Charles G. Warner and Joseph Boyce spoke of the "processes of political, commercial and industrial evolution" in restoring national harmony. "In business and in the professions the soldiers of the sixties are now the leaders," the letter continued. "Dead issues belong to impartial history. To be true to our past we must stand for liberty, law and order, so that our beloved country may fulfill her mission in the van of humanity's progress."[92]

While the society may well have fostered reconciliationist feeling between the white veterans of St. Louis, its more immediate purpose was to cultivate patronage. Membership in the Veterans of the Blue and Gray made good business sense. In this regard the Veterans of the Blue and Gray was like other late nineteenth-century fraternal organizations, particularly the GAR. According to historian Stuart McConnell, the GAR embodied "businessman's fraternalism." Posts served as ideal places for businessmen to network with like-minded individuals and to "build alliances, reward subordinates, [and] cultivate customers."[93] This made the marginalization of black Missourians within the GAR particularly biting as it further limited their social contacts and economic opportunities. To all indications, the membership of the Veterans of the Blue and Gray was restricted to whites only. Considering the elite circles in which the members moved, it is unsurprising that it was segregated.

Despite the exclusive nature of the Veterans of the Blue and Gray, its members not only thought of themselves as the class most able to accomplish reconciliation but also believed that Missouri was the logical home of this new, progressive organization. They recognized that Missourians felt keenly the full tragedy of sectional division. Thus, they were uniquely suited to be the greatest champions of reconciliation. The *St. Louis Republic* anticipated that the successful reconciliation of St Louis veterans would inspire a national movement. The newspaper boasted, "To St. Louis will be given the credit of having inaugurated a new social order that has for its cardinal principle good fellowship and the wiping out of every vestige of embitterment that remains to mar the peaceful relations of men who would have them obliterated forever."[94] During the society's 1897 annual meeting, member David Patterson Dyer credited Missouri's divisive history with facilitating reconciliation. "People who lived in the far South," he explained, "or in the far North at the beginning of the War could not understand the situation in which brave and conscientious men were placed in Missouri, where the line of division was of necessity sharply drawn, and those of us who lived here only could understand how the truest and the best of friends had to separate according to their honest convictions."[95] Taking up this theme at the first annual banquet of the Veterans of the Blue and Gray, the toastmaster proclaimed that it was precisely because of its painful past that Missouri offered the most fertile ground for reconciliation to take root. "It followed naturally, therefore," he said, "that on the soil of this State should be taken the first practical step toward the entire rehabilitation in citizenship of the fighting men on the losing side at the hands of the fighting men on the winning side."[96] It was a bit of a backhanded jab—implying former Confederates needed "rehabilitation"—but if anyone took offense, the official report made no mention of it. Still, it was an intriguing slip, revealing that while the Veterans of the Blue and Gray reconciled around a shared identity as Missourians, its members retained their wartime biases.

Still, the Veterans of the Blue and Gray made every attempt to appeal to both Union and Confederate Missourians. It reassured prospective members that the society expected "no abatement or surrender of self respect, no apologies for convictions which any man honestly held and maintained at the peril of life and all that he held dear."[97] As its uniform, the Veterans of the Blue and Gray adopted a dark blue coat, with buttons modeled on the Missouri state seal, and gray trousers.[98] Its emblem depicted a shield quartered into blue and gray segments behind the U.S. flag, giving both sides "equal prominence to show that we meet on common ground and in a fraternal feeling of equality."[99] Such gestures appear to have worked. At its height, the organization numbered about a hundred members, with only marginally more Union than Confederate veterans. The roster even included a few familiar names, like James O. Broadhead (who so adamantly opposed secession at the 1861 state convention), James B. Gantt (Missouri supreme court justice and one of the state's most active UCV members), Robert McCulloch (the "live Johnnie" who sang "Auld Lang Syne" with the Ransom Post GAR), Harvey W. Salmon (who was moved by the donations of three Union veterans to the Springfield Confederate monument), Jo Shelby (Confederate general), and Leroy B. Valliant (Missouri supreme court justice and UCV member). The society also claimed celebrated generals James Longstreet, John M. Schofield, John B. Gordon, and Oliver O. Howard as honorary members.[100]

While the Veterans envisioned their organization as spawning a movement to restore peace and patriotism among all Americans, their mission was fulfilled from another quarter. In February 1899, the *St. Louis Globe-Democrat* observed, "The last twelve months of our history . . . have done more to unite us than any events that have heretofore intervened since the war of the rebellion. Our sons have fought side by side against a common foe for liberty, justice and humanity."[101] As far as the Veterans of the Blue and Gray were concerned, the Spanish-American War obviated the need for the society. The members suspended their annual banquet and closed their organization. "The chief purposes for which . . . this organization was formed," they insisted, "have been accomplished: That the late war with Spain . . . affords the crowning proof that former animosities are extinguished, and that the survivors of the Union and Confederate armies and navies . . . are now true comrades in arms, united in defense of the Constitution and laws of the United States."[102] In the minds of the Veterans of the Blue and Gray, the Spanish-American War reunified the country in a real and permanent sense. Still, these veterans took pride in having laid the groundwork for reconciliation. "As is so often the case," founding member Edward D. Meier wrote, "St. Louis was a little in advance of the rest of the country in feeling and voicing the patriotic sentiments which found their full expression at Santiago and Manila."[103]

For these men, as for others of their race and class in Missouri, reconciliation in the wake of the Civil War was not only an abstract national goal but an immediate economic, political, and social necessity. Through the creation of this remarkable organization, former enemies turned fellow businessmen laid out a new vision for their city, state, and nation on the foundation of their troubled past. By insisting they understood the tragedy of the Civil War better than most Americans, members of the St. Louis Veterans of the Blue and Gray positioned themselves as exemplars of the promise of reconciliation. In the process, they embodied a distinctive form of Civil War memory taking shape in Missouri—a reconciliationist memory that evoked the state's antebellum compromise tradition. While acknowledging the bitter divisions left by the war, these veterans identified as fellow Missourians and foresaw potential for reconciliation through a mutual investment in economic development.

The Veterans of the Blue and Gray, however, were not the only such society in Missouri. While the primary motivation for the kind of reconciliation promoted by the Veterans of the Blue and Gray was economic, other veterans endorsed reconciliation for political goals. This was particularly the case with the Kansas City Old Soldiers' Association of the Blue and Gray. Just as the Veterans of the Blue and Gray consolidated the economic influence of the St. Louis elite, the Old Soldiers' Association forwarded the political agenda of Kansas City's white veterans. As much as a vehicle for reconciliation, the Old Soldiers' Association was a practical mechanism to prioritize veterans' affairs and imperialism in Missouri politics.

Like St. Louis, turn-of-the-century Kansas City was on the verge of tremendous demographic and economic development. Between 1860 and 1900, the population of the city reached 163,752, an increase of 37 percent.[104] Much of this population increase was due to immigration and the arrival of black southerners as a part of the Exoduster movement. These new arrivals were attracted by the flourishing economic life of the city, much of it driven by the railroads and stockyards.[105] Kansas City became a critical hub for transcontinental commerce. "The field for product is practically the entire West," one promotion bragged, "and it would be impossible to obtain a more central location, or one endowed with greater natural or other advantages than those enjoyed by Kansas City."[106] Business thrived. By 1900, Kansas City's industrial output ranked fifteenth in the nation.[107]

At the same time, these rapid changes unsettled the political landscape of the city. The close of the nineteenth century inaugurated the Pendergast era and the rise of machine politics in Kansas City. From the neglected and impoverished "West Bottoms" neighborhood inhabited by the city's immigrant and African American communities emerged James F. "Big Jim" Pendergast. Although the Pendergast political machine is more often associated with Thomas J. "Boss Tom" Pendergast, "Big Jim's" younger brother, it was James Pendergast who laid the groundwork for Missouri's most notorious political dynasty. The Pendergast era began in 1892 when "Big Jim" took office as alderman of the city's first ward, including the West Bottoms. Pendergast, a first-generation Irish American, consolidated a Democratic voting bloc among the immigrant and African American working class by providing community services and championing civic improvement. By 1900, Pendergast had extended his reach and seemed poised to become the boss of Kansas City.[108] His bourgeoning machine illustrated to Kansas City's veteran population the virtues of organization.

It was in this milieu that the Kansas City Old Soldiers' Association of the Blue and Gray was formed. Founded on June 22, 1898, it was much larger than its St. Louis counterpart. Unlike the St. Louis society, whose membership remained small and exclusive, the Kansas City Association expanded into four camps, or chapters, in Kansas City and the surrounding area, including Independence and Blue Springs.[109] According to Union veteran Colonel Theodore S. Case, the association boasted some eight hundred members.[110] The *Kansas City Journal* put the number as high as 3,600—its ranks equally divided between Union and Confederate veterans. Membership was not limited to Civil War survivors either, but also included recently demobilized Spanish-American War veterans. Beyond their immediate membership, the association claimed to represent the interests of five thousand veterans in the Kansas City area.[111]

Inspired by the reconciliationist atmosphere of the Spanish-American War, the Old Soldiers' Association hoped to build on that goodwill. Its "prime object," the *Kansas City Journal* reported, was "to cement still stronger the union of the blue and gray."[112] In part, the association functioned as a social club, modeled on GAR encampments, but it had charitable goals as well. The association hosted a number of vaudeville entertainments on behalf of social reform causes, including benefits for orphans and needy children of veterans.[113] Most of its activities, however, were directed at influencing the 1898 state elections. According to the *Kansas City Journal*, "The organization has been founded with the frank purpose of benefitting the old soldiers financially and politically."[114] As such, it claimed to be nonpartisan and solely interested in veterans' concerns.[115]

Newspaper coverage does not indicate whether the association admitted black members, although black men and women were an important part of civic life in Kansas City. By 1900, an influx of African American migration from the local countryside and from the Deep South brought the black population of the city to more than 10 percent.[116] While the city's black residents faced racial discrimination, there were as yet no Jim Crow laws in force. They enjoyed unrestricted access to public transportation and lived in diverse neighborhoods. Black men exercised their franchise relatively freely and navigated the city's deep partisan divides in pursuit of patronage and civil rights.[117] Party leaders understood the black vote could turn the tide in the hotly contested arena of local politics. The association must have understood this too, but whether or not they attempted to take advantage of this is unclear.

In its efforts to foreground veterans' concerns in the 1898 elections, the Old Soldiers' Association hosted debates and exerted pressure on candidates. In July, the group prepared a list of questions and asked each candidate to respond in order "to tell how much he will do for the old soldier if elected."[118] They also supported veteran candidates for office. In the 1898 congressional race, the association unanimously backed the nomination of Republican state legislator Captain Thomas H. Ijams, a Union veteran. Captain R. D. Bledsoe, a Confederate veteran and vice president of the association, attended the district Republican convention to present the organization's endorsement in person. Bledsoe asked the convention to nominate Ijams "as an act of patriotism." "[Bledsoe] explained that he had been a Democrat all of his life and had never but once voted for a Republican. But he was prepared to say for himself and other ex-Confederates that they would gladly vote for their old soldier candidate for congress."[119] Despite Bledsoe's appeal, Ijams did not receive the party's nomination.

The association not only endorsed candidates with a pro-veteran agenda but also endorsed imperialism. Indeed, its expansionist politics were on full display at a picnic in October 1898, attended by thirty Civil War veterans and their families along with an unknown number of veterans of the Spanish-American War. The *Kansas City Journal* encapsulated the mood of the picnic with a brief headline—"They Enjoy the Day Fraternally and Listen to Patriotic Speeches"—which describes veterans' reunions about as accurately and concisely as its possible to do. The veterans listened to several speeches and applauded President William McKinley's administration. McKinley, himself a Union veteran, championed reconciliation and an expansionist foreign policy. Then, two candidates for the office of Jackson County prosecuting attorney addressed the crowd. Both men espoused imperialistic rhetoric and were rewarded with the approbation of the veterans. According to the *Kansas City Journal*, "Several of the speakers declared their belief in the doctrine of expansion and the applause which greeted their professions on this subject indicated that the platform of the meeting was to 'hold all we got.'" George A. Neal, the Republican candidate, proclaimed, "I am an expansionist. I believe the destinies of our country demand that the American flag shall fly wherever our soldiers have been. It should everywhere be a guarantee that the interests of liberty and honor and justice, the world over, will be protected by the American sword."[120] Even with the veterans' support, however, Neal lost the 1898 election.[121]

Despite its claims to nonpartisanship, the Old Soldiers' Association placed itself in opposition to the tactics of the growing Pendergast machine. It expressed concern over the means Democrats used to attract voters, including providing services in neglected Kansas City neighborhoods. As Colonel John N. Southern, a Confederate veteran, asked the association in September 1898: "Don't you believe that a man who will go out on the streets and buy votes is an enemy?"[122] The association also suspected the Democrats of practicing voter suppression. In the days before the November election, the group petitioned the Jackson County court to provide two additional polling places in Independence, citing the need for "fairness" and a concern for "the old men of Blue township," who could expect to wait in line for hours to cast their ballots.[123] Judges George L. Chrisman and J. R. Marsh, who the *Kansas City Journal* accused of being part of the Democrat "gang," denied the request.[124] As the association feared, election day was miserable and rainy. After waiting in line for hours, some voters gave up. The Democrats, Judge Chrisman included, recorded widespread victories in the election.

It is not evident how long the Old Soldiers' Association remained active as apparently no organizational records have survived. Nevertheless, the history of the St. Louis Veterans of the Blue and Gray and the Kansas City Old Soldiers' Association embodied a similar ethos. Both provided a means for white veterans to further their own economic and political interests in an environment where wartime divisions could only prove a hindrance.

Still, the existence of blue and gray societies in Missouri does not mean that even white veterans universally embraced reconciliation. Indeed, reactions to a proposed national blue and gray reunion in Washington, DC, provide some insight into the conflicted feelings Missourians held about reconciliation.[125] In October 1898, the *Kansas City Journal* interviewed local veterans about their interest in the Washington reunion. By their responses, it was evident they agreed that the timing was crucial—victory in the Spanish-American War belonged to the descendants of both the blue and the gray and had laid the groundwork for reconciliation. Some commented that they already had personal friendships with their former foes, making the prospect of a larger national reconciliation seem more feasible. Several veterans expressed a generally favorable impression of the proposed reunion, even suggesting it should be held in Kansas City instead. William C. Ebert, a Union veteran, told the *Journal*:

> There is a feeling—a strong desire, I might say—among old soldiers of both sides, to get together and make some formal demonstration in the way of showing the change which has taken place in our hearts since the war with Spain began. Kansas City is the place for such a celebration, by all means. It is right here where the breach was the widest, and where, too, more of the men who fought over that breach have come together since the war and learned to know and respect each other as citizens, than in any other city of this size.[126]

Another Union veteran, Rev. Dr. H. D. Jenkins, agreed: "That Kansas City should be chosen as the place of meeting I think most fitting, both on practical and on sentimental grounds. There is no point in the United States more generally available than Kansas City, and there is no state in the Union so pre-eminently the battleground, on which we should meet to wipe out old scores, as is Missouri."[127] Like the members of the Veterans of the Blue and Gray, Ebert and Jenkins believed Missouri's unique wartime history and central location could help facilitate reconciliation on both a practical and symbolic level.

Not every local veteran, however, was so optimistic about the possibility of reconciliation. Some commented that such a reunion, whatever its intentions, could not help but resurrect painful wartime divisions and damage patriotic feelings. Others voiced more stringent opposition. One anonymous Union veteran fumed, "I don't believe in doing a thing for Confederates nor allowing them to come in on our reunions. . . . I have never seen them meet us of the Union army half way in friendly advances." According to the *Journal*, the man "was immediately taken to task" by his fellow veterans "for the sentiments he expressed." Former Confederate general James Harding was more sanguine in his lack of interest in the reunion. "Meetings of this kind are very pleasant social gatherings," he said, "but that is about all the good they do."[128]

In a state so deeply rent by the Civil War, however, sometimes sociability was an achievement in and of itself. While fraternizing at blue and gray events, including banquets, picnics, and other entertainments, white veterans cultivated important relationships. These relationships fostered business and political partnerships, which enhanced not only the individual veterans' own socioeconomic status but also the status of veterans more generally. Although their efforts were framed in the spirit of reconciliationist sentimentality, the cooperation of these men was founded on the same pragmatic realities that fueled Missouri's antebellum compromise tradition. In Missouri, the line between the blue and the gray proved a hindrance to the ambitions white veterans held for themselves and for their state. Albeit in a limited way, blue and gray societies provided veterans a means of overcoming their divisions.

Missouri Monument, Vicksburg National Military Park

The turn of the century witnessed increasing fraternization between Missouri's white Union and Confederate veterans. For this narrow, although influential group of Missourians, reconciliation became an important component of Civil War commemoration. On the national level, reconciliation stemmed largely from the shared politics, race, and gender identities of white veterans. Reconciliation in Missouri, however, was also rooted in unique local prerogatives as well as in a strong sense of regionalism. Many white veterans believed that Missouri's contributions to the Civil War were undervalued, particularly by easterners.

In the late 1890s, these feelings of marginalization became all the more pronounced as a major movement for battlefield preservation got underway. This resulted in the creation of several national military parks at the Civil War battlefields of Gettysburg, Shiloh, Chickamauga and Chattanooga, and Vicksburg. Although the selection of these battlefields, with the exception of Gettysburg, indicated an appreciation for the significance of the trans-Mississippi theater of the Civil War, no parks were initially established west of the Mississippi River. This seemingly relegated Missouri's battles to the periphery of the most decisive actions of the Civil War. Furthermore, although Missourians fought in most of these battles, they lacked representation within the existing national military parks. As battlefields gained cultural importance as sites of Civil War memory, many states erected monuments honoring the roles their soldiers played in the action. Missourians, however, were notable only for their absence.[129]

Leo Rassieur believed this state of affairs reflected poorly on Missouri. As former commander of the Department of Missouri GAR as well as one-time national commander in chief of the GAR, Rassieur insisted the state was neglecting an important duty and that, as a result, Missourians visiting the parks "had been compelled to hang their heads in shame." In Rassieur's mind, it was the equal responsibility of Union and Confederate Missourians to take pride in their history and redeem the honor of their state by placing monuments at the parks. He believed that "the time had come for the Blue and Gray . . . to make an effective appeal together for the recognition of the services of their fallen comrades . . . and thus remove the blemish of ingratitude which seemed, at present, to rest upon the people of this great State."[130] In 1906, Rassieur and the GAR petitioned the Missouri General Assembly to set aside funds to erect numerous battlefield monuments not only in Missouri but also at the national military parks.[131]

At first, the General Assembly seemed receptive to Rassieur's idea. The timing was nearly perfect as, in 1905, the federal government had disbursed approximately $475,000 to the state of Missouri in payment of ongoing war claims settlements, which reimbursed loyal citizens for requisitions made during the Civil War and for expenses incurred by the states in raising troops. Missouri's veterans felt it would be particularly appropriate to spend that money on Civil War commemoration. Some favored using the funds to construct "a Missouri soldiers memorial building" at the University of Missouri to house a museum, library, and the archives of the state historical society.[132] Both the GAR and the UCV also petitioned the General Assembly to allocate the money to a monument fund. In spite of their efforts, commander of the Department of Missouri GAR John M. Williams noted bitterly, "The entire half million dollars . . . was given to the road fund. The old soldier, his services and his sacrifices were forgotten. Years hence these monuments may be erected," Williams added, "but I have no hope of seeing them in this present life."[133]

Undeterred by the state government's lack of interest, veterans continued to press for action. They particularly directed their attention to Vicksburg National Military Park in Mississippi. The Battle of Vicksburg, more accurately described as a siege, lasted forty-seven days between May and July 1863 and resulted in one of the most decisive Union victories of the Civil War. Vicksburg held a special place in the memories of both Union and Confederate Missourians because of the numbers involved. Missouri sent more regiments and batteries into the action than any state besides Illinois. During the siege, Union and Confederate Missourians directly fought one another, perfectly illustrating the tragedy of a war that pitted brother against brother. If any battlefield merited a Missouri monument, this was it.

Rassieur, himself a veteran of the siege, spearheaded the effort to erect a Missouri monument at Vicksburg. From the beginning, he conceived of it as a "common" monument to both the Union and Confederate troops engaged in the siege—not unlike the Wolfe-Montcalm monument in Quebec. In 1910, acting under pressure from the Department of Missouri GAR and Missouri Division UCV, Representatives M. Jackson Jones and Oliver T. Remmers introduced a bill to the state legislature proposing a $50,000 appropriation to place a monument and various smaller markers on the battlefield. On March 1, 1911, Rassieur wrote a particularly impassioned letter to the General Assembly in support of the bill, reminding the legislators of the significance of such a measure for the people of Missouri. He stated,

> The great State of Missouri . . . cannot afford to remain inactive any longer in a matter of so much moment. Nor will you, as the legislative body of our State, postpone action when such postponement will . . . reflect upon the good name and patriotism of our State, which was represented by the second largest number of organizations in that siege. The present generation will gladly bear this small burden and have the great satisfaction of erecting a monument which will be unique, inasmuch as it will manifest equal gratitude for the courage and valor displayed by those who wore the Gray as well as those who wore the Blue, and thus still further heal the wounds wrought by the Civil War.[134]

Rassieur's letter helped produce the desired result. In 1911, the General Assembly approved the appropriation and authorized the creation of the Missouri-Vicksburg National Military Park Commission. As an indication of the reconciliationist spirit behind the monument, the commission consisted of five members, including two Union veterans and two Confederate veterans—all of whom had served in the battle.[135] The commission planned to construct its monument at the very site where Missourians had met in battle. It would commemorate both sides, the commission decided, "in order to foster the atmosphere of brotherhood and reconciliation" cultivated by the Vicksburg National Military Park. It was a remarkable and almost entirely unprecedented idea. At that time, no other monument on the battlefield commemorated both sides.[136]

The commission invited a competition for the design of the monument. They confined the contestants to a budget of $40,000 and instructed them to "give fitting artistic expression to the gratitude of the State to its sons, both Union and Confederate, for their heroic services and sacrifices in contending for their honest convictions."[137] Sixteen artists from around the country sent scale models of their prospective monuments to the commission, but the winning submission came from a team of St. Louis architects, Hellmuth & Hellmuth, and sculptor Victor S. Holm, a teacher at the St. Louis School of Fine Arts.[138]

Holm imbued his design with powerful symbolism pertinent to Missouri's role in the Battle of Vicksburg. Finished in Missouri red granite, the completed monument stands forty-two feet high, representing the total number of Missouri units engaged on the battlefield—twenty-seven Union and fifteen Confederate. The central shaft is topped by a relief carving of the state seal and fronted by an allegorical personification of the "Spirit of the Republic." This figure is flanked by two bronze panels depicting Missouri soldiers meeting one another in battle. The monument is inscribed,

> To commemorate and perpetuate
> The heroic services
> The unselfish devotion to duty
> And the exalted patriotism
> Of the Missouri soldiers
> Union and Confederate
> Who were engaged in the
> Campaign, siege and defense of Vicksburg.[139]

The monument was completed in time for the Vicksburg Peace Jubilee on October 16–19, 1917. The organizers hoped the jubilee would emulate the success of the 1913 Gettysburg reunion, although they anticipated it would be smaller in scale. Nevertheless, they intended it "to give the Western veterans an opportunity of coming together on a Western battlefield of like importance."[140] The Peace Jubilee, however, was terribly overshadowed by World War I. Held within days of the arrival of the first American troops on the Western Front, the Peace Jubilee commanded nowhere near the publicity of the 1913 Gettysburg reunion. As World War I prepared to enter its fourth year, reaching an unimaginable scale of death and destruction, commentators could not help but consider this nineteenth-century foray into trench warfare quaint, romantic, and even trivial by comparison. At Vicksburg, the *St. Louis Star and Times* claimed, "The men in the opposing trenches . . . were fighting for principle, not for territory nor world dominion, and did

Figure 5. Missouri monument at Vicksburg National Military Park. Courtesy of National Park Service, Washington, DC

not hate each other." Whereas the indiscriminate use of lethal new weapons technologies in World War I led to the deaths of millions in Europe, soldiers and civilians alike, northerners and southerners carried out the Civil War "as near the standards of Christianity as war has ever been made to come." According to the paper, their shared American identity and the surety that they had waged a just war meant "these 'Yanks' and 'Johnny Rebs' can meet again, their difference of principle settled, in mutual response and love and in joint loyalty to a common country, a common flag and common high ideals of citizenship and human rights." It predicted no such reconciliation would be possible between the belligerent nations of World War I.[141]

As the first American "doughboys" approached the Western Front in Europe, a small group of Missourians gathered on the afternoon of October 17 to celebrate the dedication of their monument and the placement of fifty smaller granite markers identifying the various positions of Missouri troops during the siege. Rassieur, as president of the monument commission, presented the work to Captain William T. Rigby, who accepted on behalf of the federal government and the Vicksburg National Military Park. In his remarks, Rigby said the monument would inspire the young Missourians now preparing for combat in France, "whether his parent wore the Union

Figure 6. Dedication of Missouri monument during the Peace Jubilee, October 17, 1917, Vicksburg National Military Park. Courtesy of National Park Service, Washington, DC

blue or the Confederate Gray on the Vicksburg battle lines."[142] It was not a monument to the North or the South, the *St. Louis Star and Times* reflected, but "a perpetual memorial to American courage and true manhood."[143] On the whole, the dedication ceremony reiterated the importance of nationalism and militaristic masculinity to reconciliationist sentimentality.

In Missouri, as was true across the United States, reconciliation in the aftermath of the Civil War was not uncomplicated, was never complete, and was often extended only along specific racial and gender lines. In Missouri, reconciliationist feeling was most usually expressed between white men. It is quite telling that women were absent from the efforts described here until they came forward to oppose the incorporation of the Confederate and national cemeteries in Springfield. The absence of African American Missourians is also telling, confirming the larger trend that reconciliation marginalized black perspectives on the Civil War. At the same time, these reconciliationist undertakings reflect the distinct imperatives of Civil War commemoration in Missouri. While white Missourians were certainly inspired by the broader spirit of reconciliation that characterized Civil War memory at the turn of the twentieth century, they were also driven by their unique concerns and responsibilities as Missourians. As often as reconciliation evoked sentimentality, masculinity, white supremacy, and nationalism, for Missourians it was also quite pragmatic. Reconciliation recalled their affinity for compromise and served immediate needs and priorities, including caring for the dead, stimulating business, shaping politics, and increasing recognition for Missouri's contributions to the Civil War.

SIX

"Tender of Both Uniforms"

Missouri's Homes for Civil War Veterans

Our Missourian . . . went under two flags—both ways—went at once. . . . When he came home from the war his mighty mother, the state of Missouri, with a great heart, claimed him as her son, proud of his deeds, resolute to cherish his memory, magnanimous to forget his quarrel, tender of both uniforms, and mourning over the dead of war-worn and desolate confederate and federal.

—Judge Henry Lamm, *Hale v. Stimson*, June 30, 1906

IN THE HISTORY OF THE Missouri General Assembly, there were few days as dramatic as February 11, 1897. On that day, the senate voted on whether the state should assume control of Missouri's privately funded Confederate and Federal soldiers' homes. With legislators and observers spilling out of the senate chamber and into the halls of the statehouse, young senator Henry H. Hohenschild implored his fellow legislators to lay aside the bitter and divisive legacy of the Civil War. He asked them to vote in favor of the measure and, in so doing, show that a spirit of charity and reconciliation now governed the once-tortured border state. After making a final plea to his fellow Missourians to enter the twentieth century as friends and partners, Hohenschild relinquished the floor to his colleague and fellow Democrat Senator Charles H. Vandiver. A native Virginian and disabled Confederate veteran, Vandiver had relocated to Missouri in 1880 and became an early champion of the Missouri Confederate Home. As a result, he took the floor that day on its behalf. As Vandiver rose to speak, the *St. Louis Republic* observed, the empty right sleeve of the senator's jacket fell to his side—a silent argument, perhaps stronger than any he had prepared, of the hardships still endured by the state's Civil War veterans.[1]

Vandiver began by speaking about his own service in the Army of Northern Virginia. Appealing to reconciliationist sentimentality, he remembered fraternizing with Union soldiers over tobacco and coffee during the war. "We were not mad at each other," he said, but rather caught up in circumstances beyond individual control. In peace, veterans continued this tradition of fraternization. He spoke about the generous support Missouri's Union veterans had already provided the Confederate Home—as much as $10,000 in private donations. "I want to say now," Vandiver concluded, "as one who was a Confederate soldier, who followed Lee from Manassas to Gettysburg, from the Wilderness to Petersburg, was thrice wounded with his face to the foe, and left an arm to moulder in the Old Dominion, that I cast my vote for this bill."[2] It was a dramatic moment, one that sent his audience into ecstatic applause and left them fumbling for their handkerchiefs at the same time. The press recognized the powerful symbolism of the occasion. "When a one-armed soldier like Senator Vandiver stands up in a Missouri legislature and appeals for the perpetual union of the blue and gray," the *Mexico Weekly Ledger* noted, "it is convincing proof that the war is over and that sectional sentiment[s] are rapidly being lost sight of."[3] Such optimism was not misplaced. The bills passed with only one dissenting vote, leaving those present feeling encouraged about the prospect of reconciliation in their state. For Vandiver, it "was like laying a joint tribute on the altar of forgetfulness and forgiveness."[4]

Missouri's deeply conflicted identity, as exemplified by the history of the two homes, made this legislation all the more profound. Despite their competing agendas, white Missourians appealed to their shared regional identity and compromise tradition to band together in support of both the state's Union and Confederate veterans. "I congratulate myself that I am . . . a citizen of a state," Hohenschild said, "that . . . is endeavoring to link all sections and bind all sentiments by caring for the old soldiers of both armies."[5] "I am proud of grand old Missouri that has shown a spirit broad enough and a liberal policy in this respect," Vandiver echoed. "She is the first State in the Union to become mother of 'Twin Soldiers' Homes.' Old soldiers without shelters are provided for in our glorious State, whether they wore blue or gray."[6] "The passage of the two bills at one and the same time constituted a significant object-lesson," the *Iron County Register* proclaimed. "The war is over. Nowhere did it range with more desperate fierceness than in Missouri. It is Missouri that now sets the example of forgetting the bitterness and helpfully remembering the claims of the brave soldiers who fought faithfully and well under either flag."[7]

Thus, white Union and Confederate veterans, the wartime generation and their descendants, became allies in a monumental effort in Civil War commemoration. Although the reconciliationist spirit demonstrated by the incorporation of the Springfield cemeteries, the organization of blue and gray veterans' societies, and the construction of the Vicksburg monument were remarkable and unprecedented, that work paled in comparison to the effort and expense committed to the state's two veterans' homes. "A people carves its own image in the monuments of its generosity," Hohenschild said.[8] And in the case of the Missouri homes for Civil War veterans, it was the literal truth. Few historians have recognized the centrality of soldiers' homes to the project of Civil War commemoration and yet they quite literally kept the memory of the war alive.[9] Part nursing home and part shrine, they were "living monuments" that provide insight into how white Missourians remembered their Civil War.[10]

For white Missourians, the Confederate and Federal Homes were a testament to the long process of personal and national healing in the aftermath of the Civil War, but more specifically, to the uniqueness of its legacy in Missouri. The history of Missouri's veterans' homes demonstrates the frequent collaboration and persistent tension that characterized the efforts of Missourians to commemorate the Civil War. It also demonstrates the uneven process of reconciliation in the state, which was often grounded more in pragmatism than in ideological agreement. In this case, the inability of private fundraising efforts to meet the needs of Civil War veterans drove white Missourians into a reconciliationist effort to seek state intervention. In order to secure it, they recalled the state's compromise tradition and claimed a responsibility as Missourians to foster reconciliation. In the process, however, they ran not only against contentious Civil War memories but also against competing ideas about gender, state power, and welfare. In the end, the veterans' homes reveal the particular concerns that shaped Civil War commemoration in Missouri.

The idea of providing care to war veterans was not unique to Missouri. In fact, the U.S. Navy established the first veterans' home in 1811, and in 1851 the U.S. Soldiers' Home opened in Washington, DC. The unprecedented size of Civil War armies, however, threatened to strain the existing system. During the course of the Civil War, the U.S. Sanitary Commission and patriotic private citizens maintained convalescent homes for wounded soldiers. Unfortunately, this provided only a temporary solution.[11] As early as 1864, President Abraham Lincoln understood something more needed to be done. In his Second Inaugural Address, he urged Americans not only "to finish the work we are in" but also "to bind up the nation's wounds, to care for him who shall have borne the battle and for his widow and his orphan."[12] In response, the U.S. Soldier's Home expanded into a nationwide enterprise, the National Home for Disabled Volunteer Soldiers. With ten branches across the United States, it was the culmination of Lincoln's vision.

The National Home only extended eligibility to Union veterans, however, and no branches existed in Missouri. In 1887, the Missouri General Assembly began considering a remedy to this situation when Representative John Daniel introduced House Bill 137 to establish a soldiers' home in Missouri.[13] Although the precise details of this bill are unclear—its text was destroyed in a major fire that gutted the statehouse in 1911—it requested an appropriation of $100,000 to construct a home for Union veterans. The press coverage of the proposed legislation was generally favorable. The *Holt County Sentinel*, for example, suggested a Missouri soldiers' home was long overdue: "While many of the states of the Union have organized soldiers' homes upon their own soil Missouri, the fifth state in wealth and population, has not yet moved in the matter."[14] Following up the story a week later, the paper added, "There is no good reason why there should not be a soldier's home in this state."[15]

Within the ranks of the Department of Missouri Grand Army of the Republic (GAR), however, the proposition met with distrust. Upon consideration of whether the department ought to endorse the bill, some members insisted it was a matter for national, not state, funding. Others voiced concerns about the influence former Confederates might have had on the legislation. Representing the General Joe Bailey Post, Charles Germman Burton urged caution: "I desire to say that . . . I was informed by a member of the Legislature that it was his intention to offer an amendment to the bill, making it applicable to Confederate soldiers and sailors who live in Missouri. I want to understand just how much of that bill we are endorsing." Comrade W. H. Day of the W. S. Hancock Post agreed: "It will be necessary for us to be extremely careful how we endorse the bill, as by our action we may place the Confederate soldiers on an equal footing with the Federal soldiers of Missouri." William Page of the Bates County Post raised an additional point of concern: "I want to ask whether or not the man who introduced this bill was a Confederate soldier?" Upon hearing that yes, "he was," Page added, "Then I would not like to trust them. It strikes me that it is a kind of Trojan horse brought in here to entrap the Grand Army."[16] In reality, it is not clear that Daniel hoped his proposed home would admit Confederates or that he even was a Civil War veteran. While Daniel registered with the U.S. provost marshal's office for the draft in 1863, he does not appear to have served in either army.[17] His failure to volunteer for the Union Army, whether or not he sympathized with the Confederacy, was enough to sow doubts about his loyalty. Despite the concerns over Daniel's motives, however, the Ransom Post ultimately passed a resolution endorsing the bill.

Back in the General Assembly, the debate surrounding the bill grew heated. Indeed, it was a complicated proposition. Missourians like Representative Daniel may have felt a duty to provide aid for their Civil War veterans, but this proved to be a contentious proposition in a border state. Besides serving in the regular Union and Confederate Armies, Missourians also enlisted in various Union militia units and the southern-sympathizing State Guard, and unknown numbers joined the ranks of the guerrillas. This presented Missourians with a difficult political situation: it was unclear which veterans should qualify for assistance. The state could not easily justify providing for some without alienating others. Furthermore, the legislators, among them a number of Union and Confederate veterans, disagreed as much over the merits of welfare as they did on the legacy of the war itself. The debate over Daniel's bill raised questions about the nature of government aid, state power, and contemporary gender stereotypes. In the late nineteenth century, most Americans regarded needy individuals as either "deserving" or "undeserving." Only those in desperate circumstances beyond their control "deserved" charity. Widespread recognition of the sacrifices incurred through military service classed most veterans among the "deserving." Even so, for a veteran to accept government aid or commit himself to institutional care served as a public admission of his inability to provide for himself and his dependents, which called into question his masculinity and character.[18]

As a result, the debate surrounding House Bill 137 did not fall neatly along wartime divisions. There were larger social and political forces at work. Validating the worst fears of the GAR, Democrat John H. Babcock, a Union veteran, proposed amending the bill so that Confederate veterans could be admitted to the home. At least one other Union veteran in the assembly endorsed Babcock's amendment.[19] Interestingly, it was Representative Henry A. Newman, a former Confederate, who expressed the most determined resistance to the amendment. Newman praised the magnanimity of his Union fellows but insisted Confederate veterans did not need the state to validate their service by providing for their welfare. According to an account in the *Butler Weekly Times*:

> Mr. Newman . . . disclaimed on behalf of the Confederates of Missouri, any desire to be provided with a home at public expense. He said the Confederates did not want it. They never went begging for anything. They did

> not need anything. One-legged or one-armed, they were able to take care of themselves. . . . [The Confederate] has no palatial "home" maintained by public taxation. He has no pension for exposing himself to the leaden hail, but he can point . . . to a hundred well-fought fields and feel glorious. . . . The confederate soldier was wrapped in a halo of glory and romance, and he (Newman) would not dim it by making him a pensioner.[20]

Newman did not dispute the reality that many veterans needed assistance to support themselves and their families. In fact, he was heavily involved with the ongoing effort of the Ex-Confederate Association to construct a privately funded Confederate Home in Missouri. Rather, his opposition reflected the pervasive stigma attached to public welfare initiatives in the nineteenth century, which were fraught with classist and gendered undertones. Newman likely felt Confederate masculinity, already wounded by defeat, could not bear the added humiliation of a mercenary bid for government assistance. Such behavior ran counter to the dictates of militaristic masculinity, which viewed military service as driven by duty rather than the expectation of reward.[21] Confederates like Newman, however, were not the only representatives who harbored this gendered bias. When Union veteran and Republican representative Joseph T. Moore told the assembly "he had a supreme contempt for Union soldiers who opposed the bill," Democrat William O. L. Jewett, another Union veteran, responded by saying, "He had a supreme contempt for the man who fought on the winning side and came before the people as a beggar." According to the *St. Joseph Weekly Gazette*, Jewett went so far as to call the bill "a useless expenditure."[22] Ultimately, Daniel's bill failed by a vote of sixty-nine to sixty-two.[23]

Thus, the debate surrounding the soldiers' home bill succumbed to the complicated legacy of Missouri's Civil War and to gendered attitudes about welfare legislation. Although the idea of admitting Confederates to the proposed soldiers' home met with resistance in the GAR, Union veterans in the legislature evinced a ready willingness to accommodate their one-time enemies. It was not only wartime hostilities that killed the measure, therefore, but also a discomfiture with government spending on veterans and its attendant social implications. Opposed to the expansion of state power and concerned that placing veterans under government care would effectively emasculate them, Union and Confederate veterans in the Missouri legislature deferred the issue. In 1887, when most veterans were still in their forties, they could afford to do so. The ever-advancing age of the state's veteran population, however, ensured the matter would only increase in urgency and importance.

The rejection of the soldiers' home bill did not end the conversation about the needs of veterans in Missouri nor did it deter ongoing efforts by the Ex-Confederate Association to construct a private home for Confederate veterans in the state. The association believed providing private care served to lessen the stigma of charity and best preserved the dignity of needy men. It felt private funding would demonstrate popular "gratitude . . . and true sympathy" for the veterans without making "them a charge upon the public and a burden to the community."[24] These veterans would not be "charity cases" or wards of the state but rather charges of their loving comrades.

As a result, when the Ex-Confederate Association of Missouri formed in 1881, it committed to building and maintaining a Missouri Home for Confederate Veterans. In 1889, the Ex-Confederates organized the Confederate Home Association to put this plan into action.[25] The group understood that in the case of needy Confederate veterans, the duty of care fell squarely on its members. As one Confederate Home employee observed much later: "While they endured all the hardships, faced all the dangers and fought as bravely as any soldiers who ever marched to the field of battle, their cause was lost, and no Federal Home awaits their coming, when old age and poverty overtakes them."[26] Although the association did not expect or necessarily want state assistance, it understood the construction of a Missouri Confederate Home would not only meet a real need but also legitimize the veteran status of former Confederates. Therefore, sympathetic Missourians imagined the Confederate Home as more than a necessity; for them, it was "justice which has been too long delayed."[27]

However high-minded and symbolic its intensions were, the Confederate Home Association nevertheless struggled to gather financial support among Missourians. Over time, as the needs of veterans grew, its efforts garnered more attention. "Gradually," Ex-Confederate W. P. Barlow remembered, "as public confidence increased, and as the helpless increased in number, grew the sentiment that we must have a Home, and agitation began." With the help of a statewide fundraising effort led by Missouri schoolchildren, the Ex-Confederates raised $13,000.[28] In 1890, the association used these funds to purchase roughly 360 acres of farmland near Higginsville as a prospective site for the home. Situated in Lafayette County, about fifty miles east of Kansas City, Higginsville lies at the heart of Little Dixie. Establishing the home there linked the effort even more strongly to Confederate memory.

Despite the region's reputation as a bastion of the Lost Cause, however, the Ex-Confederate Association could not immediately raise enough money to begin construction. O. H. P. Catron, one of the Ex-Confederates, complained that there were too "few Confederates in this portion of

Missouri" to support the home.[29] In fact, work stalled until the Daughters of the Confederacy, later the Missouri Division United Daughters of the Confederacy (UDC), launched a renewed fundraising campaign on behalf of the Confederate Home. This effort aligned with the benevolent mission of the Daughters. According to historian Karen L. Cox, its members "strongly committed to providing for the aging and indigent . . . in their midst" and "were vehemently opposed to placing their ancestors in almshouses or on poor farms."[30] The Missouri Daughters shared the desire of the Ex-Confederate Association to provide a place where, as Confederate veteran F. P. Bronaugh put it, "destitute comrades and their families can pass the remainder of their lives, secure from the ever-present danger of the poor-house."[31] Trading on traditional stereotypes that cast women as caretakers, the Missouri Daughters took the reins of the fundraising effort and proved dramatically more successful than its male colleagues.[32] "In two counties, where the men could not raise a dollar," the *Confederate Veteran* pointed out, "the local [Daughters of the Confederacy] raised over a thousand dollars each."[33] The women left no stone unturned. They raised collections in schools; hosted dances, picnics, and socials; and sold bricks.[34] They even petitioned the state government, proposing a resolution that every state employee donate a day's pay on behalf of the home. According to W. P. Barlow, the measure passed unanimously, with "a large audience of ladies being given woman suffrage for that occasion."[35] Ultimately, the Daughters raised as much as $100,000, enough to start work on the main building of the home.[36] "The women, God bless them! have nobly done their part. . . . Without them," Catron confessed, "the Confederate Home of Missouri would never have been built."[37] While men wrestled with the stigmatization of charity, late nineteenth-century gender conventions made it seem natural and appropriate that women would take the lead in the care of Confederate veterans, and women reaped the rewards. It is important to remember, however, that the Daughters envisioned the Confederate Home not only as a charitable institution but also as testament to future generations of its members' reverence for the Confederacy.[38]

The Missouri Daughters owed a portion of its success to the generosity of the state's white Union veterans. Across the state, members of the GAR helped raise money and even hosted fundraising initiatives in their communities on behalf of the Confederate Home.[39] As one Ex-Confederate reported, "In many counties ex-Union soldiers have accepted the position of treasurer and of township collectors, modesty alone preventing their taking higher positions. It has been no unusual thing to see the members of a G. A. R. Post come marching to our meetings in full uniform, taking reserved seats, while their officers came upon the platform and introduced the speakers in words that cheered the hearts of every ex-Confederate present."[40]

It is hard to know the motives of the GAR men. Perhaps they were moved by the bonds of militaristic masculinity to provide aid for other needy soldiers or perhaps they were governed by more romantic considerations. As historian Nina Silber has demonstrated, marriages between Union veterans and Confederate women advanced the sentimental appeal of reconciliation.[41] This was certainly the case for Major James Adams, a Union veteran whose wife was an active member of the Missouri Daughters. According to the *St. Louis Republic*, "Adams was a gallant Federal soldier and is a prominent member of the GAR but he ably seconds his wife in her work for the Confederate Home as do a number of the GARs of Edina and vicinity."[42]

Of course, the support of Union veterans for the home may have also indicated some political agreement with former Confederates. In fact, the Higginsville site belonged to a Union veteran, Grove Young, who reduced his asking price by $5,000 as a goodwill gesture toward the Ex-Confederates.[43] Young also left a small endowment to help support the home. According to the UDC, "The actions of carpetbaggers and other Northern actions after the war had made him sympathetic for the South."[44] Grove was not alone among Union veterans. Racist opposition to the policies of the Radical Republicans and suspicions over the expansion of federal power during Reconstruction led more than one Yankee to identify with his former enemies.

Whatever the motivations of Union veterans who aided the Confederate Home, the local press enthused over their contributions. "Past differences of opinion are having no influence in the matter," the *Boonville Weekly Advertiser* proclaimed, "but the old Union veteran and his friends are coming with open hands and cheerful liberality to help those who started the enterprise."[45] Attributing their generosity to bonds forged in combat, the *Sedalia Weekly Bazoo* insisted that although the veterans had once been bitter enemies, they "now remember only that they were soldiers and by their bravery won a right to a haven of rest in their old age."[46] Still others understood the importance of Missouri's historical context in these reconciliationist actions. The assistance of Union veterans, the *Confederate Veteran* observed, transformed the Confederate Home into "a monument attesting peace and Christian charity in a State where war was waged more bitterly than ever before on American soil."[47] It gave at least one Missourian reason to hope, nearly thirty years after its conclusion, that "the war is about over."[48]

The cooperation of Union veterans seemed to herald the reconciliation of the white members of Missouri's Civil War generation. In reality, however, wartime tensions were never too far beneath the surface. Some, like

Young, may have joined the ranks of the "belated Confederates," but many Missourians remained unable to forgive or forget, and lingering hostilities strained their tolerance for one another. While individual Union veterans sympathized with the plight of needy Confederates, the Department of Missouri GAR wanted it to be clear it did not wish to honor the cause for which those men fought. In 1891, the Ransom Post warned its members against responding to calls for help from the Confederate Home Association "when such solicitations are accompanied with a manifest attempt to honor the Lost Cause, or by a display of the folds or figure of the rebel flag." In particular, the post condemned the use of the Confederate flag on the association's stationery, expressing regret "that those most prominent and active in behalf of the home seem either unable or unwilling to separate feelings of charity towards worthy living persons from feelings of esteem for the unworthy dead cause for which they so gallantly fought."[49] That same year, the Justi Post passed resolutions calling the Confederate flag an "emblem of *treason* and Rebellion" and insisted "it is in bad taste and ill advised zeal to come in Charity's name, flaunting that flag in any form or manner, and however small, it is an insult to the G. A. R.." The post promised, however, to "cheerfully aid and assist the Ex-Confederate Soldiers as far as we are able, to secure a home under our flag."[50] In one Sedalia newspaper, an anonymous contributor voiced his "disapprov[al] of the mingling of union soldiers with ex-confederates" and "discourage[d] contributions to the ex-confederate home by speaking contemptuously of it." "Sectional hatred is not quite dead, yet," the piece acknowledged. "But it is rapidly dying out."[51] The GAR's opposition to the use of Confederate iconography in the promotion of the home reveals the limits of reconciliationist sentiment in the state. Despite the conservatism of many white Missourians and despite their sympathy for the needs of aging veterans, they did not necessarily wish to endorse the Lost Cause.

The Missouri Confederate Home was undoubtedly a shrine to the Lost Cause, as manifested in its very architecture. At its dedication on June 8, 1893, guests sat on its wide porches, deliberately designed to evoke a plantation aesthetic that had never really existed on the Missouri frontier. Inside, veterans circulated in rooms named in honor of Missouri's Confederate heroes, including John Sappington Marmaduke and Claiborne Fox Jackson, while portraits of Jefferson Davis, Robert E. Lee, and Stonewall Jackson decked the walls.[52] Eventually, the pictures of these famed Confederates were joined by one of Grove Young, identified as "A Federal Soldier and a worthy Patron of the Confederate Home."[53] In all, the design and decor

Figure 7. Missouri Confederate Home, Higginsville. Courtesy of Confederate Home, Higginsville, Photographs (P1046). 2. The State Historical Society of Missouri, Photograph Collection

of the home illustrated the complexities of Confederate commemoration in Missouri. The home's features paid homage to both the eastern and western Confederacy and, by acknowledging Young, hinted at how much Confederates owed the state's Union majority.

This tension was also evident in a pamphlet produced by the Confederate Home Association in 1893 entitled *Missouri of Today: Progress and Prospects of the Great Commercial State and Center of Population.* The pamphlet provided a brief history of the Civil War in Missouri, biographies of famous leaders, and an overview of the operations of the Confederate Home. It also highlighted Missouri's burgeoning industries, featured in dozens of advertisements for railways, beer, shoes, and colleges and universities. It included detailed descriptions of St. Louis, Kansas City, and St. Joseph designed to appeal to potential investors. Indeed, the pamphlet was dedicated not to Confederate veterans, as might be expected, but "to the Merchants, Manufacturers and Bankers of the splendid and progressive cities of Missouri." *Missouri of Today* did not call for a return to the state's antebellum past but looked forward to development and growth.

More importantly, *Missouri of Today* accentuated the state's unique regional perspective on the Lost Cause. Its account of Missouri's Civil War history harkened back to the themes commonly espoused by Missouri's Confederates: an emphasis on the state's complex geographic position and on the profound sacrifices of its people. Missourians had not wanted war, the pamphlet insisted, but extremists forced the conflict, and Missouri's geography made it impossible to avoid. "Whichever way they decided," the tract read, "ruin and desolation of themselves and their homes was inevitable. The unfortunate geographic position of Missouri placed them between the upper and nether millstone of a great civil war, and no human intellect could save them." "Unhappy people," it deplored, "placed midway between two sections equally determined upon war." This situation was particularly problematic for Missouri's Confederates who, the pamphlet noted, "fought in the Confederate army with no hope of regaining their homes even if the Confederacy gained its cause. The 'consciousness of duty faithfully performed' was to be their only reward, and they knew it." This emphasis on sacrifice on behalf of the Confederate war effort was intrinsic to Missouri's Lost Cause and challenged southern assumptions that the border state had only half-heartedly committed to the Confederacy. Still, *Missouri of Today* stressed that former Confederates were not clinging to the past. "The ex-Confederates of Missouri can now see that the benefits of the struggle are worth all it cost," it vowed. "In a civil war the vanquished lose only a little more than the victors. All participate in the gains. The wonderful progress of our united country proves this."[54]

Indeed, the Confederate Home administration went to pains to position itself within the narrative of national reconciliation. Expressions of pride in the residents' Confederate service were often accompanied by acknowledgments of the bravery of Union soldiers. In one report, the board of the Confederate Home spoke with respect for "the brave Federal soldier," evoking the bonds of militaristic masculinity. "It was the admiration and wonder of the on-looking world," the board claimed, "to note how quickly the bitter feelings and wounds engendered by this internecine strife were healed by the men who wore the blue and those who wore the gray, being chivalrous and magnanimous enough to revere and recognize the strength and purity of their adversaries' principles."[55] As a testament to the renewed patriotism of its residents, the "stars and stripes" flew over the home, not the "stars and bars" or the Confederate battle flag. In 1896, administrators "erected a flagstaff on the highest top of the main building of the home," they explained, "'so that the flag of our united common country can be unfurled to the breezes.'"[56] This tradition continued throughout the life of the home. In 1922, the *Kansas City Journal-Post* reported with pride:

> One of the sights at the home is to see J. R. (Rocky) Moore . . . raise the American flag each morning and haul it down at sunset. Never greater love shown in a man's face than in his when he takes Old Glory out to let the breeze caress her colors. Never greater reverence glows in any man's eyes than in his when he carefully lifts her from the staff, keeping her hem from touching the round, and bears her away to her resting place for the night. Hero of a bitter war, enemy of the flag he now guards so carefully.[57]

In fact, use of the Confederate flag was reserved for special occasions, typically funerals.[58] The U.S. flag signified that the Confederate veterans saw themselves as "a great army of now loyal American citizens."[59] Anxious to prove their rebellion had not been a betrayal of the American republic but rather an effort to restore it to its founding principles, Confederate veterans used the American flag to signal their unblemished patriotism.

Meanwhile, Missouri's Unionists busied themselves in planning their own Federal Soldiers' Home. The Woman's Relief Corps (WRC) first proposed the idea in 1890, but it was four years before they made any significant progress. The WRC's motives and strategies were not unlike those employed by the UDC on behalf of the Confederate Home, except it not only sought to venerate the wartime contributions of men but of women as well. For example, the WRC intended the Federal Soldiers' Home to accommodate army nurses, imbuing them with veteran status. Distressed by the fact that the National Home and its branches excluded women, a provision they believed prevented many married veterans from applying, the WRC "determined on establishing a Home, where Veterans and their Wives might spend the remnant of their lives together."[60] For a generation that already bore so much suffering, the WRC believed separating husbands and wives to be unnecessarily cruel. In 1894, with that purpose in mind, the WRC established the Missouri Soldiers' Home Association and began raising money.

The WRC regarded the prospect of building a Missouri soldiers' home with optimism. With only a modest donation from every sympathetic citizen, the WRC believed "a grand building, a monument . . . and shelter and home for those who have born the burden and heat of the day when the nation was in peril, would be built somewhere in this great state."[61] Progress, however, continued slowly. Frustrated by a general apathy surrounding the project, the WRC felt more than a little aggrieved. Given the support GAR members lavished on the Confederate Home, the WRC's inability to generate similar generosity was particularly galling. As WRC member Belle M. Satterly pointedly observed, "I feel sure that if the Grand Army of the Republic will give to the Woman's Relief Corps in this enterprise the support that they have given to another home in the State of Missouri that we shall soon have a soldiers' home."[62] The women also understood, however, that Missouri's history as a border state meant they could expect only limited sympathy for their endeavor. "We must remember," WRC president Orpha R. Bronson later acknowledged, "we are living in a state that does not sympathize with our boys in blue as they do in the East; thus there is more need for the Woman's Relief Corps to do in this state for the Union veterans than in any of the Eastern states."[63] For his part, GAR commander Louis Benecke placed the blame for the lack of initiative on the state government. "Grand old Missouri ought not to be an exception" to "patriotic sentiments," he wrote in 1895. "Yet . . . not one cent is appropriated to provide a home for the aged and infirm Veterans by our State."[64] Given the failure of House Bill 137 less than ten years before, Benecke perhaps should not have been surprised. A reluctance to exacerbate wartime divisions and a stigmatized view of public welfare initiatives prevented the government from rallying behind the WRC.

In the fall of 1893, feeling desperate at the prospect of yet another winter approaching without a Federal Home, some GAR members proposed modifying an abandoned St. Louis arsenal into a temporary shelter for veterans. The women of the WRC, however, held out for a more fitting space.[65] They realized, Sarah J. Martin said, "every undertaking of this proportion requires time, thought and energy to get it started."[66] In 1895, the WRC finally received the help it needed when the citizens of Phelps County offered to purchase the thirty-four-room Dunmoor Mansion in St. James, at the price of $20,000, on behalf of the Federal Home. Situated on nearly sixty acres with rooms ready for immediate occupancy, it seemed an ideal solution, but the mansion needed extensive repairs and there were other cities vying for the location of the home.[67]

Indeed, the proposition of establishing the home in St. James garnered some criticism. Unlike the selection of Higginsville for the Confederate Home, St. James and its environs offered little significance in Union memory. In addition, it was an inconvenient location, nearly one hundred miles from St. Louis. Established in 1857 and nestled among the foothills of the Ozark Mountains, Phelps County was only sparsely populated at the outbreak of the Civil War. It was a predominately rural area, mostly made up of small farms with minimal reliance on enslaved labor. The region witnessed some unrest in the aftermath of the war, as the remnants of local guerrilla bands in the area turned to terror campaigns of looting and robbery. As a result, the Bald Knobbers—an antivigilante counterinsurgency largely made up of Union militia veterans—formed to curb the lawlessness of the guerrillas and the Ku Klux Klan (KKK).[68] By 1890, however, the violence in the Ozarks had largely subsided.

In the spring of 1895, at the annual WRC encampment in Macon, the Federal Soldiers' Home Association convened in order to finally decide on the location of the home. Because voting membership only cost one dollar, a large delegation arrived from nearby La Plata, hoping to turn the vote in favor of a one-hundred-acre piece of empty farmland in their community. Fearful that the St. James mansion would be voted down, association president Hollen E. Day preemptively forced the meeting to adjournment and the WRC accepted the deed for Dunmoor before all the proposals had even been heard. While a slightly underhanded move, as WRC president Adah Goss Briggs explained, "For years, we had thought and hoped and planned and worked for a home for aged veterans and their dependent ones. . . . Was it strange, that we should take this munificent gift? The sentiment was that we would at least have a home!"[69]

It would be a full year, however, before the WRC and the Federal Soldiers' Home Association could meet and complete the transfer of the deed. In the meantime, the WRC footed the entire financial burden of maintaining Dunmoor. "I began to be seriously worried as to our ability to even pay taxes and insurance on this Home of ours," Briggs wrote.[70] She admitted the WRC had exceeded its authority in accepting the deed, but she urged the association to cooperate: "Having accepted the gift, we owe it to the good people of St. James, who have exemplified their patriotism [l]oyalty and gratitude in so striking a manner, to fit it as soon as possible for occupancy. We owe it also to the old soldiers to whom a month's delay may mean privation and suffering. What the Woman's Relief Corps expects to do for the Union Veterans, must be done quickly, kindly and generously."[71] Finally, on July 1, 1896, the association agreed to the transfer.[72]

The Federal Home formally opened on October 25, 1896, at a lavish dedication ceremony. The WRC planned for thousands of guests and even booked a special excursion train for the convenience of attendees traveling from St. Louis. That morning, the train left St. Louis and barreled through its first stop, unaware that mistake put them on a collision course with another train coming from the opposite direction. Near Kirkwood, barely thirteen miles outside the city, the two trains crashed head-on. According to a St.

Paul, Minnesota, newspaper, "The collision was terrific, both engines being demolished and a number of cars telescoped. The wreckage was piled high on the track, and above the sound of the escaping steam could be heard the cries of the frightened and injured passengers."[73] News of the tragedy soon arrived in St. James by telegraph, as well as the grim pronouncement that the wreck had left eight passengers dead and at least twenty injured.[74] "This had a tendency to put quite a damper upon the occasion," the *St. James Journal* reported dryly, "and for a while it was a question whether the dedication should take place or not, but the crowd was so great, and had come so far to take part in the opening of the home that, after deliberation, it was decided to proceed with the ceremonies."[75] A crowd of five thousand, led by three hundred schoolgirls marching in the shape of a "human flag," formed a mile-long parade to the home. As they walked, the crowd sang favorite Union war songs like "Marching through Georgia" and "The Battle Cry of Freedom" as well as the rebel anthem "Dixie."[76] Whether this selection was intended as a gesture of reconciliationist feeling or simply an indication of the popularity of the Confederate anthem is unclear. As a matter of course, officials gave speeches, vaunting patriotism and praising the WRC, after which the new superintendent accepted the keys, raised the U.S. flag, and opened the home.[77]

Figure 8. Missouri State Federal Soldiers' Home, St. James. Courtesy of Benecke Family Papers (C3825). f7572-5. The State Historical Society of Missouri, Photograph Collection

Not all of the bitterness surrounding the location of the Federal Home had passed, however. The citizens of St. James raised nearly all the money necessary for the purchase of the Dunmoor Mansion, but their motives were certainly self-interested. The Federal Home promised to stimulate the local economy. Even still, the *Taney County Republican* observed, "The town is not very friendly to the home, and does not care much for the inmates outside of their pension checks." "It was mistakenly located here in the first place," the paper complained, "in the wrong town, in the wrong county, among a people who never had much sympathy for the old federal soldier."[78]

Despite the competing wartime allegiances that necessitated the creation of two separate veterans' homes, their operations were broadly similar. The Federal Home offered admission to any honorably discharged U.S. combat veteran as long as he had lived in the state for one year. Applicants to the Confederate Home needed to prove two years of residence in Missouri. Confederate veterans likewise had to present evidence of an honorable discharge but not necessarily from a Missouri regiment. In fact, the population of the Confederate Home included individuals from nearly every former Confederate state. Veterans at both homes also had to demonstrate an inability to support themselves due to disability "not the result of any vicious habit or illegal act," chronic disease, or insanity.[79] This important qualification on eligibility stemmed from popular prejudice against the "undeserving." Neither home would permit association with addicts, criminals, or the mentally ill to sully the reputation of veterans.

Still, the unique nature of Missouri's Civil War experience presented challenges in determining the eligibility of residents. While the rules made it clear the Confederate Home only accepted applications from veterans of the regular army, they nevertheless discretely admitted ex-guerrillas.[80] As a matter of fact, the home's first superintendent, Mark Belt, rode under guerrilla chieftain Dave Pool.[81] Some guerrillas, Belt included, claimed eligibility based on previous service in the Confederate Army. Many served under General Sterling Price during his failed 1862 campaign and remained in the state following his departure; some deserted, and others were paroled as prisoners of war before joining a guerrilla band. The exact number of guerrilla residents at the Confederate Home remains unclear, although in a 2011 report the *Kansas City Star* claimed as many as fourteen lie buried on the grounds—including the partial remains of notorious guerrilla William Clarke Quantrill, interred long after the home closed.[82]

The fractious history of the border state complicated eligibility requirements at the Federal Home as well. Assessing the loyalty of applicants could be problematic. For this reason, the Federal Home initially excluded veterans of the Enrolled Missouri Militia (EMM) on the basis that they had served as state, not federal, soldiers and were ineligible for federal pensions. Increasingly, however, the Federal Home board regarded this as unfair. After all, President Louis Benecke insisted, the EMM had "performed valuable service and were exposed to the hardships incident to the war in border states. . . . As they were Missourians serving in a Missouri Military organization it seems to me that amendment to the law should be enacted providing that such ex-members of the [EMM] . . . may be permitted to enjoy the benefits of our Missouri Home."[83] When the board did admit EMM veterans, they did not necessarily enter on equal terms. One EMM veteran complained that he and his wife received unfair treatment because they came from Higginsville, the site of the Confederate Home. The superintendent admitted that "some one may have referred to him, questioning his loyalty or calling him a rebel," but the superintendent attributed it to this man's service in the militia and not the regular army.[84] This was an expression of the old prejudice against Missouri's Union militia men, many of whom were conscripted and found their loyalty under scrutiny as a result.[85]

The number of German-born veterans in Missouri presented a further complication for the Federal Home. Anxious to prove their patriotism and generally opposed to slavery, German Americans rallied to the Union cause during the Civil War and served with distinction. Nevertheless, anti-immigrant prejudice persisted after the war. Even though German-born veterans made up roughly a quarter of the population of the home and German-born Louis Benecke even served as president of the Board of Trustees, they were not spared from nativist bigotry. One resident complained he overheard a member of staff telling the superintendent's wife "she ought to poison all the ---- dutch."[86] The Confederates shared this prejudice. In *Missouri of Today,* the Confederate Home Association admitted German Americans often suffered abuse but regretted that many continued to celebrate the fall of Camp Jackson. "Good citizens as they are, [they] lack some of the virtues transmitted by the Latin races to English-speaking people. Honestly ignorant are they of the stigma attached to this accident, as is proven by their still annually celebrating the 10th of May, while their well-wishers are trying to forget it."[87]

Despite prevalent prejudice, German Americans found refuge at the Federal Home. African Americans, on the other hand, were barred entirely. There is no evidence of the presence of African Americans at the home either as staff or residents. According to the 1875 state constitution, Missouri only officially segregated its school facilities. De facto segregation existed in most public spaces, however, including the veterans' homes.[88] The Federal Home rules never explicitly excluded black veterans, but there were certainly indications they were not welcome. In 1900, resident Jerry Keller claimed that the local KKK actually made its headquarters in the home. The extent and efficacy of its organization is unclear, though Keller reported klansmen left notes in the home threatening to lynch himself and another resident, Frederick Bokamper.[89] Although Keller and Bokamper were both white, the KKK may have targeted Bokamper because he was a German-born immigrant.[90]

Doubtless, the threat of intimidation and violence posed by the KKK kept black veterans out. Years later, in 1921, the Missouri State Board of Charities and Corrections conducted a report on the conditions of black citizens in state eleemosynary institutions. At that time, the Federal Home administration unapologetically informed the board, they had "no arrangements or quarters" for black residents.[91] This kind of policy put black veterans in an incredibly difficult position. In addition to the many problems facing aging Civil War veterans, they had to navigate a system that neither prohibited nor accommodated them. According to the state report, it was an all too common problem: "In Missouri there is no statute which restrains negroes from receiving the benefits from all its public institutions, but there is a sort of indifference which permits many embarrassing handicaps. Somehow," the author urged, "men and women, white and black, must develop conviction, courage, faith and vision to tackle the problems for the general welfare as human problems, regardless of . . . color or social standing."[92] Until that time, some black Missourians may have sought admission to branches of the National Home, but it is likely they depended on the strength of their own communities, churches, and societies for support.

There is no evidence the Confederate Home admitted black residents either, though other state Confederate homes occasionally did. Black Missourians did, however, serve on the staff.[93] Although African Americans certainly had their own reasons for taking jobs in the Confederate Home, former Confederates interpreted their service in the context of the Lost Cause. In 1932, for example, the Confederate Home superintendent woefully reported the death of Sam Benton, an African American who had worked at the home for nearly thirty years until he was struck and killed by a train. "Sam Benton was loyal to the Confederate Home and faithful to the members and never failed to assist any of them in any way possible," he wrote. "[Benton] was admired by every man and woman here."[94] Mired in the mythology of the Lost Cause, which emphasized the supposedly benevolent nature of slavery, former Confederates celebrated men like Benton as evidence of their harmonious relationships with African Americans. There can be no better example of this point than an account of a reunion on the Confederate Home grounds during which UDC member B. R. Ireland watched an African American woman help an elderly white woman into a chair. This scene "carried me back to the black mammy days," Ireland rhapsodized. Then, referring to the African American woman, Ireland proclaimed, "She is a Confederate, . . . and proves her allegiance by her works. . . . One left! . . . of the many faithful."[95] Still, the Confederate Home hardly offered a model of racial tolerance. On another occasion, the board expelled a veteran for insisting "a Negro was as good as a white man."[96]

As a testament to the critical contributions of women to their creation, both homes extended admission to the wives and widows of veterans, albeit with some stipulations. At the Federal Home, only wives over fifty and widows over sixty were allowed admission. Remarkably, from the time it opened, the Federal Home also extended applications to army nurses.[97] By contrast, the National Home did not admit nurses to its branches until 1928.[98] The inclusion of army nurses certainly represented the intervention of the WRC and their vital role in shaping the Federal Home. Thus, the admission of women was not only a means of commemorating their wartime contributions but also an indication of the importance of women to the construction and operation of the homes.

Only the Confederate Home provided for veterans and their entire families, including children under the age of fourteen.[99] This policy arose from a stigmatized view of poverty that equated financial and moral bankruptcy. Missouri's Confederates could not allow needy and delinquent children to besmirch the reputation of their veteran fathers. "We have resolved," F. P. Bronaugh wrote in the *Boonville Weekly Advertiser*, "that the future criminals shall not be recruited from the descendants of men who braved death for a point of honor."[100] Therefore, allowing dependent children to accompany their parents into the home seemed the best solution. For the privacy and comfort of these families, the UDC built several small cottages on the grounds and "encouraged [residents] to live just as if their little home belonged to them."[101] The possibility of maintaining a normal family life in spite of their disadvantages must have been tremendously appealing to Missouri's Confederate veterans.

Beyond the challenge of determining and administering their admissions criteria, both the Confederate and Federal homes suffered persistent financial problems. As the nineteenth century drew to a close, the onset of a national economic crisis and the advancing age of veterans made it more difficult for them to support themselves. Both homes exceeded their capacity, and neither could afford to run efficiently on private charity. "Depending entirely upon voluntary contributions, our need for funds increased, while the receipts decreased," Confederate veteran Harvey W. Salmon explained. "This condition grew steadily worse until it became unbearable." As a solution, the General Assembly drafted two bills proposing the transfer of the veterans' homes to the state of Missouri. Coming a decade after the failure of House Bill 137, this new initiative reflected the growing need of Missouri's veterans and the increasing popularity of reconciliationist remembrances of the war. "There is a pathetic beauty and touching appropriateness in the fact . . . that the two acts . . . were companion bills," Charles H. Vandiver remarked.[102]

After receiving approval from the House, the bills came to a vote in the Senate in February 1897. There, Hohenschild and Vandiver led the measures to success by praising the common bravery of Union and Confederate Missourians and offering the adoption of the homes as an important step toward reconciliation. Significant legal and financial challenges, however, clouded the harmonious feelings engendered by the state's adoption of the homes. Now in competition for funding, staff at both homes expressed suspicion over official partiality. Administrators at the Federal Home believed the state was appropriating more money for the Confederate Home—a fact that Missouri's Confederates did not deny. "The State of Missouri is not only doing something for the relief of Confederate soldiers," the *Confederate Veteran* observed, "but is being very liberal in its appropriations, so that the Confederates have been kindly treated by the State at large."[103] Nonetheless, in his biennial report, Federal Home superintendent Wilbur F. Henry complained, "It seems quite reasonable that appropriation for salaries for this Institution should be nearly or quite as much as for the Confederate Home at Higginsville. While the membership of that Institution is slightly greater than ours, yet with the same officers and help we now have we could care for as many as are in the Confederate Home." He begged "the Legislature . . . to treat these institutions fairly."[104] In their defense, the Confederates pointed out that while they did receive a larger state appropriation, the Federal Home benefited from additional support from the federal government amounting to one hundred dollars a year for every Union veteran in residence. That federal money did not extend to women or militia veterans residing at the home, however, so they still depended on state funding. Regardless, as the Federal Home Board later admitted, there was no real evidence of favoritism toward the Confederate Home.

While both homes sustained and cultivated competing versions of Civil War memory, they operated in a similar fashion. They both reflected the particular challenges posed by Missouri's unique location and complex history.

They also espoused a similar vision of welfare. Of course, caring for the veterans themselves served as the underlying purpose of both homes. To that end, they made provisions to meet their residents' every need. Each home grew into a large campus with multiple buildings including dormitories, hospitals, and chapels. The staff provided meals, health care, and laundry service. They organized entertainment, maintained libraries, and arranged visiting hours. In all, they strove to create a comfortable atmosphere. Superintendent F. P. Bronaugh pronounced the Confederate Home "the grandest charity in the country," while the Federal Home proudly proclaimed, "Who enters here—leaves care behind."[105]

Like most nursing homes, however, veterans' homes earned a reputation as places where once brave men went to languish away, suffering what one veteran described as "a *death-in-life* in a Soldiers' Home." In an open letter to the nation's veterans' homes, including the Missouri Federal Soldiers' Home, this man articulated the fears many veterans had of institutionalization: "A Soldiers' Home! There, my keen sympathies would be harassed, for my associates would be dear fellows who have lost their grip on life, having only one remaining purpose—to slide down a buttered plank into the grave. And what will I do with my mental activity? May I not well fear that, like many others, I will drivel into insanity? . . . Better, it now seems to me, that I had met a soldier's fate where our unnamed demi-gods yielded their lives."[106] In a climate of Civil War commemoration that venerated the war dead, survivors like this man often felt like outcasts—reduced to the ignominy of dependency alongside "undeserving" criminals, the disabled, and the mentally ill. Veterans' homes, including those in Missouri, were often a last resort for desperate individuals without better options.

Both the Confederate and Federal Homes were conscious of how the stigma of institutionalization impacted their residents and worked to help them preserve their sense of masculinity and self-worth. "I know what idleness will do," Confederate veteran and Missouri senator George Graham Vest remarked. "I have for years in Washington seen one of the most successful Federal Homes for G. A. R. men in the country, and there is not a month that the inmates do not escape from the Home as they would from a jail. . . . What they want is to be well-cared for, but they must not be kept idle." As a solution, both homes put veterans to work. On the model of most Progressive-era charitable institutions, the homes maintained a self-sufficient operation by utilizing resident labor. The grounds of both homes largely remained open farmland, where veterans raised livestock, tended orchards, and grew crops. This work not only served as a practical way to run such large institutions but also helped the residents feel useful. "There are no drones in Missouri's Confederate Home," Ex-Confederate Association president James Bannerman reflected with pride. "The rough-and-ready lessons of the war made self-reliant, industrious men, and the boys who have turned their swords into plow-shares, and their bayonets into pruning hooks have . . . shown that they can do a little foraging of the peaceful kind."[107] The GAR adopted a similar view of resident labor. "The stigma of pauper is not allowed by word or act to humiliate," Commander Ira T. Bronson observed, "but the inmates are treated rather as boarders, causing them to realize they are receiving no more than their just dues, earned by sacrifices and hardships that can never be told."[108]

Administrators professed reverence for veterans as living embodiments of Civil War memory but managed their charges with the imposition of arbitrary discipline. As residents of state institutions and beneficiaries of government aid, veterans were expected to adhere strictly to administrative mandates. Staff at both homes referred to their residents as "inmates" and required the veterans to wear uniforms, gray in Higginsville and blue in St. James.[109] They also held residents to a strict code of rules, prohibiting everything from profanity and fighting to skipping church and leaving without permission. Anyone who failed to cooperate with these rules risked expulsion, though that threat did not always serve to prevent problems. Louis Benecke, president of the Federal Home Board, acknowledged that "among a lot of men there are always some who are not satisfied with their surroundings and the old Veterans at the Home are no exception to this rule."[110] In his monthly report, one Confederate Home superintendent admitted the residents constantly argued with one another. "You cannot force them to respect each other," he wrote, "and it is out of the question to attempt to try it."[111] In some cases, misbehavior was quite trivial. For example, the Federal Home Board expelled one resident for refusing to participate in prayer before meals.[112] Other disputes were typical of the problems arising between individuals living in close quarters, as when one Confederate veteran struck his roommate over the head with a cane for leaving a light on too late at night. A more serious incident occurred at the Confederate Home when two residents disagreed over the election of officers at the state reunion of Confederate veterans and one attacked the other with a knife. Upon recovery, both men faced expulsion.[113]

Both homes also experienced persistent problems with alcoholism, despite the fact that the rules expressly prohibited alcohol except for medicinal purposes. This was certainly a reflection of the values of Progressive-era reformers, who supported state welfare initiatives while advocating for temperance and prohibition. To legitimize the needy as "deserving" of government aid, reformers had to establish that the recipients' difficulties were not of their own making. Preventing alcohol consumption at the veterans' homes, however, proved to be a challenge. There is some evidence that veterans at the Federal Home ran an illicit moonshine ring, distributing alcohol to the surrounding community, though the administration quickly denied such rumors.[114] "We cannot afford to have the report to go out that our Home is the resort of drunken men," Benecke wrote.[115] In spite of the staff's best efforts, the biennial reports of both homes reveal the constant battle administrators waged against alcohol and, occasionally, against opium as well.[116] Substance abuse among the veterans may have been a response to the dull routine of institutional life, chronic pain, depression, or even war-related trauma.[117] Unprepared to treat mental health conditions, both of Missouri's veterans' homes immediately expelled or transferred mentally ill residents to one of the state's asylums.

In truth, life at the veterans' homes could be quite bleak. Despite the administrators' attempts to provide comfort, structure, and purpose, death loomed before the veterans at all times. "These old men *come to stay*," one Confederate Home staff member observed frankly. "They have nothing but the graveyard before them."[118] This reality did not escape the veterans either—death was a part of their routine. Surgeons at both homes dutifully recorded the deaths of every one of their residents, usually citing natural causes including old age, heart disease, and cancer. More suggestive entries appeared as well. For example, over the course of several years, Confederate Home surgeons listed two separate men as "killed by train," while two more "fell from porch," another "died from a fall," and still another death was reported simply as "suicide."[119] The frequency of suicides in the Missouri veterans' homes can only be speculated at but, given the lack of mental health care for these men, it certainly occurred.

Among the indignities suffered by Missouri veterans who entered the homes, the blow to their masculinity was particularly severe. Institutionalization not only carried an overt impingement to their gender identity; it also threatened their status as citizens. Once adopted by the state, the two homes fell under the control of the eleemosynary board—which governed the state asylums, schools for the deaf and blind, and reform schools—effectively making the veterans wards of the state. As such, a question emerged over whether the veterans could legally retain their right to vote. According to the 1875 Missouri constitution, "No person, while kept at . . . public expense, . . . shall be entitled to vote at any election under the laws of this state."[120] Upon the acquisition of the two homes, the Missouri General Assembly immediately passed a revised "qualification of voters" bill to protect the franchise of the residents of the veterans' homes, but the legislature did not amend the constitution itself.[121]

This oversight prompted a controversy in Phelps County in 1904 during a race for the office of county collector. Republican candidate William Stimson initially won, but the Democratic candidate, A. B. Hale, contested his victory. In short order, the election became a concatenation of the peculiar problems associated with the legacy of Missouri's Civil War. In this case, wartime hostilities, partisan politics, and gendered attitudes about welfare all intruded on the matter. For example, William Nelson Evans, the local circuit judge, decided the election. He was not exactly a neutral party. Besides being the state Democratic Party chairman, Evans was a Confederate veteran and member of the Jo Shelby Camp United Confederate Veterans (UCV). Evans may have also cherished more than usual resentment against Union veterans. His father had served in the Confederate Army and died at Illinois's Rock Island prison camp. Evans certainly remained unreconstructed in regard to race. Returning to school shortly after the Civil War and finding a black woman in charge, he promptly walked out of class.[122]

In the contested election, Evans discounted all the votes cast by the veterans in the Federal Home because, according to the state constitution, they were kept at "public expense" and were therefore "government paupers and not entitled to vote."[123] "It was not the intension of the framers of the constitution to humiliate the inmates of eleemosynary institutions," Evans explained by way of justification, "but for the purpose of protecting the public against an inclination that would naturally grow up in these institutions to control local affairs."[124] Evans then ordered a recount, and the Democratic candidate emerged victorious.

Missourians followed the unfolding case with interest. One paper said it "is receiving more consideration at this time than any other public matter in the state."[125] Evans's decision immediately drew suspicion over party favoritism and reawakened simmering Civil War hostilities in the border state. "We understand the confederates at Higginsville voted," one paper noted bitterly.[126] In reality, the decision affected both homes, and the veterans worked together to seek its reversal. Colonel Henry Fairback, commander of the Department of Missouri GAR, insisted the matter concerned "every . . . old soldier in the state" and their "comrades who may now be, or who may hereafter become members of either of the homes. Therefore, the question is not a partisan one to be made a football of between contending political parties."[127] More than thirty years after the repeal of the Iron Clad Oath, the prospect of denying American veterans their right to vote—even former Confederates—found little support. As Fairback observed, "There is a pent-up feeling of wrath and indignation which prevails over the State."[128] He asked the posts of the Department of Missouri to raise money to defend the veterans, saying, "While we are not interested one way or another in the contested election case in which this ruling was made, we are vitally interested in securing all the rights of American citizens to our old comrades in arms. They are citizens of this State, entitled to their rights as such, which they have not forfeited because compelled by their infirmities in their old age to seek the refuge of a Soldier's Home. They should not be classed with either paupers or felons."[129]

As Hale and Stimson formed legal teams and prepared to present the case to the state Supreme Court, Missourians took sides. Stimson's opponents seem to have been motivated by a strange mixture of political partisanship and racial animosity. Former Missouri Supreme Court justice Thomas Adiel Sherwood, defending Evans's decision, reportedly said, "The inmates of the federal soldiers' home at St. James have no rights which a white man is bound to respect."[130] This was almost a direct quote of Roger Taney's opinion in the landmark U.S. Supreme Court case *Scott v. Sandford* (1857), in which Taney ruled that enslaved African Americans had no claims to citizenship and therefore could not bring cases before the court. It was a curious remark, not least because there were no black veterans in the Federal Home. It must, therefore, be interpreted in light of the pervasive, stigmatized view of veterans' care in the era. Sherwood felt that, as recipients of government aid, the veterans sacrificed their entitlement as citizens.

The Supreme Court of Missouri finally heard the case in 1906.[131] In his opinion, Judge Henry Lamm—although not a veteran himself—recognized the sensitivity of the matter. He acknowledged that in this case, "memories obtrude themselves of no light significance." Lamm elaborated on the complicated legacy bequeathed to Missouri by the Civil War and on the circumstances that made the construction of two separate homes necessary in the first place. He went on to insist the state of Missouri had taken on the veterans' homes out of "patriotic duty" and "sentimental beauty" and owed the residents an obligation. Lamm argued the veterans had earned "the privilege of a home in the evening of their days" and reminded the court that their "right to vote was bought and paid for with a great price." He consciously refused to weigh the fact that half of those veterans once willingly renounced their citizenship. "Nor do we care to split hairs over the question of which cause the inmates of these homes fought for," he continued. Then, espousing the reconciliationist rhetoric so characteristic of turn-of-the-century Missouri, Lamm observed, "Our Missourian . . . went under two flags—both ways—went at once. . . . When he came home from the war his mighty mother, the state of Missouri, with a great heart, claimed him as her son, proud of his deeds, resolute to cherish his memory, magnanimous to forget his quarrel, tender of both uniforms, and mourning over the dead of war-worn and desolate confederate and federal."[132] In the end, Lamm overturned Evans's decision and restored the veterans' right to vote. The other judges on the court, including Confederate veterans James Gantt and Leroy Valliant, unanimously supported Lamm's ruling.

While the veterans' right to vote was restored, state oversight also presented problems for the female residents of the Federal Home. When the homes transitioned from private, female-driven charitable enterprises to extensions of the male sphere of the state, women's power diminished. Now under the control of the state eleemosynary board, each home still maintained separate governing boards, usually composed of veteran officeholders, who supervised the management of both facilities. Despite its longstanding dedication to the Federal Home, the WRC found itself excluded under the new administration. On March 9, 1903, the General Assembly and the governor voted to remove the WRC from the Federal Home Board of Trustees.[133] In light of all its work on behalf of the home, the WRC not only felt tremendously insulted by this action but also deeply concerned about the consequences for women at the Federal Home. "The purpose for which it was created has been defeated," President Hollen E. Day lamented. "We are denied any voice in the management of an institution which was created by us by long years of earnest endeavour." When WRC president Francis H. D. VanSlyke wrote Governor Alexander Dockery in 1904 asking him to reconsider, "he replied that there were no vacancies on the Board of Managers of the Federal Soldiers' Home at St. James, and would not be during his administration; therefore, we should present our views to his successor."[134]

The tension between the WRC and the state government only escalated as a flood of new admissions taxed the Federal Soldiers' Home to its limits. Indeed, the home often had more residents than beds. The staff understood this problem would only get worse with the passage of time. "When we take into consideration the number of old veterans, their wives, widows in the State . . . and that each year is adding to their infirmities," they pointed out, "the time is near by when they can no longer keep the wolf from the door but will be forced to accept help from some other source."[135] "If all our members were present at one time," home administrators later confessed, "we would not have room enough to accommodate them."[136]

As far as the board was concerned, the significant population of female residents at the Federal Home exacerbated this problem. The home was already crowded and the nearly equal proportion of male and female residents hurt the bottom line.[137] Veteran residents brought a government subsidy into the home with them; women did not. As a consequence, the WRC suspected the administration delayed and rejected female applicants as an attempt to lessen the strain on the Federal Home. In one case, the WRC independently cared for a widow for an entire year before the board finally admitted her. "The main object of establishing this home was to have a refuge for the Union veteran, his wife and widow," Hollen E. Day complained, "and now we can hardly get a woman into the home; they don't want the widows because the national government pays $100 per year for the support of each veteran in the home."[138] The WRC became convinced this extra financial incentive only served to privilege the applications of men over women. Its ultimate fear was realized in 1910, when the Federal Home Board refused to accept any more applications from widows. In fact, the administration claimed, the home never technically had the authority to do so. While the board promised "those widows now in the home will not be turned out," it insisted "no more will be accepted."[139]

The board further defended its refusal to admit widows by insisting they abused the benefits of the home. Administrators claimed women often married elderly veterans just to qualify for admission. In one case, after obtaining permission for a short visit to St. Louis, an eighty-year-old resident married a woman twenty years his junior. Shortly thereafter, he passed away and "his 'widow' applied promptly for membership in the Home." Wary of the "machinations" of such "a designing woman," the board revised the rules, now requiring a couple to be married six years before they could apply for admission together. "No one is likely to question the right of any sound man to become a husband, if he finds that to be in his interest," Board President S. D. Webster conceded. But, he continued, "Very few will have the hardihood to maintain that a man . . . has either a moral or a legal right, by entering the bonds of matrimony, . . . to confer upon her an eligibility to membership in such an institution."[140]

Against this backdrop of legal, financial, and administrative difficulties, the Confederate and Federal Homes continued to function as sites of Civil War memory. Over time, however, Missouri's Civil War generation felt their control slipping away. At the Federal Home, the state not only curtailed the influence of the WRC but also expanded admission to include Spanish-American War veterans. Despite the thinning ranks of Civil War survivors, the WRC and the UDC worked even more feverishly to preserve the legacy of the Civil War at the veterans' homes. By hosting reunions on the grounds, maintaining cemeteries, and erecting monuments, they anchored the veterans' homes to Missouri's multifaceted Civil War memories.

The WRC in particular refused to abandon its charges at the Federal Home, despite its exclusion from the board. "I wish to remind the Woman's Relief Corps," President Carrie R. Sparklin wrote, "that this Home is of their creation, and while it has been turned over to the state . . . our responsibility by no means is ended." "It is true," member Orpha Bronson acknowledged, "that the wants of the living should be looked after. . . . Yet, we should not stop there, but should by every means in our power perpetuate their patriotic sacrifices. We not only live in the present, but should so live and so work that our deeds may live on."[141] To that end, the WRC organized special events on the grounds, including celebrations of Lincoln's birthday, Memorial Day, and the Fourth of July, and infused them with the mythology of the Union Cause.[142] On these occasions, veterans commemorated the preservation of the Union and reified the Union soldier as the guardian of America's founding principles. During one Fourth of July festival, for instance, veterans heard speeches "on what the G.A.R. had accomplished for the veterans their wifes [sic] and army nurses" and reflected on "the old war time both Continental and rebellion."[143] In a testament to the Union Cause, the veterans linked the war that birthed the Union to the war that saved it.

The WRC also devoted its attention to the Federal Home cemetery, which remained the organization's property even after the state transfer. Badly neglected, by the turn of the century it apparently more closely resembled a cornfield than hallowed ground. The WRC relished this kind of project. "Now, my sisters," the WRC president proclaimed, "here is work for the Woman's Relief Corps to do . . . to make the place where the men [rest] . . . beautiful with flowers and walks where . . . people will love to go, and the Union soldier and what he did will be brought to mind." To that end, the WRC manicured the cemetery lawn, paved paths through it, and erected a new fence around the perimeter.[144] The women also built a memorial fountain on the grounds.[145] Such efforts ensured the Federal Home remained a testament not just to Missouri's Union Cause but to the WRC. "The Soldiers' Home at St. James will ever be to your memory," WRC president Lucinda A. Scott proudly told her members, "a monument that you conceived, reared and constructed to the noblest type of manhood, the maimed and decrepit Union veteran."[146]

The UDC also maintained its commitment to caring for Missouri's Confederate veterans following the state transfer. The UDC continued to send the veterans reading material, snacks, tobacco, clothing, and linens, which the men received with gratitude. "These donations are expressive of the spirit of fraternity which exists toward the inmates of the Home, and often cheer a sad heart," one staff member wrote.[147] Every year, the UDC prepared special holiday dinners for the veterans, brought them Christmas presents, and decorated their Christmas tree. The highlight of the year was the Confederate reunion held on the grounds every fall. At one such reunion in 1895, the *Kansas City Daily Journal* estimated as many as eight thousand people attended—including prominent local Confederates, who delivered "enthusiastic addresses on memories of the past." On this occasion, the Lost Cause was wrapped in a mantle of American nationalism. "The stars and stripes floated from nearly every business house in the city," the *Journal* reported.[148] As with their decision to fly the U.S. flag over the home, former Confederates intended such displays to disavow the idea that their rebellion amounted to treason and to signal their commitment to the reunited nation.

Like the WRC, the UDC turned its attention toward caring for the dead. They raised $5,000 for the beautification of the Confederate Home cemetery and for the construction of a monument in honor of the veterans buried there.[149] The UDC hired Kansas City sculptor M. H. Rice to design the monument, who drew his inspiration from the famous Swiss monument the Lion of Lucerne. According to the *Confederate Veteran*, "Mr. Rice rightly conceived that if a lion wounded unto death well represented the brave Swiss who fell defending a foreign place, better would it represent the deathless courage of the Confederates." As many as five thousand people attended the dedication of the monument on June 2, 1906. One resident said of it simply, "We ought to be proud of it. It is good enough for anybody."[150] It was an offhand comment, but it spoke to the determination of Missouri's Confederates to be taken seriously by their southern comrades. By virtue of the successful operation of the Confederate Home, the service it provided for veterans, and the symbolic weight added by the monument and by reunions held on the grounds, no one could claim Missourians had turned their backs on the Lost Cause.

As time wore on, however, the Confederates struggled to retain a presence on their Board of Managers. During the 1920s, the Republican Party returned to power in the state, stirring old fears about the alignment of wartime hostilities and partisan politics in Missouri. The Confederates, in particular, became especially wary of government oversight. In that period, some believed "disinterested representatives" in the Republican administration "stinted" and "neglected" the Confederate Home.[151] Disgruntled employees at the home also accused the state government of appointing board members who were less than "honest to God ex-Confederates."[152] In 1921, their fears became realized when Governor Arthur Mastick Hyde proposed consolidating both veterans' homes under the direction of a single board. Hyde's advisors cautioned him about the sensitivity of this issue: "We cannot afford to make a mistake about this Home," one wrote. "It is a delicate question for Republicans to handle and we should proceed carefully with changes."[153] "I realize," Hyde conceded, "that there are certain sentimental attachments applying to the Confederate and Federal Homes, which do not apply to other Institutions in the state," but he hoped Missourians would "realize that the class of those qualified under the present statues to be Trustees of these Homes is rapidly narrowing and . . . there will be few, who can . . . act on these boards."[154] Missouri's surviving Confederates, however, refused to hand over their last vestige of control over the Confederate Home. They continued to insist that only Confederate veterans, preferably members of the Confederate Home Association, could serve on the board. "The Board of Managers of these two institutions should be made up of men who had served with them as soldiers," secretary Maecenas E. Benton insisted, "on the theory that they would better understand than men who had not been soldiers in either army."[155] The implication that they would accept veteran board members from "either army" was an interesting testament to the bonds of militaristic masculinity. Evidently, the Confederates trusted Union veterans to represent their interests better than civilian bureaucrats.

Despite their suspicions about the Republican administration, the Confederates found the state government fully receptive to a plan they devised to create a new Confederate memorial park. As the Confederate Home aged and enrollment declined, the institution threatened to fall into disuse and neglect. As a result, the UDC proposed turning a portion of the grounds into a memorial park. In 1925, the General Assembly unanimously approved the plan, dedicating ninety-two acres of home land for that purpose. It was a unique idea, especially fitting because it would commemorate both Confederate soldiers and preserve the memory of the Confederate Home, now quickly outlasting its usefulness. The UDC believed "a more beautiful location, with rolling knobs, shining lakes, winding drives, trees, shrubs, and flowers could never have been selected for a park."[156] Not content with the natural beauty of the grounds, the UDC added thousands of shrubs and native trees and dug at least six new lakes, which they stocked with fish. They imagined it as a place Missourians would come for generations, both to enjoy the outdoors and pay tribute to the Lost Cause—a kind of "historical playground."[157] "The park will be a constant drawing card to those lovers of nature in the great out door life," the *Higginsville Advance* explained, "who by their very coming to the park itself, throughout the ages to come, will be reminded of the valor which was unquestionably exhibited during the years of 1861 to 1865."[158] "We feel that as time goes on and this beautiful landscaped park, with its circling drives and shaded lanes, comes to its full maturity," they continued, "it will express increasingly our love for these veterans and our reverence for the memory of those who have gone."[159] The more time passed, the more imperative that mission became. In 1931, during the dedication of a stone gateway to the park, one visitor remembered, "as the crimson Missouri sun sank into the purple hills, and the first cool shades of night began to stretch along the ground, the Missourians sang 'Dixie' with all the fervor of their souls."[160] In effect, it was the requiem of the Confederate Home.

Indeed, by the mid-1920s, the heyday of Missouri's veterans' homes was nearing its end. "In a few years," the *Columbia Missourian* lamented, "homes for Civil War veterans will be uninhabited. . . . Soon the stories of famous battles of the sixties' will be but memories and will be superseded by wild tales of the Argonne and the Marne."[161] That prediction was surprisingly accurate. In 1923, with admissions dwindling, the Federal Home Board relented and began readmitting widows. By 1929, Civil War veterans fell into the minority of residents at the home and finally, in 1944, the last Union veteran passed away. Meanwhile, more and more ex-Confederates died every year, and few remained to take their place. In the fall of 1940, with only four surviving male residents, the Confederate Home converted some of its space for use as a hospital for disabled children.[162] Continual budget and staff cuts, however, led to deteriorating conditions. Veterans complained that falling plaster in the dormitories struck them in their beds, and eventually the board voted to shutter the main building and administration building entirely.[163]

In 1945, the General Assembly passed a bill to transfer the Confederate Home property to the federal government for the purpose of creating a U.S. veterans' facility.[164] The bill met with support from some of Missouri's veterans, including President Harry Truman. One newspaper report claimed the Veterans Administration had already inspected the property and would recommend its acceptance.[165] Some felt this was a fitting end for a home that owed so much to the generosity of Union veterans and that it would serve as a final testament to the reconciliation of the wartime generation. One man wrote Democratic governor Phil M. Donnelly: "I firmly believe governor if Grove Young the public spirited citizen who gave this land for this home were living he would want the war veterans to have it, and after all we are descendants of union and confederate soldiers."[166] Ultimately, Donnelly vetoed the legislation, saying it would be a breach of the state's promise to maintain the Confederate Memorial Park.[167] Donnelly believed the Confederate Home property should remain available in case it was needed to accommodate overflow from the state hospitals. On behalf of the national UCV, Missourian W. Scott Hancock thanked Donnelly for his opposition to the plan. "In so doing," Hancock wrote, "not only do you maintain the contractual obligation of the State of Missouri but also preserve a landmark significant of high human value."[168] Here again, the limitations of reconciliation were evident. Eighty years after the conclusion of the Civil War, Missouri's Confederates were yet unwilling to entirely relinquish their own distinct commemorative tradition.

That same year, the Confederate Home board disbanded and turned its management over to the Board of Managers of the State Eleemosynary Institutions.[169] The state of Missouri then made plans to convert a portion of the property into a permanent state park. They chose to preserve "one suitable building closely associated with the care of the Confederate veterans and their survivors as a memorial building, in addition to the Memorial Park, . . . and to select and purchase a suitable commemorative stone to be erected upon the grounds of the Memorial Park, which . . . shall stand as a perpetual memorial to the valor of those who served the Confederacy in the war between the States."[170] Only a few years later, in 1950, the last Confederate veteran in the home passed away, and the state transferred the surviving widows to nearby nursing homes.[171]

Although born of competing impulses inherent to the conflicted border state, Missouri's homes for Confederate and Union veterans shared many similarities. Both owed their existence to the monumental efforts of Missouri women in not only creating but sustaining them. Both also provide insight into the gendered considerations that undergirded Civil War commemoration, particularly with regard to veterans' welfare. At their most basic level, both homes served as nursing homes governed through sentimental devotion and strict discipline—illustrating the tension between commemorative and administrative imperatives. The residents of both homes struggled with old age, alcoholism, and the physical and mental scars of war.[172] More than merely refuges for needy individuals, however, Missouri's veterans' homes were also both important sites of Civil War memory. The two homes symbolized the wartime fractures that continued to divide the border state. They illustrated the willingness of white Missourians to pursue reconciliation as a practical solution to the challenge of funding and operating these competing enterprises. At the same time, they embodied the determination of white Union and Confederate veterans to maintain their separate memorial traditions even into the mid-twentieth century. As a result, they remain important reminders of Missourian's attempts to derive meaning from their devisive and brutal Civil War.

Epilogue

We ought not to live in the past, and we cannot live on memories, but there is a right use of the past. There are ways in which it may be made to yield blessing, help, and good in the life of the present.

—Judge James B. Gantt (CSA), Kansas City, May 30, 1902

FOR MISSOURIANS, CIVIL WAR COMMEMORATION was a fraught undertaking complicated by their state's unique geographic location and complex history. In the Civil War era, Missouri emerged as the "Gateway to the West" and the heartland of the growing republic. The state embodied centrality not only in terms of geography but also in terms of politics. White Missourians embraced a political tradition of compromise that sought to bridge sectional interests. As westward expansion precipitated violent and divisive controversies over slavery, white Missourians struggled to reconcile their commitment to slaveholding with their dedication to the Union. At the outbreak of the Civil War, many white Missourians desired neutrality but soon found themselves on opposing sides of the conflict. During the war, Missourians' professions of neutrality disintegrated into factionalism. Divided as they were over the issues of slavery and emancipation, Missourians nevertheless repudiated secession and remained loyal to the Union. Missouri's seemingly contradictory record of proslavery, pro-Union politics, however, proved a poor foundation for Civil War commemoration.

As they constructed Civil War memories, Missourians encountered similar frustrations and embraced similar strategies. White Unionists worked to commemorate the Union Cause in Missouri in the face of resistance from their Confederate neighbors and in spite of dismissal by their eastern comrades. Missouri's Unionists sought to redeem their state's tarnished loyalty and divest it of Confederate remembrances. Often marginalized within white commemoration of the Union Cause, African Americans mobilized Civil War memory on behalf of mutual aid and racial uplift. In defiance of discrimination and segregation, they established the first schools for African

Americans in Missouri and made the history of slavery, emancipation, and black military service a well-spring of race pride. In their efforts to lay claim to the Lost Cause, Confederate Missourians refused to be outshone by their more numerous and better organized Union rivals. They appealed to Missouri's cultural ties to the South and to their state's wartime martyrdom under Union occupation in order to demonstrate their devotion to the Confederacy. Ultimately, however, Missouri remained on the periphery of the Lost Cause.

Despite their inevitable and persistent confrontations, white Missourians discovered that they had a distinct perspective on the Civil War and a proclivity for compromise. They found some solace in their shared identity as Missourians, as well as in the racialized, gendered, and nationalistic impulses that popularized reconciliation. As a result, some white veterans encouraged reconciliation out of necessity, for the sake of economic and political patronage, for the prestige of their state, or to secure government aid for veterans. Their most remarkable overture toward reconciliation came through the simultaneous adoption of Missouri's Confederate and Federal Soldiers' Homes by the state. While the homes each nurtured discrete remembrances of the Civil War, at critical moments their residents and representatives acted as allies to secure the rights and wellbeing of Missouri's veterans. On the whole, both homes served as testaments to Missouri's complicated relationship to the legacy of the Civil War.

After the passing of the Civil War generation, Missourians remained active in the commemoration of the conflict. Descendant societies, including the Sons of Union Veterans, Woman's Relief Corps (WRC), Ladies of the Grand Army of the Republic (LGAR), Sons of Confederate Veterans (SCV), and the United Daughters of the Confederacy (UDC) carried on the work begun by the Grand Army of the Republic (GAR) and the United Confederate Veterans (UCV). While commemorations in Missouri continued to emphasize the state's distinctive regional perspective on the Civil War, they also evidenced the survival of persistent hostilities.

The Lincoln Institute, renamed Lincoln University in 1921, still thrived as a center of education and racial uplift. As the veterans who founded it had hoped, it served as a training school for teachers and expanded educational opportunities for black Missourians.[1] Among its most famous alumni is Lloyd L. Gaines. After receiving a bachelor's degree from Lincoln, Gaines sued for admission into the all-white University of Missouri law school. In the 1938 U.S. Supreme Court case *Gaines v. Canada*, the court ruled that unless the state could provide a law school for black students in keeping with its "separate but equal" precedent in *Plessy v. Ferguson*, the University of Missouri must admit Gaines. Gaines won the suit but mysteriously vanished before he could enroll. Although *Gaines v. Canada* did not end racial segregation, the case still helped draw attention to the fundamental fiction of the "separate but equal" doctrine. It also bridged the efforts of black Civil War veterans to perpetuate the Emancipation Cause with the modern civil rights movement. Today, the legacy of the African American veterans who established Lincoln University is commemorated by a memorial on campus. It is an unconventional monument, composed of life-size bronze statues of black Civil War soldiers approaching and assisting one another onto a stone plinth. It is a compelling tribute to the accomplishments of black Missourians but also a reminder that the work they began on behalf of racial equality remains incomplete.

The Civil War centennial provided Missourians with yet another opportunity to assess the legacy of the Civil War. In 1958, Governor John T. Blair, Jr., authorized the creation of the Civil War Centennial Commission of Missouri. He viewed the centennial as an occasion for remembering the state's history and, as Blair put it, fostering "a new understanding of the importance of the preservation of the American Union as an instrumentality of freedom."[2] Blair, who was sympathetic to the civil rights movement, clearly believed the memory of emancipation should figure into centennial commemorations. Ultimately, however, Missourians invested very little in such projects. The state only appropriated $10,000 for the first two years of the centennial, a miniscule amount compared to other states. Neighboring Arkansas, for example, budgeted twice that amount, while Virginia allocated $1,387,000.[3]

Missouri's Civil War Centennial commissioner, James R. Fuchs, doubted his ability to accomplish much. He complained that the centennial generated little interest and admitted his work was likely "doomed to failure."[4] As he began coordinating centennial observances, Fuchs encountered the same problems that so frustrated the Civil War generation: apathy, hostility, and lack of funds. This was readily evident in Fuch's November 1960, schedule of "Commemorative Events for the First Civil War Centennial Year in the State of Missouri":

> 1) May 10, 1961—Capture of Camp Jackson, St. Louis—ceremony dedicating marker (now because of a controversy involving site this event may not be held[)]. . . .
>
> 2) May 18, 1961—Battle of Lexington re-enactment. . . .

> 3) July 5, 1961—dedication of memorial to Union Gen. [Franz] Sigel and Confederate governor Claiborne F. Jackson—this event, which requires the raising of some $23,000 may not reach fruition? . . .
>
> 4) Aug. 10, 1961—Ceremony dedicating Wilson's Creek Battlefield National Park—if money for land not forthcoming, park may not actually be a reality by then. . . .
>
> 5) Oct. 21, 1961—Meeting of rump session of Mo. Legislature—passing of Act of Secession on Oct. 28— . . . appropriate ceremony no doubt will be held—plans haven't jelled yet.[5]

It was only November; Fuchs still had months to coordinate these events, but he evidently anticipated complications. The controversy Fuchs mentioned at the Camp Jackson site, for instance, involved the relocation of a monument to Union general Nathaniel Lyon at the behest of Harriet Frost Fordyce. Fordyce was the daughter of Confederate general Daniel M. Frost, who Lyon arrested at Camp Jackson, and the passage of nearly a century had not cooled her resentment. In exchange for a substantial donation to St. Louis University, Fordyce had the Lyon monument moved.[6] Aware of the potential for centennial events to reawaken old bitterness, Fuchs made an effort to appease Missourians by commemorating individuals and events significant to both sides. Perhaps because of the difficulty of such a proposition, the commission ultimately focused primarily on collecting and preserving archival material. It was certainly a less controversial approach. "This," Fuchs believed, "will result in a very lasting effect of the commemorative effort that we expect to put forth."[7]

Despite Fuchs's skepticism, the Civil War Centennial Commission of Missouri achieved some impressive results. For example, it helped establish a museum at the Lone Jack battlefield near Kansas City. It also held observances of several notable events, including the Battles of Lexington and Carthage. Its greatest success, however, was securing Wilson's Creek as a national battlefield park. This was the fulfillment of an ambition long cherished by Missourians and lent a stamp of legitimacy both to Missouri's Civil War and to the western theater as a whole.

To ensure the park became a reality, the Missouri General Assembly and the citizens of Springfield raised funds and secured nearly forty acres of battlefield land, which they gifted to the federal government.[8] President Dwight D. Eisenhower signed the legislation creating the park on April 26, 1960, ending, as one of the park's leading advocates observed, "75 years of almost continuous effort to gain proper recognition by Congress of one of the significant battles of the War."[9] It was the kind of recognition veterans of the western theater in general and Missourians in particular had sought for so long. Roughly fifty to sixty thousand people attended a parade commemorating the anniversary of the battle in nearby Springfield the morning of its dedication on August 11, 1961, while three thousand attended ceremonies at the park itself.[10]

It is interesting to note, however, that the most famous monument dedicated in Missouri during the centennial period was not related to the Civil War at all. It was, of course, the St. Louis Gateway Arch. As the focal point of the Jefferson National Expansion Memorial, which encompasses the site of the historic French settlement at St. Louis, the arch commemorates the Louisiana Purchase and St. Louis's role as the "Gateway to the West." While the creation of the memorial was not a centennial project, having been conceived in the early 1930s as a plan for the revitalization of the St. Louis riverfront, the arch itself was constructed between 1963 and 1965. At one of the most important anniversaries in American history, Missourians remembered not only their participation in the Civil War but also their key place in the narrative of westward expansion.

Still, Missourians had not entirely put the Civil War behind them. In the late twentieth century, the Springfield National Cemetery once again made news. Over the decades, burials in the cemetery expanded into the vacant land previously owned by the Confederate Cemetery Association. By 1980, however, it was once again running out of room. The Veterans Administration asked the Missouri Division UDC to release the 485 empty burial plots located within the walls of the Confederate cemetery to the federal government. The UDC unanimously agreed to the proposal, but with two conditions intended to preserve the historic character of the cemetery. First, the group asked that the stone wall surrounding the Confederate section remain intact. Second, it insisted that any new grave markers should be installed flush with the ground.[11] The Veterans Administration agreed, adding that they were "deeply conscious of the necessity to preserve this enclave in a manner which is consistent with the spirit in which it was established."[12] Although the UDC promised its cooperation, some individual members took issue with the plan. Mary M. Haydon, for example, said the date the UDC relinquished the plots would "be a day of infamy and shame." She insisted she "had no part in 'selling out' my Confederate ancestors last resting place."[13] Despite Haydon's objections, Congress passed legislation authorizing new burials in the Confederate cemetery in February 1984, and President Ronald Reagan signed it into law.[14]

Like the Springfield National Cemetery, Missouri's Civil War veterans' homes continued to operate in one form or another. On November 10, 1996, the Federal Soldiers' Home, now the Missouri Veterans' Home, celebrated its centennial, though local newspapers largely ignored the occasion and its connection to the Civil War went entirely unmentioned. As the Federal Home admitted veterans from other wars, its significance as a site of Civil War memory faded. In the end, however, perhaps there was no better means of commemorating the Union Cause than by continuing to provide care for American soldiers involved in the ongoing defense of the nation.

Missouri's Confederate Home, on the other hand, "remained forever Confederate"—inextricably linked to the Civil War.[15] In fact, the Confederate Home still represents an uncomfortable reminder for some Missourians of their state's contributions to the Confederacy. Now known as Confederate Memorial State Historic Site, the home often attracts debates over the appropriate use of Confederate symbols in Missouri. In 2003, the park garnered national attention in an episode that forced the removal of a Confederate flag flying on the grounds. At that time, Representative Richard A. Gephardt, a Democratic hopeful in the 2004 presidential race, weighed in on the longstanding controversy surrounding the display of a Confederate flag on the South Carolina statehouse grounds.[16] "My own personal feeling," Gephardt said, "is that the Confederate flag no longer has a place flying any time, anywhere in our great nation."[17] Gephardt was unaware that the Confederate flag flew at two historic sites in his home state, at the Confederate Home and at Fort Davidson Historic Site in Pilot Knob. After the press brought this fact to public attention, the director of the Missouri Department of Natural Resources and Governor Bob Holden asked the historic sites to remove the flags.[18] The Missouri Division SCV protested this decision in a demonstration before the governor's mansion in Jefferson City. They also placed small Confederate flags on each individual grave in the Confederate Home cemetery. Governor Matt Blunt yielded some ground in 2005, allowing the Confederate flag to be flown on Confederate Memorial Day, but as recently as 2014, the SCV petitioned lawmakers to let the flag return permanently.[19]

In all, the flag debacle speaks to the prevailing confusion Missourians still felt about their relationship to the Civil War and to the southern Confederacy. Some Missourians, like Gephardt, were surprised to learn the Confederate flag flew anywhere in the state. Others, as many as 45 percent according to one poll, believed Governor Holden made the wrong decision in removing the flags.[20] Clearly, Missouri's vexed and conflicted place within the history and memory of the Civil War continued to confound not only outsiders but Missourians themselves.

The sesquicentennial of the Civil War initiated a thorough reevaluation of the meaning of the conflict for Missourians. It not only encompassed traditional acts of commemoration, particularly the observance of important anniversaries, but also encouraged careful reflection about how popular interpretations of the Civil War have been constructed and manipulated over time. In particular, the sesquicentennial provided African Americans the opportunity to draw increased attention to the persistent marginalization of their perspectives on the Civil War. Additionally, the advent of the Black Lives Matter movement accentuated how the Lost Cause narrative of the Civil War perpetuated damaging racial stereotypes and propped up institutionalized racism.

In 2014, Missouri became the epicenter of a serious national controversy that again revealed the complicated internal dynamics of the state. When police officer Darren Wilson shot and killed Michael Brown, an unarmed African American teenager in the St. Louis suburb of Ferguson, black Missourians demanded accountability. The National Association for the Advancement of Colored People organized a protest march, called the Journey for Justice, from St. Louis to Jefferson City. There, the group planned to press state leadership for measures against institutionalized racism and police brutality, and for recognition that "Black Lives Matter." Along their march, in the tiny mid-Missouri township of Rosebud, the protesters met with a jeering, all-white crowd who taunted them with racially charged objects including fried chicken, a watermelon, and a Confederate flag.[21]

The death of Michael Brown, compounded by months of civil unrest, attracted the attention of the national news media to Missouri. One article, complete with a blood-spattered graphic of a Confederate flag shaped like the state, reminded its readers that Missouri was a former slave state and that St. Louis had a long and checkered history of segregation and racial violence.[22] Aljazeera America explicitly linked current events to the state's turbulent Civil War history. "The rifts that plague [Ferguson] originate," the journal insisted, "from Missouri's long-standing identity crisis, still unresolved 150 years after the American Civil War."[23]

Perhaps in hope of facilitating some form of healing for his city in the wake of so much discord, St. Louis mayor Francis Slay asked his constituents to consider removing the Confederate monument in Forest Park. Echoing the men of the Ransom Post GAR one hundred years before, Slay pointed out that the monument had always been controversial and asked "whether, with the benefit of a longer view of history, the monument is appropriately situated in Forest Park . . . or whether it should be relocated to a more appropriate setting."[24] For Slay, Confederate symbolism did not represent the city or its history as he knew it. One of the monument's defenders wrote the *St. Louis Post-Dispatch*, however, asking its readers to remember that "Confederate lives matter, too."[25]

While St. Louis considered the fate of its Confederate monument, national events were unfolding that heralded a dramatic reappraisal of the Civil War in American memory. The 2015 murders of nine members of the predominately African American Emanuel AME Church in Charleston, South Carolina, served as a bloody epilogue to the Civil War sesquicentennial. The widely circulated photographs of shooter Dylan Roof posing with Confederate flags exposed the deep-seated link between Confederate symbolism and white supremacy. Across the nation, states, counties, towns, and schools disavowed Confederate iconography and dismantled Confederate memorials.

Many Missourians were moved by these racially motivated murders. In St. Louis, vandals spray-painted "Black Lives Matter" across the Forest Park Confederate monument.[26] Calls for its removal gained renewed momentum. Rather than see it destroyed, the newly founded Missouri Civil War Museum at nearby Jefferson Barracks expressed a willingness to accept the monument into its collections. But the tremendous expense of moving the massive thirty-two-foot-tall, forty-ton granite and bronze monument delayed its acquisition. The *St. Louis Post-Dispatch* estimated the cost of relocation at roughly $400,000.[27] As a result, the monument remained in Forest Park, suffering repeated vandalism. Meanwhile, the UDC and the Missouri Civil War Museum squabbled with city officials over who actually owned the monument and how much control they would exercise over its future exhibition. Having been gifted the monument by the UDC, the Missouri Civil War Museum filed a lawsuit against the city to secure full control over its unwieldy and provocative new artifact. Ultimately, the city and the museum settled the case out of court. Finally, on June 25, 2017, the city announced plans to remove the monument and place it in storage at the museum, where it currently remains.[28]

Confederate monuments in Missouri continued to attract criticism, however, particularly in the aftermath of the "Unite the Right" rally in Charlottesville, Virginia, in August 2017. This protest, surrounding the proposed removal of a statue to Confederate general Robert E. Lee, resulted in the murder of antiracist activist Heather Heyer. Heyer's death, coupled with the unbridled racism expressed by the protesters, shocked many Americans. Not for generations had the nation's attention been so fixed on the memory of the American Civil War, nor had the debates surrounding it proven so divisive and deadly.

In the wake of Charlottesville, sporadic acts of vandalism were directed at Confederate monuments in Missouri. In Kansas City, vandals tagged a 1934 monument to "Women of the Old South." In response, the UDC announced its intention to remove the monument for its own safety. With all expenses paid by a private donor, the UDC dismantled the monument and placed it in storage.[29] Two Confederate monuments in the Springfield National Cemetery were also vandalized, including the monument to the Confederate dead erected in 1901. In response to this act, Missouri representative Warren Love tweeted, "This is totally against the law. I hope they are found & hung from a tall tree with a long rope." Love, a Republican from Osceola, faced criticism for seemingly endorsing lynching. The House Ethics Committee called a hearing on the matter, but Love emerged without any formal punishment.[30] In fact, Love later introduced a piece of legislation in the General Assembly that would make it more difficult to remove Confederate monuments. Democratic senator Jamilah Nasheed from St. Louis responded by presenting a competing bill that recommended moving all Confederate monuments to the Confederate Memorial State Historic Site and banning the display of Confederate flags on state property. Neither bill moved forward to a vote, but their proposals—made more than one hundred years after the state adopted the veterans' homes—indicate how futile Hohenschild's hope had been that the twentieth century would find Missourians united in "friendship, love and patriotism, to differ never more."[31]

Missouri has long been a place of conflict and contradictions. Its old sources of division—political, racial, rural, urban, Union, Confederate—continue to resurface. In 1989, historian William E. Foley observed, "It is little wonder that confusion still exists concerning Missouri's proper identity. . . . Not clearly situated in any of the four national geographic sections, and yet a part of all, Missouri and its people personify American pluralism."[32] As a result, Missouri continues to confound neat characterization, and Missourians still grapple with the meaning of the Civil War.

As Missourians and as Americans persist in contesting Civil War memories, it is useful to remember where these debates originated. Understanding the challenges faced and compromises wrought by the Civil War generation in their efforts to commemorate the Civil War lends informative context to contemporary conversations about Civil War memory. First, they reveal Civil War commemoration was never undertaken for objective purposes. Even before the end of this devastating and transformative conflict, Americans on both sides took a profound interest in how history would reflect on their participation. As a result, the Civil War generation worked diligently to record their wartime experiences. Their efforts produced competing interpretations of Civil War history, which can reveal how people thought of themselves, the past, and their place in it. For both white and black Missourians, Civil War commemoration served to further their particular economic, political, and social goals. Second, although Civil War memorials have recently reemerged as major news items, acts of Civil War commemoration have long been controversial. Missourians antagonized and frustrated one another as they attempted to variously enshrine the Union, Emancipation, and Lost Causes in their state. Although significant reevaluation and reappraisal of the legacy of the Civil War might be expected from the distance of more than 150 years, the concerns now popularly raised about Civil War memorials—Confederate memorials, in particular—are nothing new.

The legacy of Civil War commemoration in Missouri, however, represents more than a mere reminder of how the cultural, political, and racial divides that marred the Civil War generation have persisted into twenty-first-century life. It also speaks to the ways in which Civil War commemoration unified some Missourians around a regional identity rooted in their shared history and values. It reveals that Civil War commemoration empowered African Americans and women, challenged prevalent assumptions about gender, and expanded the role of the state in education and welfare. In the words of Confederate veteran James Gantt, "We ought not to live in the past, and we cannot live on memories, but there is a right use of the past. There are ways in which it may be made to yield blessing, help, and good in the life of the present."[33] Through acts of commemoration, Civil War–era Missourians accomplished some good, and it may be that their descendants can do so again.

Notes

Acknowledgments

Epigraph. Proceedings of the Fourteenth Annual Encampment of the Department of Missouri, Grand Army of the Republic, 1895, 90.

Introduction

Epigraph. The *Confederate Veteran* mistakenly credited the speech to "Garrett" instead of Gantt. "Confederate Monument at Kansas City," *Confederate Veteran,* June 1902, 276.

1. "Homes for the Veterans," *Mexico Weekly Ledger*, February 25, 1897.

2. *Souvenir of the Missouri Legislature,* [59].

3. *Kansas City Journal*, February 18, 1897.

4. *Palmyra Spectator*, February 18, 1897.

5. Scholars use the term "memory" to refer to social constructions of the past that emphasize particular historical narratives to the exclusion of others in the interests of consolidating group identity. Memory is preserved and perpetuated across generations through "landmarks" or "sites of memory," including archives, monuments, and cultural celebrations. See Halbwachs, *On Collective Memory*; Nora, "Between Memory and History"; Klein, "On the Emergence of *Memory* in Historical Discourse"; Anderson, *Imagined Communities*; and Kammen, *Mystic Chords of Memory*.

6. Kammen, *Mystic Chords of Memory*, 1.

7. "Confederate Monument at Kansas City," 276.

8. These categories of Civil War memory are informed by the work of a number of historians; see Gallagher, *Causes Won, Lost, and Forgotten*, 2; Blight, *Race and Reunion*; and Cook, *Civil War Memories*, 4–6. See also Neff, *Honoring the Civil War Dead*; and Janney, *Remembering the Civil War.*

9. Stanley, *The Loyal West*, 2.

10. Kammen, *Mystic Chords of Memory*, 14.

11. Marshall, *Creating a Confederate Kentucky*, 7.

12. See Monaghan, *Civil War on the Western Border*; Fellman, *Inside War*; Gerteis, *Civil War St. Louis*, Etcheson, *Bleeding Kansas*; Neely, *The Border between Them*; Earle and Burke, eds., *Bleeding Kansas, Bleeding Missouri*; Gerteis, *The Civil War in Missouri*; Phillips, *The Rivers Ran Backward.*

13. Fellman, *Inside War.*

14. See Sutherland, "Sideshow No Longer." Other histories of Missouri's guerrilla war include Beilein, *Bushwhackers*; Brownlee, *Gray Ghosts of the Confederacy*; Geiger, *Financial Fraud and Guerrilla Violence in Missouri's Civil War*; Goodrich, *Black Flag*; and Sutherland, *A Savage Conflict*. For the impact of the guerrilla war on Missouri women, see Whites, "Forty Shirts and a Wagonload of Wheat"; and Whites and Long, eds., *Occupied Women.*

15. LeeAnn Whites, "You Can't Change History by Moving a Rock: Gender, Race, and the Cultural Politics of Confederate Memorialization," in Fahs and Waugh, eds., *The Memory of the Civil War in American Culture*, 216; Hulbert, "Constructing Guerrilla Memory," 61, 72; Hulbert, "How to Remember 'This Damnable Guerrilla Warfare,'" 145–148.

16. Marshall, *Creating a Confederate Kentucky*, 2–4.

17. Astor, *Rebels on the Border*, 5, 194–201. See also Marshall, *Creating a Confederate Kentucky*, 4.

18. Stanley, *The Loyal West*, 4, 130–152, 10.

19. Aron, *American Confluence*, xxi; Foley, *The Genesis of Missouri*, 299.

20. See Berger, *St. Louis and Empire*, 2, 28; and Richardson, *West from Appomattox*, 108–147.

21. West, *The Last Indian War*, xix. See also Kelman, *A Misplaced Massacre.*

22. The construct of the West applied here has been informed by scholarship on the "frontier," "middle ground," "borderlands," and "shatter-zones." See Weber, "Turner, the Boltonians, and the Borderlands"; Bradshaw, *Regions and Regionalism in the United States*; White, *The Middle Ground*; Ayers et al., *All Over the Map*; Cayton and Teute, eds., *Contact Points*; and Stephen Aron, "The Making of the First American West and the Unmaking of Other Realms," in Deverell, ed., *A Companion to the American West*, 5–24.

23. Aron, "The Making of the First American West and the Unmaking of Other Realms," 6.

24. Nash, *Creating the West*, 134; Meinig, "American Wests"; Hausladen, ed., *Western Places, American Myths*, 1. See also Athearn, *The Mythic West in Twentieth-Century America*; and Smith, *Virgin Land.*

25. Phillips, "The Crime against Missouri," 61. See also Phillips, *The Rivers Ran Backward*; Phillips, "'The Chrysalis State': Slavery, Confederate Identity, and the Creation of the Border South," in Gordon and Inscoe, eds., *Inside the Confederate Nation,* 147–166; and Phillips, *Missouri's Confederate.*

26. Phillips, *The Rivers Ran Backward*, 8, 299–302. For more on Civil War memory in the Midwest, see Stanley, *The Loyal West.*

27. Hulbert, *The Ghosts of Guerrilla Memory*, 11, 183.

28. Marshall, *Creating a Confederate Kentucky*, 2.

29. Neely, *The Border between Them*, 5, 246–247; Jonathan Earle and Diane Mutti Burke, "Revisiting the Long Civil War on the Border," in Earle and Burke, eds., *Bleeding Kansas, Bleeding Missouri*, 10.

30. Neely, *The Border between Them*, 246–247.

One: "Cradled in a Compromise"

Epigraph. Journal and Proceedings of the Missouri State Convention, 36.

1. 1850 U.S. Census, St. Louis County, Missouri, slave schedule, St. Louis, 67, National Archives and Records Administration microfilm publication M432, www.FamilySearch.org.

2. Quoted in Boman, *Lincoln's Resolute Unionist*, 92.

3. *Journal and Proceedings of the Missouri State Convention*, 34–36.

4. Arenson, *The Great Heart of the Republic*, 2.

5. Foley, *The Genesis of Missouri*, 299; Aron, *American Confluence*, xxi.

6. John Mack Faragher, "'More Motley Than Mackinaw': From Ethnic Mixing to Ethnic Cleansing on the Frontier of the Lower Missouri, 1783–1833," in Cayton and Teute, eds., *Contact Points*, 316.

7. Phillips, *Missouri's Confederate*, 51.

8. Burke, *On Slavery's Border*, 29. See also Astor, *Rebels on the Border*, 29–32.

9. For more on the experience of enslaved people in the settlement of Missouri, see Burke, *On Slavery's Border*, 38–44. For the legacy of French and Spanish colonization and Indian removal in shaping slavery in Missouri, see Epps, *Slavery on the Periphery*, 13–44.

10. Epps, *Slavery on the Periphery*, 16; McCandless, *A History of Missouri*, 7.

11. Burke, *On Slavery's Border*, 5, 49, 57.

12. Epps, *Slavery on the Periphery*, 17, 47.

13. Neely, *The Border between Them*, 82.

14. Phillips, *Missouri's Confederate*, xii. According to Adam Arenson, at this time the West included the "residents of a vast region—including parts of Arkansas, Indiana, Illinois, Kentucky, and Michigan as well as California, Missouri, Iowa, Wisconsin, and federal territories from Minnesota to Oregon to New Mexico—[who] considered themselves westerners." See Arenson, *The Great Heart of the Republic*, 3.

15. *Missourian*, June 24, 1820.

16. *Missourian*, September 5, 1821.

17. West, *The Last Indian War*, 47.

18. Billington, *Westward Expansion*, 469.

19. Merk, *Manifest Destiny and Mission in American History*, 24.

20. *Missourian*, July 22, 1820.

21. *Democratic Banner*, July 12, 1847; Arenson, *The Great Heart of the Republic*, 12. For more on how Missourians envisioned their role in Indian removal, westward expansion, and empire, and in particular how Senator Thomas Hart Benton worked to make this a reality, see Berger, *St. Louis and Empire*, 19–25.

22. Rash, *The Painting and Politics of George Caleb Bingham*, 76–90.

23. *Grand River Chronicle*, May 14, 1849.

24. *Western Union*, May 29, 1851.

25. *Hannibal Journal*, March 22, 1853.

26. Mering, *The Whig Party in Missouri*, 167.

27. McCandless, *A History of Missouri*, 246.

28. Phillips, *The Rivers Ran Backward*, 87, 96.

29. *Missouri Statesman*, March 16, 1849.

30. Rash, *The Painting and Politics of George Caleb Bingham*, 105–106, 115.

31. Burke, *On Slavery's Border*, 263. See also Aron, *American Confluence*, 202; and James Neal Primm, "Missouri, St. Louis, and the Secession Crisis," in *Germans for a Free Missouri*, 4.

32. Schurz, *The Reminiscences of Carl Schurz, 1852–1863*, 38, 48, 39.

33. Epps, *Slavery on the Periphery*, 67.

34. McLaurin, *Celia*, xii–xiii, 107.

35. Phillips, "The Crime against Missouri," 73.

36. Epps, *Slavery on the Periphery*, 57–58, 14–15.

37. *Glasgow Weekly Times*, June 22, 1854.

38. *Weekly Jefferson Inquirer*, August 26, 1856.

39. Aron, *American Confluence*, xxi.

40. Fellman, *Inside War*, 3; Burke, *On Slavery's Border*, 264.

41. Phillips, "The Crime against Missouri," 65–66. See also Phillips, *The Rivers Ran Backward*, 86; and Epps, *Slavery on the Periphery*, 111–112.

42. Epps, *Slavery on the Periphery*, 112.

43. Schurz, *The Reminiscences of Carl Schurz, 1852–1863*, 39.

44. *Glasgow Weekly Times*, May 24, 1860. Although it initially garnered very little attention in Missouri, Dred Scott began his suit for freedom in this same period. While the Missouri Supreme Court had often ruled in favor of enslaved people in similar cases, they decided against Scott, forcing him to take his case to the U.S. Supreme Court. Again, Missouri was at the center of a national controversy that strengthened the institution of slavery and abridged the rights of enslaved people.

45. Yancey was a prominent secessionist from Alabama. *Glasgow Weekly Times*, May 24, 1860.

46. Astor, *Rebels on the Border*, 50, 48.

47. Astor, *Rebels on the Border*, 49. See also Robinson, *A Union Indivisible*, 69.

48. Robinson, *A Union Indivisible*, 65, 72.

49. *Weekly California News*, October 6, 13, 20; November 3, 1860.

50. *Anzeiger des Westens*, October 29, 1860, in *Germans for a Free Missouri*, 137.

51. Burke, *On Slavery's Border*, 266.

52. *Weekly Jefferson Inquirer*, November 10, 1860.

53. *Daily Missouri Republican*, November 8, 1860.

54. *Weekly Jefferson Inquirer*, November 10, 1860.

55. *Weekly California News*, November 17, 1860.

56. *Weekly Jefferson Inquirer*, December 1, 1860.

57. *St. Joseph Weekly Free Democrat*, December 1, 1861.

58. *St. Joseph Weekly Free Democrat*, December 1, 1861.

59. *Daily Missouri Republican*, November 11, 1860.

60. *Anzeiger des Westens*, December 10, 1860 (for December 6, 1860), in *Germans for a Free Missouri*, 145.

61. *Randolph Citizen*, February 7, 1861.

62. *Randolph Citizen*, November 29, 1860.

63. *Weekly Jefferson Inquirer*, December 22, 1860.
64. *Weekly Jefferson Inquirer*, January 12, 1861.
65. *Weekly California News*, December 22, 1860.
66. *St. Joseph Weekly Free Democrat*, December 1, 1860.
67. *Weekly Jefferson Inquirer*, January 12, 1861. See also Burke, *On Slavery's Border*, 266.
68. *Mississippi Blätter*, January 27, 1861, in *Germans for a Free Missouri*, 161–162.
69. *Randolph Citizen*, February 14, 1861. See also *Daily Missouri Republican*, November 11, 1860.
70. See *Randolph Citizen*, February 7, 14, 1861.
71. *Anzeiger des Westens*, December 17, 1860 (for December 12, 1860), in *Germans for a Free Missouri*, 148.
72. *Weekly Jefferson Inquirer*, December 22, 1860.
73. Phillips, "The Crime against Missouri," 67.
74. *Daily Missouri Republican*, November 5, 1860.
75. *Weekly Jefferson Inquirer*, December 29, 1860.
76. *Weekly Jefferson Inquirer*, January 12, 1861.
77. *Weekly Jefferson Inquirer*, January 12, 1861.
78. *Weekly Jefferson Inquirer*, January 12, 1861.
79. *Anzeiger des Westens*, February 4, 1861 (for January 29, 1861), in *Germans for a Free Missouri*, 165.
80. *Journal and Proceedings of the Missouri State Convention*, 122. For more on the convention, see Parrish, *Turbulent Partnership*, 9–14.
81. *Journal and Proceedings of the Missouri State Convention*, 35–36.
82. *Journal and Proceedings of the Missouri State Convention*, 122, 127.
83. *Journal and Proceedings of the Missouri State Convention*, 68, 26, 82–83.
84. *Journal and Proceedings of the Missouri State Convention*, 16.
85. *Journal and Proceedings of the Missouri State Convention*, 36, 50, 176.
86. Gerteis, *The Civil War in Missouri*, 22–26; Parrish, *Turbulent Partnership*, 22–23.
87. Phillips, *Missouri's Confederate*, 268; Parrish, *Turbulent Partnership*, 34; Kirkpatrick, "The Admission of Missouri to the Confederacy."
88. Gerteis, *The Civil War in Missouri*, 1–4.
89. Drake, *Missouri Voters' Oath*, 7.
90. Gerteis, *The Civil War in Missouri*, 1.
91. Greene, Holland, and Kremer, "The Role of the Negro in Missouri History," 9.
92. Parrish, *Missouri under Radical Rule*, 3; Parrish, *Turbulent Partnership*, 35–47.
93. Parrish, *Turbulent Partnership*, 57.
94. Brownlee, *Gray Ghosts of the Confederacy*, 143.
95. S. T. Ruffner, "War in Missouri Began at Camp Jackson," *Confederate Veteran*, January 1912, 27.
96. *OR*, series 2, 1:221–222.
97. Parrish, *Turbulent Partnership*, 78–79.
98. Parrish, *A History of Missouri*, 44–45, 67–68.
99. *OR*, series 2, 1:221.

100. Fellman, *Inside War*, 11; Parrish, *Turbulent Partnership*, 60–62.

101. Burke, *On Slavery's Border*, 289. See also Romeo, *Gender and the Jubilee*, 3, 28, 48–49, 80–84.

102. Boyd, "The Exigencies of War," 47–50; Romeo, *Gender and the Jubilee*, 42–44.

103. Burke, *On Slavery's Border*, 285, 283.

104. Bingham to Rollins and Hall, February 12, 1862, James S. Rollins Papers, The State Historical Society of Missouri.

105. Bingham to Rollins, February 12, 1862, James S. Rollins Papers.

106. Romeo, *Gender and the Jubilee*, 4, 47.

107. Parrish, *Missouri under Radical Rule*, 2; Astor, *Rebels on the Border*, 175–176; Parrish, *Turbulent Partnership*, 149–177.

108. Drake, *"Camp Jackson: Its History and Significance,"* 12.

109. For more on the relationship of the provisional government to emancipation, see Parrish, *Turbulent Partnership*, 123–148.

110. Parrish, *Missouri under Radical Rule*, 4; Epps, *Slavery on the Periphery*, 185.

111. Drake, *The Missouri State Convention, and Its Ordinance of Emancipation*, 5.

112. Phillips, *The Rivers Ran Backward*, 283; Parrish, *Turbulent Partnership*, 178–207.

113. Fellman, *Inside War*, 136.

114. See Stiles, *Jesse James*, 160–165, 191–192; and Hernando, *Faces Like Devils*, 14–15, 33–34, 43–44, 65, 78, 212–213.

115. Historian Peter S. Carmichael has observed that "the Civil War did not revolutionize American culture" or "alter the trajectory of . . . thought or create a crisis in values." See Carmichael, *The War for the Common Soldier*, 314.

Two: "Poor Old Missouri"

Epigraph. Grover, "Civil War in Missouri," 11.

1. Stiles, *Jesse James*, 38; Astor, *Rebels on the Border*, 12–13; Burke, *On Slavery's Border*, 48, 95; McCandless, *A History of Missouri*, 59–60. See also Hurt, *Agriculture and Slavery in Missouri's Little Dixie*.

2. *National Tribune*, November 10, 1892.

3. Gerteis, *The Civil War in Missouri*, 106–109.

4. *Lexington Intelligencer*, May 21, 1904. At least 365 veterans arrived by train.

5. *Proceedings of the Twenty-Third Annual Encampment of the Department of Missouri, Grand Army of the Republic*, 1904, 5.

6. *Proceedings of the Twenty-Third Annual Encampment of the Department of Missouri, GAR*, 55. See also *Lexington Intelligencer*, May 21, 1904.

7. *Lexington Intelligencer*, May 21, 1904.

8. Gallagher, *Causes Won, Lost, and Forgotten*, 2–3; Warren, *The Legacy of the Civil War*, 59–66; Neff, *Honoring the Civil War Dead*, 8–9; Gannon, *The Won Cause*, 5–8.

9. Blight, *Race and Reunion*, 2. Caroline E. Janney offers a strident counterargument to Blight's claim, insisting it overlooks important aspects of Union memory. See Janney, *Remembering the Civil War*, 9.

10. Silber, *This War Ain't Over*, 17; Janney, *Remembering the Civil War*, 10; Cook, *Civil War Memories*, 70.

11. Janney, *Remembering the Civil War*, 10.

12. Neff, *Honoring the Civil War Dead*, 8–10; Gallagher, *Causes Won, Lost, and Forgotten*, 2, 25–29.

13. Carmichael, *The War for the Common Soldier*, 270–271.

14. Cleveland, *Alexander H. Stephens in Public and Private with Letters and Speeches*, 721.

15. Astor, *Rebels on the Border*, 5. For similar interpretations of Missouri's compromised Union memory, see Stanley, *The Loyal West*, 2; and Phillips, *The Rivers Ran Backward*, 299–302, 320, 330–332.

16. Astor, *Rebels on the Border*, 195, 197.

17. See Stanley, *The Loyal West*, 154–161; and Phillips, *The Rivers Ran Backward*, 307.

18. Missouri Constitution (1865), art. 2, sec. 3–14; art. 13, sec. 6, Missouri Constitutions, 1820–1945, Missouri State Archives. See also Parrish, *Missouri under Radical Rule*, 27–37; Parrish, *A History of Missouri*, 121–122.

19. *Missouri State Times*, April 22, 1865, quoted in Parrish, *Missouri under Radical Rule*, 45.

20. Parrish, *Missouri under Radical Rule*, 185–186.

21. Fellman, *Inside War*, 243–244.

22. Parrish, *Missouri under Radical Rule*, 7; Primm, "The G.A.R. in Missouri," 357–361.

23. *Missouri Democrat*, July 13, 1866.

24. Parrish, *Missouri under Radical Rule*, 83.

25. McConnell, *Glorious Contentment*, 24–25.

26. Primm, "The G.A.R. in Missouri," 368.

27. *Missouri Democrat*, November 5, 1866.

28. *Missouri Republican*, April 7, July 1, 1867, cited in Primm, "The G.A.R. in Missouri," 368.

29. *Missouri Republican*, August 25, 26, 1868, cited in Primm, "The G.A.R. in Missouri," 373.

30. Primm, "The G.A.R. in Missouri," 373.

31. *Missouri Republican*, March 2, 1868, cited in Primm, "The G.A.R. in Missouri," 370.

32. Schurz, *The Reminiscences of Carl Schurz, 1863–1869*, 292–293.

33. Carl Schurz, "On Being Chosen United States Senator," in Bancroft, ed., *Speeches, Correspondence and Political Papers of Carl Schurz*, 476.

34. Richardson, *West from Appomattox*, 122.

35. Schurz, *The Reminiscences of Carl Schurz, 1863–1869*, 285; *Missouri Democrat*, September 3, 1870; Parrish, *Missouri under Radical Rule*, 295.

36. Carl Schurz, "Address to the People of Missouri," in Bancroft, ed., *Speeches, Correspondence and Political Papers of Carl Schurz*, 512.

37. Bancroft and Dunning, "A Sketch of Carl Schurz's Political Career," 332.

38. Parrish, *Missouri under Radical Rule*, 319.

39. Schurz, "Address to the People of Missouri," 516.

40. Richardson, *West from Appomattox*, 116–117, 270–271.

41. Phillips, *The Rivers Ran Backward*, 308–309.

42. Quoted in the *Weekly Caucasian*, September 24, 1870.

43. Stiles, *Jesse James*, 220–222, 228.

44. Richardson, *West from Appomattox*, 270–271, 155, 116; Parrish, *Missouri under Radical Rule*, 323–324.

45. "Missouri Democracy," *St. Louis Dispatch*, May 13 [n.d.], Ira B. Hyde Papers, vol. 3a, The State Historical Society of Missouri.

46. Parrish, *A History of Missouri*, 238, 243.

47. *Mexico Weekly Ledger*, October 2, 1884.

48. *Sedalia Weekly Bazoo*, August 19, 1884; *Weekly Graphic*, September 26, 1884.

49. *Butler Weekly Times*, August 27, 1884.

50. Christopher Phillips puts forth a strong counterargument about the composition of Missouri's Democratic Party. According to Phillips, wartime allegiances overwhelmingly dictated party allegiances in postwar Missouri. The Democrats who drafted Missouri's 1875 constitution and subsequently dominated state offices were mostly southern-born, and many of them were ex-Confederates. As evidence of their pro-southern perspective, Phillips cites changes to the 1875 constitution. He points out that it "passed measures making it difficult for any government, whether federal or state, to restrict individual rights, by disallowing the suspension of habeas corpus, tightening definitions of treasonable activity, and prohibiting the state government from confiscating property." Such policies, however, were very much in keeping with those of wartime conservative Unionists in other parts of the country, particularly in "the Loyal West." Missourians espoused white supremacy, jealously guarded their self-determination, and feared restrictions on their civil liberties but did not necessarily embrace a Confederate identity. See Phillips, *The Rivers Ran Backward*, 301–302; and Stanley, *The Loyal West*, 98–129, 159–160.

51. *Butler Weekly Times*, April 25, 1888.

52. *Omaha Daily Bee*, August 29, 1889.

53. *Chariton Courier*, July 26, 1888.

54. *Chariton Courier*, April 17, 1890.

55. Until 1882, the Missouri GAR operated under the Department of Kansas. "A Brief History of the Organization of the Grand Army of the Republic in Missouri," in *Proceedings of the Second Annual Encampment of the Department of Missouri, Grand Army of the Republic*, 1883, 3; *Souvenir of Frank P. Blair Post No. 1, Department of Missouri, G. A. R.* (St. Louis: A. Whipple, 1894), 6.

56. William Warner, "Report of Department Commander," in *Proceedings of the Second Annual Encampment of the Department of Missouri, GAR*, 20.

57. Warner, "Report of Department Commander," 20.

58. McConnell, *Glorious Contentment*, 86; Dearing, *Veterans in Politics*, 208.

59. "Address of Department Commander," in *Proceedings of the Third Annual Encampment of the Department of Missouri, Grand Army of the Republic*, 1884, 17.

60. Leo Rassieur, "Address of the Department Commander," April 1, 1891, in *Proceedings of the Tenth Annual Encampment of the Department of Missouri, Grand Army of the Republic*, 1891, 56.

61. "Report of the Adjutant General," in *Journal of the Seventeenth Annual Session National Encampment, Grand Army of the Republic*, 37.

62. "Unofficial Proceedings," in *Proceedings of the Seventh Annual Encampment of the Department of Missouri, Grand Army of the Republic*, 1888, 198.

63. *Proceedings of the Eighth Annual Encampment of the Department of Missouri, Grand Army of the Republic*, 1889, 154–155.

64. Thomas B. Rodgers, "General Order No. 6," September 9, 1890, in *Proceedings of the Tenth Annual Encampment of the Department of Missouri, GAR*, 196.

65. "Report of the Adjutant General," in *Journal of the Twenty-Fifth National Encampment, (Silver Anniversary) Grand Army of the Republic*, 66.

66. "Annual Report of the Inspector," in *Proceedings of the Ninth Annual Convention of the Woman's Relief Corps Auxiliary to the Grand Army of the Republic, Department of Missouri*, 1893, following p. 30.

67. "Report of National Secretary," in *Journal of the Eleventh Annual Convention of the Woman's Relief Corps, Auxiliary to the Grand Army of the Republic*, 61.

68. Armstrong, *History of the State Federal Soldiers' Home*, 37.

69. Adah Goss Briggs, "Circular Letter, No. 1," November 1, 1895, Benecke Family, G.A.R.—Woman's Relief Corps., 1894–1896, Benecke Family Papers, The State Historical Society of Missouri.

70. John P. Platt, "Address of the Department Commander," April 30, 1898, in *Proceedings of the Seventeenth Annual Encampment of the Department of Missouri, Grand Army of the Republic*, 1898, 21.

71. Thomas B. Rodgers, "Address of the Department Commander," May 10, 1897, in *Proceedings of the Sixteenth Annual Encampment of the Department of Missouri, Grand Army of the Republic*, 1897, 20.

72. *The Grand Army Blue-Book*, 22.

73. Nelson Cole, "Report of Department Commander," February 17, 1886, in *Proceedings of the Fifth Annual Encampment of the Department of Missouri, Grand Army of the Republic*, 1886, 24–25.

74. Gannon, *The Won Cause*, 5–6.

75. These included the following posts: Chandler, Collie, R. G. Shaw, Capitol City, Clay Shaw, Tipton, Whaling, Perrill, and Fletcher (possibly an integrated post). Integrated posts included Custer, Dix, and Nichols. See Gannon, *The Won Cause*, 89, 95, 205, 217.

76. McConnell, *Glorious Contentment*, 217.

77. *Proceedings of the Twenty-Second Annual Encampment of the Department of Missouri, Grand Army of the Republic*, 1903, 49–50.

78. *Proceedings of the Fourteenth Annual Encampment of the Department of Missouri, GAR*, 89.

79. *Circular Series: Grand Army of the Republic, Department of Missouri, Ransom Post No. 131*, series 1911, no. 8 (May 11, 1911).

80. "Unofficial Proceedings," in *Proceedings of the Ninth Annual Encampment of the Department of Missouri, Grand Army of the Republic*, 1890, 152.

81. *Proceedings of the Thirty-Third Annual Encampment of the Department of Missouri, Grand Army of the Republic*, 1914, 41.

82. *Proceedings of the Twentieth Annual Encampment of the Department of Missouri, Grand Army of the Republic*, 1901, 65.

83. *Proceedings of the Fifteenth Annual Encampment of the Department of Missouri, Grand Army of the Republic*, 1896, 6.

84. *Circular Series: Grand Army of the Republic, Department of Missouri, Ransom Post No. 131*, series 1911, no. 23 (December 21, 1911).

85. *Circular Series: Grand Army of the Republic, Department of Missouri, Ransom Post No. 131*, series 1915, no. 17 (September 23, 1915).

86. *Circular Series: Grand Army of the Republic, Department of Missouri, Ransom Post No. 131*, series 1917, no. 24 (January 10, 1917).

87. *Circular Series: Grand Army of the Republic, Department of Missouri, Ransom Post No. 131*, series 1915, no. 6 (April 7, 1915).

88. *Proceedings of the Nineteenth Annual Convention of the Woman's Relief Corps Auxiliary to the Grand Army of the Republic, Department of Missouri*, 1903, 40.

89. *Proceedings of the Society of the Army of the Tennessee at the Fifteenth Annual Meeting Held at St. Louis, Missouri, May 10th and 11th, 1882* (Cincinnati: N.p., 1885), 328–329; *Missouri Republican*, May 12, 1882.

90. *Proceedings of the Thirteenth Annual Encampment of the Department of Missouri, Grand Army of the Republic*, 1894, 82–83.

91. T. D. Kimball, "Address of the Department Commander," in *Proceedings of the Twenty-Seventh Annual Encampment of the Department of Missouri, Grand Army of the Republic*, 1908, 28.

92. *Cape Girardeau Democrat*, September 19, 1891.

93. *Proceedings of the Eleventh Annual Encampment of the Department of Missouri, Grand Army of the Republic*, 1892, 115, 117.

94. *Proceedings of the Eleventh Annual Encampment of the Department of Missouri, GAR*, 116.

95. Nelson Cole, "Report of Department Commander," February 1, 1887, in *Proceedings of the Sixth Annual Encampment of the Department of Missouri, Grand Army of the Republic*, 1887, 44.

96. *Proceedings of the First Annual Encampment of the Department of Missouri, Grand Army of the Republic*, 1882, 7.

97. "Unofficial Proceedings," in *Proceedings of the Ninth Annual Encampment of the Department of Missouri, GAR*, 155.

98. Historian Nick Sacco has written about the evolving legacies of Blair and Lyon in Missouri. See Sacco, "A Free Country for White Men"; and Sacco, "The Contested Memories of General Nathaniel Lyon in St. Louis."

99. *Proceedings of the Tenth Annual Encampment of the Department of Missouri, GAR*, 162.

100. *Journal of the Twentieth Annual Session of the National Encampment Grand Army of the Republic*, 235–236.

101. Cole, "Report of Department Commander," February 1, 1887, in *Proceedings of the Sixth Annual Encampment of the Department of Missouri, GAR*, 44.

102. *St. Louis Post-Dispatch*, August 27, 1887.

103. E. E. Kimball, "Address of the Department Commander," March 12, 1888, in *Proceedings of the Seventh Annual Encampment of the Department of Missouri, GAR*, 45.

104. *Butler Weekly Times*, July 13, 1887.

105. The bill would have provided a pension of twelve dollars per month to any honorably discharged Union veteran suffering from a disability, regardless of when the applicant sustained it. McConnell, *Glorious Contentment*, 150–151; Dearing, *Veterans in Politics*, 328–337. For more on the controversy surrounding Cleveland's response to the St. Louis encampment, see Dearing, *Veterans in Politics*, 337–342; and Matthew Jordan, *Marching Home*, 161–164.

106. *Butler Weekly Times*, July 13, 1887.

107. *St. Joseph Weekly Herald*, July 14, 1887.

108. *St. Louis Post-Dispatch*, October 1, 1887.

109. Cole, "Report of Department Commander," February 1, 1887, in *Proceedings of the Sixth Annual Encampment of the Department of Missouri, GAR*, 44; *St. Louis Post-Dispatch*, August 27, 1887.

110. *Souvenir and Official Programme of the 21st National Encampment Grand Army of the Republic*, 2.

111. E. E. Kimball, "Address of the Department Commander," in *Proceedings of the Seventh Annual Encampment of the Department of Missouri, GAR*, 45–46. It is worth noting that Kansas City hosted the national encampment in 1916, apparently without arousing any of the reticence that attended the St. Louis encampment.

112. Rassieur, "Address of the Department Commander," 57.

113. Grover, "Civil War in Missouri," 4–5.

114. Grover, "Civil War in Missouri," 11.

115. Rodgers, "General Order No. 6," 195.

116. Julia E. Dockery, "Report of the Delegate-at-Large," in *Proceedings of the Thirteenth Annual Convention of the Woman's Relief Corps Auxiliary to the Grand Army of the Republic, Department of Missouri*, 1897, 53.

117. Mattie E. Rich, "Report of Delegate at Large," in *Proceedings of the Twentieth Annual Convention of the Woman's Relief Corps Auxiliary to the Grand Army of the Republic, Department of Missouri*, 1904, 47.

Three: "No Longer Cowed"

Epigraph. "An Address by the Colored People of Missouri to the Friends of Equal Rights," 3, St. Louis Public Library.

1. *Proceedings of the Sixteenth Annual Encampment of the Department of Missouri, GAR*, 78–81.

2. *Stone's Hannibal City Directory, 1897-98*, 283–331, 337, 348–349.

3. *Proceedings of the Sixteenth Annual Encampment of the Department of Missouri, GAR*, 79; Gerteis, *The Civil War in Missouri*, 44–48.

4. *Proceedings of the Sixteenth Annual Encampment of the Department of Missouri, GAR*, 81.

5. *Proceedings of the Seventeenth Annual Encampment of the Department of Missouri, GAR*, 8–18.

6. Gannon, *The Won Cause*, 63–64, 93.

7. Blight, *Race and Reunion*, 2–3; Astor, *Rebels on the Border*, 199–200; Stanley, *The Loyal West*, 147–151.

8. Astor, *Rebels on the Border*, 5; Phillips, "The Crime against Missouri," 61; Whites, "You Can't Change History by Moving a Rock," 220.

9. Boyd, "'The Free People, Who Have Bought Themselves,'" 3. See also Kremer, *Race and Meaning*, 203; and Burke, *On Slavery's Border*, 292.

10. *OR*, series 3, 5:662.

11. Boyd, "'The Free People, Who Have Bought Themselves,'" 9–10. See also Romeo, *Gender and the Jubilee*, 57–62.

12. Boyd, "Exigencies of War," 4, 16.

13. See Boyd, "'The Free People, Who Have Bought Themselves,'" 7–9; Greene, Kremer, and Holland, *Missouri's Black Heritage*, 83–84; and Burke, *On Slavery's Border*, 292–297.

14. *OR*, series 1, 48, part 1:1257.

15. *OR*, series 1, 34, part 2:477.

16. Jackson and Thompson, *The Story of Mattie J. Jackson*, 30.

17. It was not until 1920 that an African American served in the Missouri General Assembly. John W. McKerley, "'We Promise to Use the Ballot as We Did the Bayonet': Black Suffrage Activism and the Limits of Loyalty in Reconstruction Missouri," in Earle and Burke, eds., *Bleeding Kansas, Bleeding Missouri*, 209–210; Kremer, *James Milton Turner*, 18.

18. Parrish, *A History of Missouri*, 151. See also Greene, Kremer, and Holland, *Missouri's Black Heritage*, 92.

19. McKerley, "'We Promise to Use the Ballot as We Did the Bayonet,'" 208.

20. McKerley, "'We Promise to Use the Ballot as We Did the Bayonet,'" 208. See also Kremer, *James Milton Turner*, 18.

21. Kremer, *James Milton Turner*, 19. For more on the work of the Missouri Equal Rights League, see McKerley, "Citizens and Strangers," 88–97.

22. Kremer, *James Milton Turner*, 8–9, 15–16.

23. Kremer, *James Milton Turner*, 16.

24. McKerley, "'We Promise to Use the Ballot as We Did the Bayonet,'" 212.

25. "An Address by the Colored People of Missouri," 3, 4. See also *Tri-Weekly Missouri Democrat,* October 16, 1865.

26. Greene, Kremer, and Holland, *Missouri's Black Heritage*, 96–97; Kremer, *James Milton Turner*, 22–23.

27. McKerley, "'We Promise to Use the Ballot as We Did the Bayonet,'" 214.

28. For more on the failure of the black suffrage movement in Missouri, see McKerley, "Citizens and Strangers," 107–123. Opposition to black male suffrage was also linked to the woman's suffrage movement; see McKerley, "Citizens and Strangers," 145–148.

29. *St. Louis Daily Missouri Democrat*, November 1, 1868, quoted in McKerley, "'We Promise to Use the Ballot as We Did the Bayonet,'" 216.

30. Astor, *Rebels on the Border*, 210, 234, 243–244.

31. Parrish, *Missouri under Radical Rule*, 118–119; Kremer, *James Milton Turner*, 25.

32. Parrish, *Missouri under Radical Rule*, 108, 123.

33. Parrish, *A History of Missouri*, 124.

34. Kremer, *Race and Meaning*, 206–210.

35. Arenson, *The Great Heart of the Republic*, 174. See also Kremer, *Race and Meaning*, 158–170; and Astor, *Rebels on the Border*, 146–154.

36. Boyd, "The Exigencies of War," 203–204.

37. Foster, *Historical Sketch of Lincoln Institute*, 6. See also Parrish, *A History of Missouri*, 166–169.

38. Jackson and Thompson, *The Story of Mattie J. Jackson*, 2, 11.

39. *Professional World*, January 10, 1902.

40. Foster, *Historical Sketch of Lincoln Institute*, 9, 12.

41. "A Soldier's Dream." It may be this legend grew from a 1911 account that claimed Jesse James gave James Milton Turner money for an African American school in Kansas City; see *St. Louis Post-Dispatch*, July 9, 1911; and Kremer, *James Milton Turner*, 210.

42. Foster, *Historical Sketch of Lincoln Institute*, 7.

43. See Arenson, *The Great Heart of the Republic*, 173.

44. Boyd, "The Exigencies of War," 196; Kremer, *James Milton Turner*, 38.

45. Parrish, *Missouri under Radical Rule*, 139.

46. *Maryland Free Press*, January 17, 1867.

47. *Weekly Caucasian*, February 29, 1868.

48. Astor, *Rebels on the Border*, 150; Parrish, *A History of Missouri*, 158–166; Parrish, *Missouri under Radical Rule*, 122.

49. Parrish, *Missouri under Radical Rule*, 123.

50. "The Freedmen of Missouri," *Semi-Weekly Louisianian*, July 27, 1871.

51. Parrish, *Missouri under Radical Rule*, 124–125; Arenson, *The Great Heart of the Republic*, 173.

52. Foster, *Historical Sketch of Lincoln Institute*, 10, 11, 12.

53. Kremer, *Race and Meaning*, 210–211; Kremer, *James Milton Turner*, 35.

54. Kremer, *James Milton Turner*, 35.

55. Foster, *Historical Sketch of Lincoln Institute*, 12.

56. Col. David Branson, "Speech of Col. David Branson," in Foster, *Historical Sketch of Lincoln Institute*, 18.

57. Branson, "Speech of Col. David Branson," 15.

58. McKerley, "'We Promise to Use the Ballot as We Did the Bayonet,'" 209.

59. Kremer, *James Milton Turner*, 28–29, 40, 42.

60. McKerley, "'We Promise to Use the Ballot as We Did the Bayonet,'" 220; Kremer, *James Milton Turner*, 41, 47; Astor, *Rebels on the Border*, 215–216.

61. *Weekly Caucasian*, September 17, 1870.

62. 1870 U.S. Census, Arrow Rock, Saline County, Missouri, population schedule, 8, National Archives and Records Administration microfilm publication M593, www.FamilySearch.org.

63. Historian John W. McKerley also attributes this to a popular conception of republicanism that vaunted "impartial manhood suffrage, with its mandate that all men, regardless of race or wartime loyalty, had the right to participate in the institutions of republican governance." McKerley, "Citizens and Strangers," 157. For more on the responses of black Missourians to the Liberal Republican movement, see Astor, *Rebels on the Border*, 236.

64. McKerley, "Citizens and Strangers," 185

65. Schirmer, *A City Divided*, 29.

66. McKerley, "Citizens and Strangers," 291, 296. For more on the relationship of black Missourians to the Democratic Party and the influence of black votes on state and local elections, see Astor, *Rebels on the Border*, 209, 219–220, 226–228. For more on restrictions on black suffrage in Missouri c. 1870s–1910s, see McKerley, "Citizens and Strangers," 243–290.

67. McKerley, "Citizens and Strangers," 8, 185.

68. Gannon, *The Won Cause*, 94.

69. Gannon, *The Won Cause*, 169.

70. Gannon, *The Won Cause*, 90–93.

71. These were the numbers of members reported in good standing in the eight African American posts identified by Gannon. *Proceedings of the Twelfth Annual Encampment of the Department of Missouri, Grand Army of the Republic*, 1893, 76–85.

72. Gannon, *The Won Cause*, 88.

73. *Leavenworth Advocate*, September 21, 1889, quoted in Gannon, *The Won Cause*, 95.

74. *Iron County Register*, July 7, 1887.

75. *St. Louis Post-Dispatch*, July 15, 1887.

76. *Proceedings of the Twenty-First Annual Encampment of the Department of Missouri, Grand Army of the Republic*, 1912, 253–255.

77. *St. Louis Post-Dispatch*, July 15, 1887.

78. *St. Louis Post-Dispatch*, June 27, 1887.

79. *Evening Star*, June 27, 1887.

80. *Evening Star*, June 27, 1887.

81. *St. Louis Post-Dispatch*, September 28, 1887.

82. *Iron County Register*, July 7, 1887.

83. *Journal of the Twenty-First Annual Session of the National Encampment, Grand Army of the Republic*, 252.

84. Gannon, *The Won Cause*, 6, 37, 58, 60, 61.

85. Delaney, *From the Darkness Cometh the Light*, 62–63. See also Romeo, *Gender and the Jubilee*, 122–123.

86. Coulter, *"Take Up the Black Man's Burden,"* 37–38.

87. Delaney, *From the Darkness Cometh the Light*, vii, v. See also Romeo, *Gender and the Jubilee*, 17.

88. Romeo, *Gender and the Jubilee*, 121.

89. *Iron County Register*, September 27, 1883.

90. *Sedalia Weekly Conservator*, July 6, 1908.

91. *Sedalia Weekly Conservator*, July 6, 1908.

92. *Sedalia Weekly Conservator*, September 14, 1908.
93. Kremer, *Race and Meaning*, 58–59.
94. McKerley, "Citizens and Strangers," 203.
95. *St. Louis Globe-Democrat*, June 1, 1892.
96. Dickson, *Manual of the International Order of Twelve of Knights and Daughters of Tabor*, 17. See also Greene, Kremer, and Holland, *Missouri's Black Heritage*, 96.
97. *Weekly Intelligencer*, August 8, 1896; *Mexico Missouri Message*, October 11, 1900; *Rising Son*, March 4, 1904; *Sedalia Weekly Conservator*, June 24, 1905.
98. *Troy Herald*, September 18, 1878; *Weekly Intelligencer*, August 8, 1896; *Weekly Graphic*, August 14, 1896.
99. *Kansas City Sun*, July 18, 1914.
100. Kremer, *Race and Meaning*, 201–202.
101. *Holt County Sentinel*, August 6, 1897.
102. *Professional World*, August 8, 1902.
103. *Holt County Sentinel*, July 30, 1897.
104. *Holt County Sentinel*, August 6, 1897.
105. *Kansas City Sun*, August 8, 1914; Parrish, *A History of Missouri*, 148, 150.
106. "Negro Celebration Poster," August 3, 1895, Negro Celebration, Poster and Program, 1895, The State Historical Society of Missouri.
107. *Macon Argus*, August 5, 1868.
108. *Holt County Sentinel*, August 11, 1905.
109. *Holt County Sentinel*, July 15, 1892.
110. *Holt County Sentinel*, August 11, 1905.
111. *Sedalia Weekly Conservator*, January 15, 1904.
112. *Holt County Sentinel*, August 6, 1897.
113. *Sedalia Weekly Conservator*, January 8, 1904.
114. *Professional World*, January 10, 1902.
115. *Macon Argus*, August 5, 1868.
116. *Sedalia Weekly Conservator*, January 15, 1904.
117. Howard, *Biographical Sketches of the Nebraska Legislature*, 177.
118. *Holt County Sentinel*, August 11, 1905.

Four: "Glory Enough for Us All"

Epigraph. Capt. James Porter, "A Missourian's Feelings on the Surrender," *Confederate Veteran,* September 1904, 430.
1. *Butler Weekly Times*, January 4, 1888.
2. Christensen and Kremer, *A History of Missouri*, 16–17.
3. *Butler Weekly Times*, January 4. 1888.
4. *State Times,* January 6, 1888.
5. *State Times*, January 6, 1888.
6. *Biographical Review of Lee County, Iowa*, 254.
7. Marshall, *Creating a Confederate Kentucky*, 4; Hulbert, "Constructing Guerrilla Memory," 61.
8. Marshall, *Creating a Confederate Kentucky*, 3, 37.
9. Porter, "A Missourian's Feelings on the Surrender," 430.

10. Edwards, *Shelby and His Men*; Edwards, *Noted Guerrillas.*

11. Hulbert, "Constructing Guerrilla Memory," 61, 63.

12. *Report of the Proceedings of the Ex-Confederate Association of Missouri, in Its Eighth Annual Meeting,* 1890, 14.

13. *Report of the Proceedings of the Ex-Confederate Association of Missouri, in Its Second Annual Meeting,* 1882, 5.

14. *Report of the Proceedings of the Ex-Confederate Association of Missouri, in Its Fourth Annual Meeting,* 1885, 9.

15. *Proceedings of the Ex-Confederate Association of Missouri, for the Years 1887 and 1888* (St. Louis: Slawson, n.d.), 11; *Journal of the Twenty-Second Annual Session of the National Encampment, Grand Army of the Republic,* 56.

16. *Proceedings of the Ex-Confederate Association of Missouri, for the Years 1887 and 1888,* 11.

17. Jeremy Neely, "The Quantrill Men Reunions: The Missouri-Kansas Border War, Fifty Years On," in Earle and Burke, eds., *Bleeding Kansas, Bleeding Missouri,* 249.

18. Fellman, *Inside War,* xix; Hulbert, "Constructing Guerrilla Memory," 62–64.

19. W. J. Courtney, "Guerrilla Warfare in Missouri," *Confederate Veteran,* March 1921, 104.

20. *St. Louis Republic,* October 2, 1898; Neely, "The Quantrill Men Reunions," 254.

21. Hulbert, *The Ghosts of Guerrilla Memory.*

22. *Iron County Register,* October 13, 1881.

23. *Report of the Proceedings of the Ex-Confederate Association of Missouri, in Its Second Annual Meeting,* 6.

24. Cox, *Dixie's Daughters,* 15–16.

25. Cox, *Dixie's Daughters,* 19–20, 26.

26. Helen Caldwell Putz, "A History of the Margaret A. E. McLure Chapter 119 U.D.C.," Alphabetical File, United Daughters of the Confederacy, folder 2, Missouri Historical Society.

27. "Appendix," in *Minutes, Missouri Division United Daughters of the Confederacy, Kansas City, October 15 and 16, 1902* (N.p.: N.p., n.d.), 1–9.

28. *Minutes of the Ninth Annual Meeting, United Daughters of the Confederacy,* 77–86.

29. *Journal of the Twentieth National Convention of the Woman's Relief Corps, Auxiliary to the Grand Army of the Republic, 1902,* 20.

30. *Proceedings of the Tenth Annual Convention of the Missouri Division, United Daughters of the Confederacy,* 1907, 27.

31. Boccardi, "Remembering in Black and White," 161–191.

32. *Official Proceedings of Fifth Annual Reunion of Missouri Division, United Confederate Veterans,* 1901, 100.

33. *Kansas City Daily Journal,* April 14, 1895.

34. *Report of the Proceedings of the Ex-Confederate Association of Missouri, in Its Seventh Annual Meeting,* 1889, 8.

35. United Confederate Veterans, Campbell Camp No. 488, Springfield, MO, Records, 1894–1915, vol. 1, July 10, 1894, The State Historical Society of Missouri.

36. *Kansas City Journal*, September 20, 1898.

37. *Proceedings of the Eighth Annual Convention of the Missouri Division, United Daughters of the Confederacy*, 1905, 9–10.

38. "Lynching in America." See also Christensen and Kremer, *A History of Missouri*, 179–180; and Pfeifer, "The Ritual of Lynching."

39. *Brownsville Daily Herald*, November 17, 1909; *Albuquerque Morning Journal*, November 16, 1909.

40. United Confederate Veterans, Campbell Camp No. 488, Springfield, MO, Record Book, 1903–1919, December [5?], 1909, The State Historical Society of Missouri.

41. W. L. Morrison, "From Across the Father of Waters," *Confederate Veteran*, April 1895, 107.

42. *Official Proceedings of Fifth Annual Reunion of Missouri Division United Confederate Veterans*, 69.

43. *Official Proceedings of Sixth Annual Reunion of Missouri Division, United Confederate Veterans*, 1902, 9.

44. "The Historical Report," in *Minutes of the Tenth Annual Meeting and Reunion of the United Confederate Veterans*, 56; *Journal of the Twenty-Fourth Annual Session of the National Encampment, Grand Army of the Republic*, 18.

45. Brownlee, *Gray Ghosts of the Confederacy*, 245. See also Hale, *The William Clarke Quantrill Men Reunions*.

46. "Survivors of Quantrell's Band," *Confederate Veteran*, November 1923, 438.

47. Neely, "The Quantrill Men Reunions," 248–249, 256.

48. *Report of the Proceedings of the Ex-Confederate Association of Missouri, in Its Second Annual Meeting*, 13.

49. *Official Proceedings of Fifth Annual Reunion of Missouri Division United Confederate Veterans*, 77.

50. *Report of the Proceedings of the Ex-Confederate Association of Missouri, in Its Second Annual Meeting*, 13.

51. *Missouri Republican*, August 30, 1886, quoted in *Report of the Proceedings of the Ex-Confederate Association of Missouri, in Its Fifth Annual Meeting*, 1886, 12.

52. *Report of the Proceedings of the Ex-Confederate Association of Missouri, in Its Eighth Annual Meeting*, 14.

53. Gen. J. B. Gantt, "Gen. J. B. Gantt's Tribute to Missourians," *Confederate Veteran*, December 1906, 537.

54. *Official Proceedings of Thirteenth Annual Reunion of Missouri Division, United Confederate Veterans*, 1909, 57.

55. Col. Bennett H. Young, "The Western Army," *Confederate Veteran*, July 1901, 312, 313.

56. *Official Proceedings of Fifth Annual Reunion of Missouri Division United Confederate Veterans*, 78–79.

57. Young, "The Western Army," 316.

58. United Confederate Veterans, Campbell Camp No. 488, Springfield, MO, Records, 1894–1915, vol. 1, December 2, 1899; April 7, 1900; April 6, 1901; December 6, 1902, The State Historical Society of Missouri.

59. United Confederate Veterans, Campbell Camp No. 488, Springfield, MO, Records, 1894–1915, vol. 1, January 31, 1904, The State Historical Society of Missouri.

60. *Proceedings of the Sixth Annual Convention of the Missouri Division, United Daughters of the Confederacy*, 1903, 29.

61. *Cassville Democrat*, n.d., quoted in *Intelligencer*, September 14, 1889.

62. United Confederate Veterans, Campbell Camp No. 488, Springfield, MO, Records, 1894–1915, vol. 1, June 16, 1897, The State Historical Society of Missouri.

63. United Confederate Veterans, Campbell Camp No. 488, Springfield, MO, Records, 1894–1915, vol. 1, July 27, 1897, The State Historical Society of Missouri.

64. United Confederate Veterans, Campbell Camp No. 488, Springfield, MO, Records, 1894–1915, vol. 1, July 27, 1897, The State Historical Society of Missouri.

65. United Confederate Veterans, Campbell Camp No. 488, Springfield, MO, Records, 1894–1915, vol. 1, July 30, 1897, The State Historical Society of Missouri.

66. United Confederate Veterans, Campbell Camp No. 488, Springfield, MO, Records, 1894–1915, vol. 1, July 30, 1897, The State Historical Society of Missouri.

67. *St. Louis Post-Dispatch*, December 8, 1905.

68. *St. Louis Post-Dispatch*, May 13, 1906.

69. *St. Louis Post-Dispatch*, December 2, 1906.

70. *St. Louis Post-Dispatch*, December 2, 1906. Campbell Camp passed a motion of thanks to the *St. Louis Republic* for condemning the GAR in its squabble with the UDC over the memorial in Forest Park. See United Confederate Veterans, Campbell Camp No. 488, Springfield, MO, Record Book, 1903–1919, December 4, 1910, The State Historical Society of Missouri.

71. *St. Louis Post-Dispatch*, December 13, 1906.

72. Unidentified news clipping, February 1902, Alphabetical File, United Daughters of the Confederacy, folder 1, Missouri Historical Society.

73. *Official Proceedings of Twelfth Annual Reunion of Missouri Division, United Confederate Veterans,* 1908, 64.

74. "An Appeal for St. Louis Monument," *Confederate Veteran,* May 1911, 216.

75. *Minutes of the Nineteenth Annual Convention of the United Daughters of the Confederacy*, 369.

76. Myers, "'Glory Stands beside Our Grief,'" 52–58.

77. S. R. McCutchen, "They Want More Than Eleven Columns," *Confederate Veteran,* February 1904, 79, 80.

78. Hulbert, "How to Remember 'This Damnable Guerrilla Warfare,'" 148.

79. *St. Louis Post-Dispatch*, November 15, 1912.

80. *University Missourian*, December 2, 1912.

81. *St. Louis Post-Dispatch*, December 6, 1912.

82. *St. Louis Post-Dispatch*, December 3, 1912.

83. *St. Louis Post-Dispatch*, December 3, 1912.

84. *St. Louis Star and Times*, December 5, 1912.

85. *Iron County Register*, December 12, 1912.

86. "Confederate Monument in St. Louis," *Confederate Veteran,* January 1915, 16.

87. Burkhardt, "The Lost Cause Ideology and Civil War Memory at the Semicentennial," 22.

88. Burkhardt, "The Lost Cause Ideology and Civil War Memory at the Semicentennial," 18.

89. Bailey, *The Confederate Monument in Forest Park,* 2, 3–4, 5, 6, 7.

90. For more on the efforts of the UDC to compose "impartial" histories of the war, see Cox, *Dixie's Daughters*, 93–117.

91. *Proceedings of the Ninth Annual Convention of the Missouri Division, United Daughters of the Confederacy*, 1906–1907, 20, 26.

92. *Reminiscences of the Women of Missouri during the Sixties.* See also Boccardi, "Remembering in Black and White," 188–189.

93. United Daughters of the Confederacy, Confederate Dames Chapter, Records, Minutes, 1918–1924, January 5, 1923, The State Historical Society of Missouri.

94. Virginia Creel, "Missouri, Dixie's Affinity," *Confederate Veteran,* February 1923, 53.

95. Mrs. George D. Baxter, "Contributions of the South to the Civilization of Missouri," *Confederate Veteran,* April 1924, 135.

96. Creel, "Missouri, Dixie's Affinity," 53.

97. Mrs. W. R. Millan, "A Confederate Association of Missouri," *Confederate Veteran,* August 1924, 317.

98. "The Rutherford History Report," *Confederate Veteran,* August 1922, 285; *Butler Weekly Times and the Bates County Record,* June 29, 1922.

99. "That Lincoln Resolution—and Some Other Things," *Confederate Veteran,* August 1922, 285.

100. Archibald A. Pearson to the *Confederate Veteran*, November 6, 1922, Alphabetical File, United Confederate Veterans, Missouri Historical Society.

101. *Evening Star*, October 31, 1922. See also *Albuquerque Morning Journal*, November 1, 1922.

102. Archibald A. Pearson to the *Confederate Veteran*, November 6, 1922, Alphabetical File, United Confederate Veterans, Missouri Historical Society.

103. "Mrs. W. Dolan" to "Miss Pope," February 20, 1923, Alphabetical File, United Confederate Veterans, Missouri Historical Society.

Five: "The Recuperative Powers of Missouri"

Epigraph. "Unofficial Proceedings," in *Proceedings of the Ninth Annual Encampment of the Department of Missouri, GAR*, 156.

1. T. D. Kimball, "Address of the Department Commander," in *Proceedings of the Twenty-Seventh Annual Encampment of the Department of Missouri, GAR*, 29.

2. Morrison and Sharples, *History of the Kimball Family in America*, 728.

3. T. D. Kimball, "Address of the Department Commander," in *Proceedings of the Twenty-Seventh Annual Encampment of the Department of Missouri, GAR*, 29.

4. Blight, *Race and Reunion, 127.*

5. Janney, *Remembering the Civil War*, 6.

6. According to Paul H. Buck, reconciliation between the North and South was accomplished by 1880. Many different factors helped facilitate reconciliation, including generational change, migration, and shared political and economic interests. See Buck, *The Road to Reunion*.

7. Reconciliation was often expressed as a metaphorical marriage between the "willful feminine entity of Dixie" and the masculine, industrious Yankee. See Silber, *The Romance of Reunion*, 6–7.

8. Gannon, *The Won Cause*, 5–8; Janney, *Remembering the Civil War*, 7–9.

9. Neely, "The Quantrill Men Reunions," 245–246. See also Stanley, *The Loyal West*, 154.

10. Neff, *Honoring the Civil War Dead*, 5; Janney, *Remembering the Civil War*, 7.

11. Neely, "The Quantrill Men Reunions," 257.

12. Neely, *The Border between Them*, 246, 252.

13. Astor, *Rebels on the Border*, 199.

14. Buck, *The Road to Reunion*, viii, 310, 318–319.

15. Buck, *The Road to Reunion*, 318–319; Silber, *The Romance of Reunion*, 162.

16. "Response to Address of Welcome by Comrade Col. George P. Gross, Asst. Adjt. Gen. of Missouri Division, U. C. V.," in *Official Proceedings of Thirteenth Annual Reunion of Missouri Division, United Confederate Veterans*, 54.

17. *Proceedings of the Twenty-Second Annual Encampment of the Department of Missouri, GAR*, 3–4.

18. Silber, *The Romance of Reunion*, 172, 174–175, 180. See also McConnell, *Glorious Contentment*, 209–219.

19. Silber, *The Romance of Reunion*, 187. See also Buck, *The Road to Reunion*, 255.

20. Frederick Jackson Turner, "The Significance of the Frontier in American History," in Faragher, ed., *Rereading Frederick Jackson Turner*, 31, 53.

21. Frederick Jackson Turner, "The Problem of the West" in Faragher, ed., *Rereading Frederick Jackson Turner*, 70, 67.

22. Silber, *The Romance of Reunion*, 168.

23. Veterans in the lower Midwest similarly foregrounded their western identity as a basis for reconciliation. See Stanley, *The Loyal West*, 171–172.

24. *Report of the Proceedings of the Ex-Confederate Association of Missouri, in Its Seventh Annual Meeting*, 7, 10.

25. *Proceedings of the Fourteenth Annual Encampment of the Department of Missouri, GAR*, 90, 92.

26. *Official Proceedings of Sixth Annual Reunion of Missouri Division United Confederate Veterans*, 32.

27. Evocations of antebellum conservative Unionism also proved effective in promoting reconciliation in the states of the lower Midwest. See Stanley, *The Loyal West*, 154–161.

28. "Unofficial Proceedings," in *Proceedings of the Ninth Annual Encampment of the Department of Missouri, GAR*, 156.

29. *Report of the Proceedings of the Ex-Confederate Association of Missouri, in Its Ninth Annual Meeting*, 1891, 9.

30. *Proceedings of the Twenty-Fifth Annual Encampment of the Department of Missouri, Grand Army of the Republic*, 1906, 5–6.

31. Peter S. Carmichael argues that wartime fraternization has been too readily dismissed by historians intent on countering romanticized and sanitized accounts of the Civil War. See Carmichael, *The War for the Common Soldier*, 247.

32. Buck, *The Road to Reunion*, 245, 255.

33. Oliver Wendell Holmes, Jr., "The Soldier's Faith," in Holmes, *An Address by Oliver Wendell Holmes,* 11. For more on the role of manhood in the context of the GAR, see McConnell, *Glorious Contentment*, 106–107, 123. See also Handley-Cousins, *Bodies in Blue*, 3–4.

34. *Official Proceedings of Fifth Annual Reunion of Missouri Division United Confederate Veterans*, 72, 82.

35. *Proceedings of the Twenty-Second Annual Encampment of the Department of Missouri, GAR*, 4.

36. *Circular Series: Grand Army of the Republic, Department of Missouri, Ransom Post No. 131*, series 1912, no. 10 (June 6, 1912).

37. Reconciliation also exerted a powerful appeal in the states of the lower Midwest. See Stanley, *The Loyal West*, 161–174.

38. Hacker, "A Census-Based Count of the Civil War Dead," 307.

39. Neff, *Honoring the Civil War Dead*, 244.

40. Janney, *Burying the Dead but Not the Past.*

41. Neff, *Honoring the Civil War Dead*, 231.

42. Capt. N. B. Hogan, "Missouri Confederate Monument," *Confederate Veteran,* July 1901, 291.

43. Unidentified, undated news clipping, reprinted from *Springfield Leader*, 1870, Historical Sketch and Newspaper Clippings, Springfield, MO, Confederate Cemetery, Civil War Collection, Missouri Historical Society.

44. Unidentified, undated history of cemetery, Historical Sketch and Newspaper Clippings, Springfield, MO, Confederate Cemetery, Civil War Collection.

45. "Former Meetings of the Association," *Missouri Republican*, October 14, 1885, quoted in *Report of the Proceedings of the Ex-Confederate Association of Missouri, in Its Fourth Annual Meeting*, 17.

46. Unidentified, undated history of cemetery, Historical Sketch and Newspaper Clippings, Springfield, MO, Confederate Cemetery, Civil War Collection.

47. Unidentified, undated history of cemetery, Historical Sketch and Newspaper Clippings, Springfield, MO, Confederate Cemetery, Civil War Collection.

48. Hogan, "Missouri Confederate Monument," 292.

49. *Windsor Review*, May 11, 1883.

50. *Report of the Proceedings of the Ex-Confederate Association of Missouri, in Its Second Annual Meeting*, 12.

51. *Report of the Proceedings of the Ex-Confederate Association of Missouri, in Its Fourth Annual Meeting*, 9.

52. *Windsor Review*, May 11, 1883.

53. "Former Meetings of the Association," in *Report of the Proceedings of the Ex-Confederate Association of Missouri, in Its Fourth Annual Meeting*, 17; *Union Record*, September 6, 1883; *Indian Chieftain*, June 2, 1887.

54. *Proceedings of the Sixth Annual Encampment of the Department of Missouri, GAR*, 106.

55. *Sedalia Weekly Bazoo*, June 9, 1891.

56. United Confederate Veterans, Campbell Camp No. 488, Springfield, MO, Records, 1894–1915, vol. 1, December 2, 1899; April 7, 1900; April 6, 1901; December 6, 1902, The State Historical Society of Missouri.

57. *Springfield Leader and Press*, February 5, 1900.

58. Hogan, "Missouri Confederate Monument," 293.

59. Laura Doan Steele, "To Complete Monument, Springfield, MO," *Confederate Veteran*, February 1901, 57.

60. "United Sons of Confederates in Missouri," *Confederate Veteran*, August 1901, 349.

61. *Official Proceedings of Fifth Annual Reunion of Missouri Division United Confederate Veterans*, 67, 68–69.

62. United Confederate Veterans, Campbell Camp No. 488, Springfield, MO, Records, 1894–1915, vol. 1, June 3, 1902, The State Historical Society of Missouri.

63. *Marshall Republican*, April 20, 1900.

64. *Mexico Weekly Ledger*, October 1, 1903.

65. "Reunion of Missouri Confederates," *Confederate Veteran*, November 1903, 491.

66. *Mexico Missouri Message*, September 26, 1907.

67. United Confederate Veterans, Campbell Camp No. 488, Springfield, MO, Record Book, 1903–1919, September 3, 21, 1904, The State Historical Society of Missouri.

68. Minnie B. Roberts, "Report of Springfield Chapter No. 625," in *Proceedings of the Tenth Annual Convention of the Missouri Division, United Daughters of the Confederacy*, 84.

69. The Confederate cemetery in Little Rock, Arkansas, became the second. It was incorporated into Fort Smith National Cemetery in 1913.

70. *Rich Hill Tribune*, October 17, 1907.

71. *Mexico Weekly Ledger*, September 26, 1907; *Official Proceedings of Fifteenth Annual Reunion of Missouri Division, United Confederate Veterans*, 1911, 26.

72. For the Henry County Veterans' Association, see *Henry County Republican*, October 6, 1898; *Henry County Democrat*, September 29, 1899; August 31, 1900; and Henry County Veteran's Association, Program, The State Historical Society of Missouri. For the Johnson County Veteran Association of the Blue and Gray, see *Windsor Review*, September 1, 1898. For the Taney County Veterans' Association, see *Taney County Republican*, September 21, 1899. For the Old Soldiers and Old Settlers' Reunion Association, see *Laclede Blade*, September 19, 1903.

73. The Old Soldiers' Association of the Blue and Gray was known variously as the Blue and Gray Association, Veteran Soldiers' Association, and Blue and Gray Veterans' Association; see *Kansas City Journal*, June 23, September 25, 1898.

74. Arenson, *The Great Heart of the Republic*, 132; Berger, *St. Louis and Empire*, 40–42; Gerteis, *Civil War St. Louis*, 175–177.

75. St. Louis elites had long cherished a vision of their city as the launching point of a prospective American Empire, but that vision gained renewed interest in the aftermath of the Civil War. See Berger, *St. Louis and Empire*, 2–4.

76. Christensen and Kremer, *A History of Missouri*, 42–43, 86; Berger, *St. Louis and Empire*, 42.

77. Parrish, *A History of Missouri*, 223; Christensen and Kremer, *A History of Missouri*, 43.

78. Christensen and Kremer, *A History of Missouri*, 43, 89.

79. Arenson, *The Great Heart of the Republic*, 155, 162.

80. Jeremy Neely argues that economic, particularly class, interests acted as a similarly essential component of reconciliation between Missouri and Kansas. Mutual interests forged over debates about railroad expansion and the emergence of "Corn Belt agriculture," Neely writes, rendered "long-standing differences between Kansans and Missourians . . . no longer as obvious or meaningful by the end of the nineteenth century." Neely, *The Border between Them*, 4, 173, 206–207, 240. See also SenGupta, *For God and Mammon*, 140–157; and Cook, *Civil War Memories*, 6.

81. *Report of the Proceedings of the Ex-Confederate Association of Missouri, in Its Ninth Annual Meeting*, 17–18, 11.

82. *Kansas City Journal*, October 10, 1898.

83. *Proceedings of the First Annual Encampment of the Department of Missouri, GAR*, 5.

84. *St. Louis Republic*, October 19, 1896.

85. Minutes, October 10, 1896, Veterans of the Blue and Gray Records, Minute Book, 1896–1900, vol. 1, 1, Missouri Historical Society.

86. *St. Louis Republic*, October 20, 1896.

87. "Report of the 1st Annual Banquet," Veterans of the Blue and Gray Records, Minute Book, 47.

88. Leonard, ed., *The Book of St. Louisans*, 124–125, 135–136, 321–322. For more on Seth W. Cobb, see Berger, *St. Louis and Empire*, 54–55.

89. Veterans of the Blue and Gray Records, Roster, 1897–1899, vol. 2.

90. McConachie, "The 'Big Cinch,'" 35, 57–59, 63, 71, 77.

91. Unsigned letter, June 10, 1897, Veterans of the Blue and Gray Records, Minute Book, 60.

92. Charles G. Warner and Joseph Boyce to "Dear Sir," October 15, 1896, Veterans of the Blue and Gray Records, Minute Book, 3.

93. McConnell, *Glorious Contentment*, 117–118.

94. *St. Louis Republic*, October 22, 1896.

95. "Minutes of the Annual Meeting," February 22, 1897, Veterans of the Blue and Gray Records, Minute Book, 38.

96. "Report of the 1st Annual Banquet," 51.

97. "Report of the 1st Annual Banquet," 47.

98. Minutes, November 26, 1896, Veterans of the Blue and Gray Records, Minute Book, 11.

99. Minutes, December 10, 1896, Veterans of the Blue and Gray Records, Minute Book, 18.

100. Unsigned letter, June 10, 1897, Veterans of the Blue and Gray Records, Minute Book, 60.

101. *St. Louis Globe-Democrat*, February 14, 1899.

102. "Report of the Executive Committee," February 12, 1900, Veterans of the Blue and Gray Records, Minute Book, 99.

103. E. D. Meier to Col. Henry Hitchcock, January 6, 1900, Veterans of the Blue and Gray Records, Minute Book, 87.

104. Coulter, *"Take Up the Black Man's Burden,"* 26.

105. Schirmer, *A City Divided*, 27; Shortridge, *Kanas City and How It Grew*, 29–60.

106. *Missouri of Today*, 181.

107. Christensen and Kremer, *A History of Missouri*, 89–90.

108. Dorsett, *The Pendergast Machine*, 3–32.

109. *Kansas City Journal*, June 23, 30, September 9, October 30, 1898.

110. *Kansas City Journal*, October 10, 1898.

111. *Kansas City Journal*, September 15, 20, 25, 1898.

112. *Kansas City Journal*, August 30, 1898.

113. *Kansas City Journal*, August 4, 1898; May 10, 1899.

114. *Kanas City Journal*, August 18, 1898.

115. *Kansas City Journal*, November 5, 1898.

116. Coulter, *"Take Up the Black Man's Burden,"* 26.

117. Coulter, *"Take Up the Black Man's Burden,"* 25, 52, 53; Schirmer, *A City Divided*, 30, 34–35; McKerley, "Citizens and Strangers," 215–228.

118. *Kansas City Journal*, July 21, 1898.

119. *Kansas City Journal*, September 20, 1898.

120. *Kansas City Journal*, October 2, 1898.

121. *Kansas City Journal*, November 10, 1898.

122. *Kansas City Journal*, September 24, 1898.

123. *Kansas City Journal*, November 5, 1898.

124. *Kansas City Journal*, November 8, 1898.

125. The proposed national reunion in Washington, DC, never took place. There was, however, a national reunion in Evansville, Indiana, in October 1899 and another in Atlanta in July 1900. At the Atlanta reunion, the limits of reconciliationist rhetoric were on full display. When John B. Gordon, one of the nation's most prominent ex-Confederates, insisted he would not teach his children the Confederacy had been wrong, Union veterans despaired of reconciliation. See *National Tribune*, July 26, August 30, 1900.

126. *Kansas City Journal*, October 10, 1898.

127. *Kansas City Journal*, October 10, 1898.

128. *Kansas City Journal*, October 10, 1898.

129. It is important to note that Missourians, particularly within the UDC, donated to monument funds all over the country. For example, the Missouri Division UDC helped raise money for a Confederate monument at Shiloh National Military Park that was dedicated just months before the Vicksburg monument described

here. In that sense, Missourians were represented at the national military parks. The important distinction, however, is that the Shiloh monument—like the others to which Missourians may have contributed—was not a Missouri monument specifically.

130. *Proceedings of the Twenty-Fifth Annual Encampment of the Department of Missouri, GAR*, 7.

131. Henry Fairback, "Address of the Department Commander," in *Proceedings of the Twenty-Fifth Annual Encampment of the Department of Missouri, GAR*, 25.

132. *Sedalia Weekly Conservator*, January 20, February 10, 1905; *Farmington Times and Herald*, February 10, 1905.

133. John M. Williams, "Address of the Department Commander," in *Proceedings of the Twenty-Sixth Annual Encampment of the Department of Missouri, Grand Army of the Republic*, 1907, 22.

134. *Proceedings of the Thirtieth Annual Encampment of the Department of Missouri, Grand Army of the Republic*, 1911, 44–45.

135. *Proceedings of the Thirtieth Annual Encampment of the Department of Missouri, GAR*, 45; Leo Rassieur to Capt. William T. Rigby, November 18, 1914, Missouri-Vicksburg National Military Park Commissioner's Minute Book, Missouri Historical Society.

136. Walker and Riggs, *Vicksburg Battlefield Monuments*, 44. In 1910, New York dedicated its "Peace Monument" on Lookout Mountain at Chickamauga and Chattanooga National Military Park. Topped by figures of a Union and a Confederate veteran shaking hands, it was one of the earliest reconciliationist battlefield monuments. See Hattaway, *Gettysburg to Vicksburg*, 61.

137. "Program for a Competition for the Erection of a Missouri Monument on the Vicksburg Battlefield by the State of Missouri," December 30, 1911, Missouri-Vicksburg National Military Park Commissioner's Minute Book, 9.

138. "Report of the Missouri-Vicksburg National Military Park Commission," Missouri-Vicksburg National Military Park Commissioner's Minute Book, 4.

139. Walker and Riggs, *Vicksburg Battlefield Monuments*, 44.

140. "Report of the Missouri-Vicksburg National Military Park Commission," 10.

141. *St. Louis Star and Times*, October 16, 1917.

142. *Vicksburg Evening Post*, October 17, 1917; *Vicksburg Herald*, October 19, 1917. See also *St. Louis Post-Dispatch*, October 15, 1917.

143. *St. Louis Star and Times*, October 16, 1917.

Six: "Tender of Both Uniforms"

Epigraph. Hale v. Stimson, in Rader, *Reports of Cases Determined in the Supreme Court of the State of Missouri*, 198:162–163.

1. "Charles H. Vandiver," *St. Louis Republic*, quoted in *Confederate Veteran*, February 1912, 78–79.

2. Hon. C. H. Vandiver, "Soldier's Homes in Missouri," *Confederate Veteran*, April 1897, 180.

3. "Homes for the Veterans."

4. Vandiver, "Soldier's Homes in Missouri," 179.

5. *Palmyra Spectator*, February 18, 1897.

6. *Official Proceedings of First Annual Reunion of Missouri Division, United Confederate Veterans,* 1897, 20.

7. "The War Is Over," *Iron County Register*, February 18, 1897.

8. *Palmyra Spectator*, February 18, 1897.

9. Rosenburg, *Living Monuments*; Marten, *Sing Not War*; McConnell, *Glorious Contentment.*

10. Rosenburg, *Living Monuments*, 3.

11. Rosenburg, *Living Monuments*, 4.

12. Abraham Lincoln, "Second Inaugural Address," March 4, 1865, in Basler, ed., *The Collected Works of Abraham Lincoln*, 3:332–333.

13. *Journal of the House of Representatives of the Thirty-Fourth General Assembly of the State of Missouri (Regular Session), 1887* (Jefferson City, MO: Tribune, 1887), 75.

14. *Holt County Sentinel*, January 28, 1887.

15. *Holt County Sentinel*, February 4, 1887.

16. *Proceedings of the Sixth Annual Encampment of the Department of Missouri, GAR*, 88–91.

17. John T. Daniel, Missouri, Sixth District, August 1863, vol. 1, 92, Consolidated Lists of Civil War Draft Registration Records, Records of the Provost Marshal General's Bureau, Record Group 110, National Archives and Records Administration, www.Ancestry.com.

18. Rosenburg, *Living Monuments*, 14; Handley-Cousins, *Bodies in Blue*, 3–4, 95–113.

19. *St. Joseph Weekly Gazette*, February 24, 1887.

20. *Butler Weekly Times*, March 2, 1887.

21. Handley-Cousins, *Bodies in Blue*, 99–100.

22. *St. Joseph Weekly Gazette*, February 24, 1887.

23. *Journal of the House of Representatives of the Thirty-Fourth General Assembly of the State of Missouri*, 546–547.

24. *Boonville Weekly Advertiser*, January 2, 1891; January 5, 1894.

25. W. P. Barlow, "History of the Missouri Confederate Home," *Confederate Veteran,* October 1893, 302.

26. "Report of State Confederate Home, Higginsville, Lafayette County," in *Journal of the House and Senate*, 42nd General Assembly, appendix, 1903, 66, General Assembly, State Documents, Missouri State Archives.

27. *Sedalia Weekly Bazoo*, June 9, 1891.

28. Barlow, "History of the Missouri Confederate Home," 302.

29. O. H. P. Catron, "Confederate Home in Missouri," *Confederate Veteran,* February l896, 61.

30. Cox, *Dixie's Daughters*, 73–74.

31. *Boonville Weekly Advertiser*, January 2, 1891.

32. Cox, *Dixie's Daughters*, 9–10.

33. Barlow, "History of the Missouri Confederate Home," 302.

34. Poppenheim et al., *The History of the United Daughters of the Confederacy*, 3. See also Cox, *Dixie's Daughters*, 15–16.

35. Barlow, "History of the Missouri Confederate Home," 302.

36. Barlow, "History of the Missouri Confederate Home," 302. For more on the role of the Daughters in establishing the Confederate Home, see Boccardi, "Remembering in Black and White," 172–178.

37. Catron, "Confederate Home in Missouri," 61.

38. Cox, *Dixie's Daughters*, 73–76.

39. Ankesheiln, *The Heart Is the Heritage*, 15.

40. *Report of the Proceedings of the Ex-Confederate Association of Missouri, in Its Ninth Annual Meeting*, 23. See also *Missouri of Today*, 47.

41. Silber, *The Romance of Reunion*.

42. Typescript from *St. Louis Republic*, August 17, 1891, Alphabetical File, United Daughters of the Confederacy, folder 1, Missouri Historical Society.

43. *Boonville Weekly Advertiser*, July 10, 1891; "History of the Confederate Home of Higginsville, Missouri," 1, Missouri Confederate Home, Higginsville, History and Cemetery Records, n.d., The State Historical Society of Missouri; Mrs. Bernard C. Hunt, "The Confederate Home of Missouri," *Confederate Veteran*, August 1928, 299–301.

44. "History of the Confederate Home of Higginsville," 1.

45. *Boonville Weekly Advertiser*, July 10, 1891.

46. *Sedalia Weekly Bazoo*, June 9, 1891.

47. Barlow, "History of the Missouri Confederate Home," 302.

48. *Chariton Courier*, December 25, 1890.

49. *Proceedings of the Eleventh Annual Encampment of the Department of Missouri, GAR*, 115.

50. *Cape Girardeau Democrat*, September 19, 1891.

51. *Sedalia Weekly Bazoo*, May 5, 1891.

52. There were cottages named in honor of John S. Bowen, William Y. Slack, Mosby M. Parsons, Henry Little, and Martin E. Greene; see Hunt, "The Confederate Home of Missouri," 299; "History of the Confederate Home of Higginsville," 3; Ankesheiln, *The Heart Is the Heritage*, 44; and "Third Biennial Report of the Board of Managers for the Years 1901 and 1902 of the Confederate Home of Missouri," in *Journal of the House and Senate*, 42nd General Assembly, appendix, 1903, 41.

53. *Report of the Seventh Annual Convention of the Missouri Division United Daughters of the Confederacy Held at St. Louis, Mo., October 10th, and 11th, 1904* (Marshall, MO: Democrat-News, n.d.), 36.

54. *Missouri of Today*, 13, 19, 43.

55. *Journal of the House and Senate*, 44th General Assembly, appendix, 1907, 49, General Assembly, State Documents.

56. *State Republican*, February 6, 1896.

57. "Establishing a Real Home for Missouri Confederate Veterans," *Kansas City Journal-Post*, November 12, 1922, Gubernatorial Series, Confederate Soldiers

Home, Higginsville, 1922, Arthur Mastick Hyde Papers, The State Historical Society of Missouri.

58. "Flags at the Confederate Home."

59. Samuel B. Shirky, "Fourteenth Biennial Report of the Confederate Soldiers' Home of Missouri," in *Journal of the House and Senate*, 53rd General Assembly, appendix, 1925, 6, General Assembly, State Documents.

60. Armstrong, *History of the State Federal Soldiers' Home*, 159, 37.

61. Armstrong, *History of the State Federal Soldiers' Home*, 46.

62. *Proceedings of the Twelfth Annual Encampment of the Department of Missouri, GAR*, 139.

63. Armstrong, *History of the State Federal Soldiers' Home*, 98.

64. Louis Benecke to Scott Sherman, Esq., November 20, 1895, Benecke Family, G.A.R., Dept. of Mo.—Letterbook, 1895–1903, Benecke Family Papers.

65. Armstrong, *History of the State Federal Soldiers' Home*, 54.

66. Armstrong, *History of the State Federal Soldiers' Home*, 56.

67. Dr. Clair V. Mann, "The Story of Dunmoor: Former Home of the William James Family," 1963, 3, Clair V. Mann Collection, The State Historical Society of Missouri; "First Biennial Report of the Board of Trustees of the Federal Soldiers' Home, at St. James, MO," in *Journal of the House and Senate*, 40th General Assembly, appendix, 1899, 4, General Assembly, State Documents; Briggs, "Circular Letter, No. 1," Benecke Family Papers; "The Relief Corps, Gleanings from National Headquarters—Notes from Departments," *National Tribune*, August 22, 1895.

68. Hernando, *Faces Like Devils*, 10–17.

69. Armstrong, *History of the State Federal Soldiers' Home*, 38, 65, 61.

70. Armstrong, *History of the State Federal Soldiers' Home*, 62.

71. Briggs, "Circular Letter, No. 1," Benecke Family Papers.

72. Armstrong, *History of the State Federal Soldiers' Home*, 65.

73. *St. Paul Globe*, October 26, 1896.

74. Mann, "The Story of Dunmoor," 7; "Death List Eight," *St. Paul Globe*, October 26, 1896.

75. *St. James Journal*, October 30, 1896.

76. Mann, "The Story of Dunmoor," 6.

77. *St. James Journal*, October 30, 1896.

78. *Taney County Republican*, January 24, 1907.

79. "The Federal Soldiers' Home of Missouri," Federal Soldiers' Home—Benecke Correspondence, 1897, Benecke Family Papers. The Federal Home changed its residency requirement to two years in 1923.

80. State Guard veterans were only admitted if they were physically disabled. Able-bodied State Guard veterans were refused admission as late as 1904; see "Rules for Admission of Inmates," in "Biennial Report, Confederate Home," in *Journal of the House and Senate*, 45th General Assembly, appendix, 1909, 6, General Assembly, State Documents.

81. Levings, "How William Quantrill Wound Up with Three Graves."

82. Levings, "How William Quantrill Wound Up with Three Graves."

83. "Seventh Biennial Report of the Board of Trustees and Officers of the Federal Soldiers' Home, St. James, Mo," in *Journal of the House and Senate*, 46th General Assembly, vol. 1, appendix, 1911, 6–7, General Assembly, State Documents.

84. W. F. Henry to Louis Benecke, December 20, 1911, Benecke Family, Federal Soldiers' Home—Benecke Correspondence, December 1911, Benecke Family Papers.

85. Parrish, *Turbulent Partnership*, 92–96.

86. C. H. Anthony to Louis Benecke, November 6, 1900, Federal Soldiers' Home—Benecke Correspondence, November 1900, Benecke Family Papers (expletive removed in original).

87. *Missouri of Today*, 29.

88. Greene, Holland, and Kremer, "The Role of the Negro in Missouri History," 11. For more on the experiences of black veterans in the National Home, see Shaffer, *After the Glory*.

89. Jerry Keller to Louis Benecke, November 14, 1900, Benecke Family, Federal Soldiers' Home—Benecke Correspondence, November 1900, Benecke Family Papers.

90. Frederick B[o]kamper, Missouri Veterans Home (St. James) Inmate Registers, vol. 1, 143, Office of Adjutant General, Record Group 133, Missouri State Archives.

91. F. T. Lane, "State Eleemosynary Institutions—What They Provide and What They Do Not Provide for the Negro," *Monthly Bulletin: State Board of Charities and Corrections* 24, no. 3 (January 1922): 89, Department of Corrections Documents Collection, 1879–present, Missouri State Archives.

92. Lane, "State Eleemosynary Institutions," 88.

93. Rosenburg, *Living Monuments*, 136.

94. "Reports and Minutes," June 1, 1952, Missouri Confederate Home, Higginsville, Records, 1897–1944, The State Historical Society of Missouri.

95. Mrs. B. R. Ireland, "Another Account of the Dedication," *Confederate Veteran*, July 1906, 295.

96. Ankesheiln, *The Heart Is the Heritage*, 102.

97. "Federal Soldiers' Home, St. James," in *Journal of the House and Senate*, 63rd General Assembly, appendix, 1945, 59, General Assembly, State Documents.

98. "History of the National Home for Disabled Soldiers."

99. Minutes, Confederate Home Board, January 2, 1932, 6, Missouri Confederate Home, Higginsville, Records.

100. *Boonville Weekly Advertiser*, January 2, 1891.

101. "Second Biennial Report of the State Board of Charities and Corrections," in *Journal of the House and Senate*, 40th General Assembly, appendix, 1901, 47–48.

102. Maj. Harvey W. Salmon, "The Confederate Home of Missouri," *Confederate Veteran*, September 1919, 331; Vandiver, "Soldier's Homes in Missouri," 179.

103. J. W. Halliburton, "Aid by States to Confederate Survivors," *Confederate Veteran*, June 1902, 254.

104. W. F. Henry, "Report of Superintendent, Federal Soldiers' Home of Missouri, St. James, December 31, 1912," in "Eighth Biennial Report of the Board of

Trustees and Officers of the Federal Soldiers' Home, St. James, Missouri," in *Journal of the House and Senate*, 47th General Assembly, vol. 2, appendix, 1913, 10, General Assembly, State Documents.

105. "History of the Confederate Home of Higginsville," 1–2; "General Information at Confederate Memorial State Historic Site"; *Boonville Weekly Advertiser*, July 13, 1894; "Eighth Biennial Report of the Board of Trustees and Officers of the Federal Soldiers' Home, St. James," 5; "Seventh Biennial Report of the Board of Trustees and Officers of the Federal Soldiers' Home," 5.

106. "Kindly Regard This as a Veteran's Personal Message to You," May 1903, Benecke Family, Federal Soldiers' Home—Benecke Correspondence, 1903, Benecke Family Papers.

107. *Report of the Proceedings of the Ex-Confederate Association of Missouri, in Its Ninth Annual Meeting*, 16, 12.

108. Ira T. Bronson, "Address of the Department Commander," in *Proceedings of the Twenty-Second Annual Encampment of the Department of Missouri, GAR*, 20.

109. Jacob A. Roof to G. W. Roof, February 18, 1902, in "Missouri's Solders' Home," *St. James Journal*, n.d., Federal Soldiers' Home—News Clippings, 1899–1902, Benecke Family Papers.

110. Louis Benecke to Hon. B. Russell, September 24, 1898, Federal Soldiers' Home—Benecke Letterbook, 1897–1901, Benecke Family Papers.

111. "Reports and Minutes," May 2, 1932, Missouri Confederate Home, Higginsville, Records.

112. Louis Benecke to Frances M. Wheeler, July 12, 1898, Federal Soldiers' Home—Benecke Letterbook, 1897–1901, Benecke Family Papers.

113. "Reports and Minutes," April 1; November 1, 1932, Missouri Confederate Home, Higginsville, Records.

114. "Rusty-Cuss" to Arthur Mastick Hyde, Federal Soldiers' Home, St. James, 1921–1922, Gubernatorial Series, Arthur Mastick Hyde Papers; Fred M. Tate to Hon. Jesse W. Barrett, March 22, 1922, Federal Soldiers' Home, St. James, 1921–1922, Gubernatorial Series, Arthur Mastick Hyde Papers.

115. Louis Benecke to Frances M. Wheeler, July 14, 1900, Federal Soldiers' Home—Benecke Letterbook, 1897–1901, Benecke Family Papers.

116. "Third Biennial Report of the Board of Managers for the Years 1901 and 1902," 38.

117. Dean, *Shook over Hell*; Jordan, *Marching Home*.

118. "Third Biennial Report of the Board of Managers for the Years 1901 and 1902," 8.

119. "Third Biennial Report of the Board of Managers for the Years 1901 and 1902," 8; "Eighth Biennial Report of the Board of Managers of the Confederate Soldiers' Home of Missouri at Higginsville," in *Journal of the House and Senate*, 47th General Assembly, vol. 2, appendix, 1913, 20–21; "Tenth Biennial Report of the Board of Managers of the Confederate Soldiers' Home of Missouri at Higginsville," in *Journal of the House and Senate*, 49th General Assembly, vol. 2, appendix, 1917,

19, General Assembly, State Documents; "Eleventh Biennial Report of the Board of Managers of the Confederate Soldiers' Home of Missouri at Higginsville," in *Journal of the House and Senate*, 50th General Assembly, vol. 3, appendix, 1918, 18, General Assembly, State Documents.

120. Missouri Constitution (1875), art. 8, sec. 8, Missouri Constitutions, 1820–1945. Soldiers on active duty could not vote either; see sec. 11.

121. "Elections: Qualifications of Voters," sec. 4670, in *Laws of Missouri Passed at the Session of the Thirty-Ninth General Assembly*, 109–110.

122. Stevens, *Centennial History of Missouri*, 242–243.

123. *Rich Hill Tribune*, December 8, 1904. See also "Restored Honor to Outraged Veterans," *Montgomery Tribune*, July 13, 1906.

124. W. N. Evans, quoted in unidentified newspaper article, Federal Soldiers' Home—News Clippings, 1899–1902, Benecke Family Papers.

125. J. W. Farris to the Editor of the *Post-Dispatch*, "Farris Defends Soldiers' Right to the Ballot," n.d., Federal Soldier's Home—News Clippings, 1903–1910, Benecke Family Papers.

126. *Rich Hill Tribune*, December 8, 1904.

127. "Claim Right to Vote," Federal Soldiers' Home—News Clippings, 1903–1910, Benecke Family Papers.

128. Fairback, "Address of the Department Commander," 25.

129. Circular Letter No. 1, July 28, 1905, Grand Army of the Republic, Erich Pape Post No. 184 Records, 1865–1913, The State Historical Society of Missouri.

130. T. A. Sherwood, quoted in unidentified newspaper article, Federal Soldiers' Home—News Clippings, 1899–1902, Benecke Family Papers.

131. It is not clear whether the veterans were allowed to vote in the intervening two years.

132. *Hale v. Stimson*, in Rader, *Reports of Cases Determined in the Supreme Court of the State of Missouri*, 134–166; "Entitled to a Vote," *Mexico Missouri Message*, July 12, 1906.

133. It appears that women did continue to serve on the board of the Confederate Home; see Unknown to Gen. Frank M. Sterrill, Federal Soldiers' Home—G.A.R. Committee Reports, 1904, Benecke Family Papers.

134. Armstrong, *History of the State Federal Soldiers' Home*, 103, 114, 110.

135. "Third Biennial Report of the Board of Trustees and Officers, Federal Soldiers' Home, St. James, Mo.," in *Journal of the House and Senate*, 42nd General Assembly, appendix, 1903, 8.

136. "Seventh Biennial Report of the Board of Trustees and Officers of the Federal Soldiers' Home," 12.

137. At the Confederate Home, the ratio of men to women was more like five to one; see "Confederate Soldiers Home," in "Report of the Committee Appointed by Governor Elliott W. Major to Visit the State Institutions of Missouri," 48th General Assembly, 1915, 40, General Assembly, State Documents.

138. Armstrong, *History of the State Federal Soldiers' Home*, 107.

139. "Why Widows Are Excluded," *Scott County Kicker*, August 27, 1910. In 1903, widows were admitted; in 1910, they were prohibited again, but in 1923 they were welcomed back. That policy stayed in place at least until 1945.

140. S. D. Webster, "President's Report," in "Fourteenth Biennial Report of State Federal Soldiers' Home," in *Journal of the House and Senate*, 53rd General Assembly, vol. 2, appendix, 1925, 6.

141. Armstrong, *History of the State Federal Soldiers' Home*, 93, 104.

142. B. Falkenhaimer to Louis Benecke, February 18, 1911, Federal Soldiers' Home—Benecke Correspondence, February–March 1911, Benecke Family Papers.

143. Henry Fairback to Louis Benecke, July 9, 1911, Federal Soldiers' Home—Benecke Correspondence, July 1911, Benecke Family Papers.

144. Armstrong, *History of the State Federal Soldiers' Home*, 101, 94, 104.

145. "Sixteenth Biennial Report of the State Federal Soldiers' Home," in *Journal of the House and Senate*, 55th General Assembly, vol. 2, appendix, 1929, 11, General Assembly, State Documents.

146. Armstrong, *History of the State Federal Soldiers' Home*, 79.

147. "Third Biennial Report of the Board of Trustees and Officers, Federal Soldiers' Home, St. James, Mo," 8.

148. "Ex-Confederate Reunion," *Kansas City Daily Journal*, August 22, 1895.

149. J. W. Halliburton, "Missouri Daughters to Build Monument," *Confederate Veteran,* April 1906, 179. See also Boccardi, "Remembering in Black and White," 182–185.

150. T. R. Carr, "Confederate Monument, Higginsville, MO.," *Confederate Veteran,* July 1906, 294.

151. "General Suggestions: Confederate Home, Higginsville," in "Report of the Committee Appointed to Visit the State Institutions," in *Journal of the House and Senate*, 51st General Assembly, 1921, 38, General Assembly, State Documents; F. H. Chambers, "Superintendent's Report," December 1, 1922, in "Thirteenth Biennial Report of Confederate Soldiers Home of Missouri," in *Journal of the House and Senate*, 52nd General Assembly, appendix, 1921–1922, 16–19, General Assembly, State Documents.

152. "Eighth Biennial Report of the Board of Trustees and Officers of the Federal Soldiers' Home, St. James," 10; Howard Gray to Arthur Mastick Hyde, May 27, 1921, Confederate Soldiers Home, Higginsville, 1920–May 1921, Gubernatorial Series, Arthur Mastick Hyde Papers.

153. Howard Gray to Arthur Mastick Hyde, May 27, 1921, Confederate Soldiers Home, Higginsville, 1920–May 1921, Gubernatorial Series, Arthur Mastick Hyde Papers.

154. Arthur Mastick Hyde to Hon. M. E. Benton, March 2, 1921, Confederate Soldiers Home, Higginsville, 1920–May 1921, Gubernatorial Series, Arthur Mastick Hyde Papers.

155. M. E. Benton to Governor A. M. Hyde, March 1, 1921, Confederate Soldiers Home, Higginsville, 1920–May 1921, Gubernatorial Series, Arthur Mastick Hyde Papers.

156. Hunt, "The Confederate Home of Missouri," 301.

157. "Fifteenth Biennial Report of the Confederate Soldiers' Home of Missouri," in *Journal of the House and Senate*, 54th General Assembly, vol. 2, appendix, 1927, 11, General Assembly, State Documents.

158. "Board of Trustees of Confederate Home," *Higginsville Advance*, November 21, 1924, Confederate Soldiers Home, Higginsville, 1924–1925, Gubernatorial Series, Arthur Mastick Hyde Papers.

159. Hunt, "The Confederate Home of Missouri," 301.

160. "Missouri Confederates in Reunion," *Confederate Veteran,* November 1931, 409.

161. "Old Soldiers Contented in State Homes," *Columbia Missourian*, August 6, 1924.

162. "History of the Confederate Home of Higginsville," 2–3; "Reports and Minutes," September 28, 1940, 1–2, Missouri Confederate Home, Higginsville, Records; *Columbia Missourian*, May 9, 1950.

163. "Fifteenth Biennial Report of the Confederate Soldiers' Home of Missouri," 10; "Report of Confederate Home," in *Journal of the House and Senate*, 63rd General Assembly, vol. 1, appendix, 1945, 13.

164. "Senate Bill No. 113," 63rd General Assembly, Legislative Correspondence, Phil M. Donnelly Papers, 1944–1957, The State Historical Society of Missouri.

165. Unidentified news clipping, 1945, Richmond Greys Chapter, United Daughters of the Confederacy, Children of the Confederacy Records, 1921–1954, The State Historical Society of Missouri.

166. Dr. B. R. Adams to Phil M. Donnelly, July 31, 1945, Legislative Correspondence, Phil M. Donnelly Papers (punctuation mine).

167. J. E. Taylor to Phil M. Donnelly, "Memorandum," July 28, 1945, Legislative Correspondence, Phil M. Donnelly Papers.

168. W. Scott Hancock to Phil M. Donnelly, August 3, 1945, Legislative Correspondence, Phil M. Donnelly Papers.

169. "Report of Confederate Home," 9.

170. "Soldiers' Homes" [S.B. 178], sec. 15131, in *Laws of Missouri Passed at the Session of the Sixty-Second General Assembly*, 954–955.

171. "History of the Confederate Home of Higginsville," 1–2; "Reports and Minutes," September 28, 1940, Missouri Confederate Home, Higginsville, Records; *Columbia Missourian*, May 9, 1950.

172. Rosenburg, *Living Monuments*, 4.

Epilogue

Epigraph. "Confederate Monument at Kansas City," 276.

1. Parrish, *Missouri under Radical Rule*, 132.

2. Proclamation of Governor John T. Blair, Jr., July 2, 1958, Civil War Centennial Commission of Missouri, Missouri State Archives.

3. Joseph Jaeger, Jr., to James Fuchs, April 10, 1959, Correspondence, Jan.–Dec. 1959, Civil War Centennial Commission of Missouri; John Alexander, "Lofty Motive for Civil War Buffs," *Kansas City Star*, May 8, 1960.

4. James Fuchs to Joseph Jaeger, Jr., October 7, 1960, Correspondence, Feb.–Nov. 1960, Civil War Centennial Commission of Missouri.

5. James Fuchs, "Commemorative Events for the First Civil War Centennial Year in the State of Missouri," November 17, 1960, Correspondence, Feb.–Nov. 1960, Civil War Centennial Commission of Missouri.

6. Sacco, "The Contested Memories of General Nathaniel Lyon in St. Louis."

7. James Fuchs to Dr. Bert Maybee, November 6, 1958, Correspondence, Jun.–Dec. 1958, Civil War Centennial Commission of Missouri.

8. "Throng for Wilson Creek Event," August 11, 1961, Newspaper Clippings Files, Centennial Events in Missouri, Civil War Centennial Commission of Missouri.

9. John K. Hulston to James Fuchs, November 9, 1960, Correspondence, Feb.–Nov. 1960, Civil War Centennial Commission of Missouri.

10. "Throng for Wilson Creek Event."

11. "A Day to Remember," *United Daughters of the Confederacy Magazine,* April 1985, 8–9, Cemeteries: Union, Elmwood, Springfield National, United Daughters of the Confederacy, Dixie Chapter No. 2188 Records, The State Historical Society of Missouri.

12. "A Day to Remember," 8–9.

13. Mary M. Haydon to Mrs. Wesley H. Bradford, June 15, 1984, Springfield National Cemetery May 12, 1981, United Daughters of the Confederacy, Dixie Chapter No. 2188 Records.

14. "A Day to Remember," 8–9; B. G. Douma, "Situation Paper: Springfield National Cemetery," May 12, 1981, Springfield National Cemetery May 12, 1981, United Daughters of the Confederacy, Dixie Chapter No. 2188 Records.

15. Rosenburg, *Living Monuments*, 5.

16. Coski, *The Confederate Battle Flag*.

17. "Missouri Removes Rebel Flag at Historic Sites."

18. "Missouri Officials Take Down Confederate Flags after Gephardt Complaint."

19. "Group Seeks to Fly Confederate Flag at Higginsville Cemetery."

20. "Missourians Back Confederate Flag, Poll Finds," *St. Louis Post-Dispatch*, February 7, 2003.

21. Schuessler, "In Missouri, Flames of the Civil War and Fires of Ferguson Are Linked."

22. Velez, "'Show Me' Missouri Racism."

23. Schuessler, "In Missouri, Flames of the Civil War and Fires of Ferguson Are Linked."

24. "Should Confederate Memorial Be Removed from Forest Park?"

25. Deal, "Confederate Lives Matter, Too."

26. O'Neil, "Everything You Need to Know."

27. O'Neil, "Everything You Need to Know."

28. McDermott, "Forest Park Confederate Monument Must Go"; O'Neil, "Everything You Need to Know"; Bott, "City, Missouri Civil War Museum at Odds Over Who Owns Confederate Monument"; Serhan, "St. Louis to Remove Its Confederate Monument"; Wicentowski, "Civil War Museum to Krewson."

29. Pekarsky, "United Daughters of the Confederacy Says Monument on Ward Parkway Will Be Removed"; Horsley and Londberg, "Daughters of the Confederacy Monument Removed Friday from Ward Parkway."

30. "Vandal Throws Paint on Confederate Statue in Springfield"; Suntrup, "Critics Demand Missouri Lawmaker Resign"; Schmitt, "No Punishment for Missouri Lawmaker."

31. Chadde, "We Won, You Know?"; *Palmyra Spectator*, February 18, 1897.

32. Foley, *The Genesis of Missouri*, 300.

33. "Confederate Monument at Kansas City," 276.

Bibliography

Archival Sources

Missouri Historical Society, St. Louis

Alphabetical Files
    Herman F. Kallman
    Clair V. Mann
    Union Veterans Legion
    United Confederate Veterans
    United Daughters of the Confederacy
Blair Monument Association
Civil War Collection
    Springfield, Missouri, Confederate Cemetery
Clubs and Societies Collection
Grand Army of the Republic Collection
Grier Family Papers
Military Order of the Loyal Legion of the United States, Commandery of the State of Missouri Records
Missouri-Vicksburg National Military Park Commissioner's Minute Book
Harvey Wallis Salmon Papers
Veterans of the Blue and Gray Records

Missouri State Archives, Jefferson City

Civil War Centennial Commission of Missouri
Department of Corrections Documents Collection
    State Board of Charities and Corrections
Department of Public Safety, Missouri Veterans Commission
    Confederate Home of Missouri at Higginsville, Biennial Reports
    Federal Soldiers Home of Missouri, Biennial Reports
General Assembly, State Documents
    Journal of the House and Senate, Missouri General Assembly, Appendices. 1903–1945.
Robert L. Hawkins, III, Collection, Winnie Davis Chapter, UDC, Jefferson City
Missouri Constitutions, 1820–1945
Missouri Veteran's Home (St. James), Inmate Registers

St. Louis Public Library, Rare Book and Manuscripts Collection

"An Address by the Colored People of Missouri to the Friends of Equal Rights." St. Louis: Missouri Democrat Print, 1865.

The State Historical Society of Missouri, Columbia, Kansas City, Rolla

African American Heroines of Jericho, Guiding Star Court No. 15 (Joplin, MO) Records, 1916-1959 (R970)

Clarence W. and Idress Head Alvord Collection, 1759-1962 (C970)

General Joe Bailey Women's Relief Corps No. 15 Nevada, Missouri Records, 1885-1918 (K0408)

Benecke Family Papers, 1816-1989 (C3825)

Bingham Family Papers, 1814-1930 (C998)

Bronaugh-Bushnell Family Papers, 1852-1930 (C0079)

A. Loyd Collins Scrapbook, 1939-1940 (C4063)

Lester E. Cox Papers, 1917-1968 (C3596)

Phil M. Donnelly Papers, 1944-1957 (C2151)

John Newman Edwards Letters, 1882-1885 (C1531)

B. James George Collection, 1887-1975 (C3564)

Todd M. George Papers, 1890-1968 (C3770)

Grand Army of the Republic, Dan McCook Post No. 312 (Leesville, MO), "Black List," 1887 (R0375)

Grand Army of the Republic, Department of Missouri, Aldrich Post No. 536, Records, 1892-1897 (C3529)

Grand Army of the Republic, Department of Missouri, A. Lincoln Post No. 5, List, n.d. (C2027)

Grand Army of the Republic, Department of Missouri, C. G. Harkas Post No. 88, Records, 1883-1907 (C2469)

Grand Army of the Republic, Department of Missouri, John A. Hayn Post No. 240, Record Books, 1885-1922 (C1112)

Grand Army of the Republic, Department of Missouri, O. P. Morton Post No. 14, Records, 1882-1943 (C0141)

Grand Army of the Republic, Department of Missouri, Smithton Post No. 417 Records, 1889-1904 (C3739)

Grand Army of the Republic, Erich Pape Post No. 184 (Zalma, Mo.), Records, 1865-1913 (R0225)

Grand Army of the Republic, Franklin Shanks Post No. 100 (Lutesville, MO), Records Book, 1883-1889 (R64)

Grand Army of the Republic, George G. Meade Post No. 48 (Lebanon, MO), Records, 1882-1937 (R81)

Grand Army of the Republic, Picket Post No. 215 (Farmington, MO), Records, 1884-1902 (R131)

Grand Army of the Republic, Tom Walker Post No. 379 (Zion, MO), Minute Book, 1888-1895 (R494)

Sarah Guitar Papers, 1931-1944 (C3563)

Henry County Veteran's Association (MO), Program, 1890 (R223)
Heroines of Jericho, St. Louis, Missouri History and Proceedings, 1891, 1903 (S0105)
Arthur Mastick Hyde Papers, 1932-1937 (C7)
Ira B. Hyde Papers, 1867-1939 (C122)
Ladies of the Grand Army of the Republic, Department of Missouri, Record Books, 1898-1937 (C1143)
Ladies of the Grand Army of the Republic, Department of Missouri, Secretary's Book, 1898-1910 (C1144)
Ladies of the Grand Army of the Republic, William H. McLane Circle No. 55 (Clinton, MO), Records, 1924-1932 (R224)
Clair V. Mann Collection, 1821-1973 (C3556)
Missouri Confederate Home, Higginsville, History and Cemetery Records, n.d. (C3498)
Missouri Confederate Home, Higginsville, Records, 1897-1944 (C0066)
Missouri Patriotic Associations Collection (C5939)
Negro Celebration, Poster and Program, 1895 (C2844)
Guy Brasfield Park Papers, 1932-1937 (C8)
James S. Rollins Papers, 1546-1968 (C1026)
Lloyd Crow Stark Papers, 1931-1941 (C4)
United Confederate Veterans, Camp No. 488 (Springfield, MO), Record Book, 1903-1919 (R273)
United Confederate Veterans, Camp No. 488 (Springfield, MO), Records, 1894-1915 (R60)
United Confederate Veterans, Camp No. 662, Nevada, Missouri, Record Book, 1895 (C1276)
United Confederate Veterans, Committee on History, Record Book, 1897 (C1277)
United Daughters of the Confederacy, Children of the Confederacy, Records, 1921-1954 (C4305)
United Daughters of the Confederacy, Confederate Dames Chapter, Records (CA2986)
United Daughters of the Confederacy, Jefferson Davis Chapter Scrapbook, 1924-1936 (K0020)
United Daughters of the Confederacy, Dixie Chapter No. 2188, Records, 1949-1989 (K1226)
United Daughters of the Confederacy, Robert E. Lee Chapter Records, 1916-1917 (K0152)
United Daughters of the Confederacy, John S. Marmaduke Chapter, Scrapbooks, 1927-1929 (C2996)
United Daughters of the Confederacy, Missouri Division, Records, n.d. (C3188)
Lucile Morris Upton Papers, 1855-1986 (C3869)
Cole Younger Papers, 1915 (C1670)
Cole and James Younger Papers, 1885-1897 (C0443)

Periodicals

All periodicals are from Missouri unless otherwise noted.

Albuquerque [NM] Morning Journal
Andrew County Republican [Savannah]
Boon's Lick Times
Boonville Weekly Advertiser
Brownsville [TX] Daily Herald
Butler Weekly Times
Butler Weekly Times and the Bates County Record
Cape Girardeau Democrat
Chariton Courier
Columbia Missourian
Columbia Missouri Statesman
Columbia Statesman
Confederate Veteran [Nashville, TN]
Daily Missouri Republican [St. Louis]
Democratic Banner [Bowling Green]
Evening Star [Washington, DC]
Farmington Times and Herald
Glasgow Weekly Times
Grand River Chronicle
Hannibal Journal
Henry County Democrat [Clinton]
Henry County Republican [Clinton]
Holt County Sentinel [Oregon]
Indian Chieftain [Vinita, Indian Territory]
Intelligencer [Lexington]
Iron County Register [Ironton]
Jefferson City Daily Tribune
Kansas City Daily Journal
Kansas City Journal
Kansas City Star
Kansas City Sun
Laclede Blade
Lexington Intelligencer
Liberty Tribune
Macon Argus
Marshall Republican
Maryland Free Press [Hagerstown]
Mexico Missouri Message
Mexico Weekly Ledger
Missourian [St. Charles]
Missouri Democrat [St. Louis]
Missouri Statesman [Columbia]
Montgomery Tribune

National Tribune [Washington, DC]
Omaha [NE] Daily Bee
Palmyra Spectator
People's Tribune [Jefferson City]
Professional World [Columbia]
Randolph Citizen
Rich Hill Tribune
Rising Son [Kansas City]
St. James Journal
St. Joseph Weekly Free Democrat
St. Joseph Weekly Gazette
St. Joseph Weekly Herald
St. Louis Globe-Democrat
St. Louis Post-Dispatch
St. Louis Republic
St. Louis Star and Times
St. Paul [MN] Globe
Scott County Kicker [Benton]
Sedalia Weekly Bazoo
Sedalia Weekly Conservator
Semi-Weekly Louisianian [New Orleans, LA]
Springfield Leader and Press
State Republican [Jefferson City]
State Times [Jefferson City]
Taney County Republican [Forsyth]
Tri-Weekly Missouri Democrat [St. Louis]
Troy Herald
Union Record
University Missourian [Columbia]
Vicksburg [MS] Evening Post
Vicksburg [MS] Herald
Weekly California News [California, MO]
Weekly Caucasian [Lexington]
Weekly Graphic [Kirksville]
Weekly Intelligencer [Lexington]
Weekly Jefferson Inquirer
Western Union [Hannibal]
Windsor Review

Published Primary Sources

Armstrong, Alice Mae. *History of the State Federal Soldiers' Home and the Work of the Department of the Missouri Woman's Relief Corps*. Kansas City: N.p., 1925.

Bailey, George W. *The Confederate Monument in Forest Park, St. Louis.* St. Louis: N.p., 1915.

Bancroft, Frederic, ed. *Speeches, Correspondence and Political Papers of Carl Schurz*, vol. 1, *October 20, 1852-November 26, 1870*. New York: Knickerbocker Press, 1913.

Basler, Ray P., ed. *The Collected Works of Abraham Lincoln*, vol. 3, *1864-1865*. New Brunswick, NJ: Rutgers University Press, 1953.

Biographical Review of Lee County, Iowa, Containing Biographical and Genealogical Sketches of Many of the Prominent Citizens of To-Day and Also of the Past. Chicago: Hobart, 1905.

Circular Series: Grand Army of the Republic, Department of Missouri, Ransom Post No. 131. 1909–1924. St. Louis: N.p., 1909–1924.

Cleveland, Henry. *Alexander H. Stephens in Public and Private with Letters and Speeches*. Philadelphia: National Publishing, 1866.

Delaney, Lucy A. *From the Darkness Cometh the Light; or, Struggles for Freedom*. St. Louis: T. J. Smith, 189[?].

Dickson, Moses. *Manual of the International Order of Twelve of Knights and Daughters of Tabor*. St. Louis: A. R. Fleming, 1891.

Drake, Charles D. "*Camp Jackson: Its History and Significance,*" *Oration of Charles D. Drake, Delivered in the City of St. Louis, May 11, 1863, on the Anniversary of the Capture of Camp Jackson.* St. Louis: Missouri Democrat, 1863.

———. *The Missouri State Convention, and Its Ordinance of Emancipation.* St. Louis: N.p., 1863.

———. *Missouri Voters' Oath: Have the People of Missouri the Right to Prescribe the Qualifications of Missouri Voters?* St. Louis: N.p., 1866.

Edwards, John Newman. *Noted Guerrillas; or, The Warfare of the Border*. St. Louis: Bryan, Brand, 1877.

———. *Shelby and His Men; or, The War in the West.* Cincinnati: Miami Printing, 1867.

Foster, R. B. *Historical Sketch of Lincoln Institute, Jefferson City, Missouri. And Speech of Col. David Branson, upon the Dedication of the New Building, July 4th, 1871.* N.p.: N.p., c. 1871.

Gentzler, Lynn Wolf, ed. *"But I Forget That I Am a Painter and Not a Politician": The Letters of George Caleb Bingham*. Compiled by Roger E. Robinson. Columbia: The State Historical Society of Missouri, 2011.

Germans for a Free Missouri: Translations from the St. Louis Radical Press, 1857-1862. Selected and translated by Steve Rowan, with an introduction and commentary by James Neal Primm. Columbia: University of Missouri Press, 1983.

The Grand Army Blue-Book: Containing the Rules and Regulations of the Grand Army of the Republic, and Official Decisions and Opinions Thereon, as Reported to and Approved by the National Encampment to September 13, 1895. Philadelphia: J. B. Lippincott, 1896.

Grover, George S. "Civil War in Missouri." Speech, Warrensburg, Missouri, November 4, 1893. Reprinted in *Missouri Historical Review* 3, no. 1 (October 1913): 1-28.

Hale, Donald R. *The William Clarke Quantrill Men Reunions, 1898-1928*. Independence, MO: Blue and Grey Book Shoppe, 2001.

Holmes, Oliver Wendell, Jr. *An Address by Oliver Wendell Holmes*. Boston: Little, Brown, 1895.

Howard, W. A. *Biographical Sketches of the Nebraska Legislature and National and State Officers of Nebraska*. Lincoln: Jacob North, 1895.

Jackson, Mattie, and Dr. L. S. Thompson. *The Story of Mattie J. Jackson; Her Parentage—Experience of Eighteen Years in Slavery—Incidents during the War—Her Escape from Slavery. A True Story*. Lawrence, MA: Sentinel Office, 1866.

Journal and Proceedings of the Missouri State Convention, Held at Jefferson City and St. Louis, March, 1861. St. Louis: George Knapp, 1861.

Journal of the Eleventh Annual Convention of the Woman's Relief Corps, Auxiliary to the Grand Army of the Republic, Indianapolis, Indiana, September 6th, 7th and 8th, 1893. Boston: E. B. Stillings, 1893.

Journal of the Seventeenth Annual Session National Encampment, Grand Army of the Republic, Denver, Colorado, July 25, 1883. Omaha, NE: Republican Book and Job Printing House, 1883.

Journal of the Twentieth Annual Session of the National Encampment Grand Army of the Republic, San Francisco California, August 4th, 5th, and 6th, 1886. Washington, DC: Gibson Brothers, 1886.

Journal of the Twentieth National Convention of the Woman's Relief Corps, Auxiliary to the Grand Army of the Republic, Washington, D.C., October 9th and 10th, 1902. Boston: Griffith-Stillings, 1902.

Journal of the Twenty-Fifth National Encampment, (Silver Anniversary) Grand Army of the Republic, Detroit, Michigan, August 5th, 6th, and 7th, 1891. Rutland, VT: Tuttle, 1891.

Journal of the Twenty-First Annual Session of the National Encampment, Grand Army of the Republic, St. Louis, Missouri, September 28th, 29th, 30th, 1887. Milwaukee: Burdick and Armitage, 1887.

Journal of the Twenty-Fourth Annual Session of the National Encampment, Grand Army of the Republic, Boston, Mass., August 13th and 14th, 1890. Detroit: Richmond and Backus, 1890.

Journal of the Twenty-Second Annual Session of the National Encampment, Grand Army of the Republic, Columbus, Ohio, September 12th, 13th and 14th, 1888. Minneapolis: Harrison and Smith, 1888.

Laws of Missouri Passed at the Session of the Sixty-Second General Assembly. Compiled by Dwight H. Brown. N.p.: N.p., 1943.

Laws of Missouri Passed at the Session of the Thirty-Ninth General Assembly. Jefferson City, MO: Tribune, 1897.

Leonard, John W., ed. *The Book of St. Louisans: A Biographical Dictionary of Leading Living Men of the City of St. Louis*. St. Louis: St. Louis Republic, 1906.

Minutes of the Nineteenth Annual Convention of the United Daughters of the Confederacy Held in Washington, D. C., Nov. 13-16, 1912. Jackson, TN: McCowat Mercer, n.d.

Minutes of the Ninth Annual Meeting, United Daughters of the Confederacy, Held in New Orleans, Louisiana, November 12-15, 1902. Nashville: Foster and Webb, 1903.

Minutes of the Tenth Annual Meeting and Reunion of the United Confederate Veterans, Held at Louisville, Ky. on May 30th, 31st and June 1st, 2nd and 3rd, 1900. N.p.: N.p., n.d.

Missouri of Today: Progress and Prospects of the Great Commercial State and Center of Population. St. Louis: Confederate Home Association of Missouri, 1893.

Morrison, Leonard Allison, and Stephen Paschall Sharples. *History of the Kimball Family in America, and of Its Ancestor the Kemballs or Kemboldes of England.* Boston: Damrell and Upham, 1897.

Official Proceedings of [First–Fifteenth] Annual Reunion of Missouri Division, United Confederate Veterans [title varies]. 1897–1911. Various publishers, 1897–1911.

Poppenheim, Mary B., et al. *The History of the United Daughters of the Confederacy.* Richmond, VA: Garrett and Massie, 1938.

Proceedings of the [First–Thirty-Second] Annual Convention of the Ladies of the Grand Army of the Republic, Department of Missouri. 1898-1929. Various publishers, 1898-1929.

Proceedings of the [Fourth–Fifteenth] Annual Convention of the Missouri Division, United Daughters of the Confederacy [title varies]. 1895-1917. Various publishers, 1895-1917.

Proceedings of the [First–Twenty-First] Annual Convention of the Woman's Relief Corps Auxiliary to the Grand Army of the Republic, Department of Missouri [title varies]. 1890-1905. Various publishers, 1890-1905.

Proceedings of the [First–Thirty-Third] Annual Encampment of the Department of Missouri, Grand Army of the Republic. 1882-1914 [title varies]. Various publishers, 1882-1914.

Rader, Perry S. *Reports of Cases Determined in the Supreme Court of the State of Missouri between June 20, and October 19, 1906.* Vol. 198. Columbia, MO: E. W. Stephens, 1907.

Reminiscences of the Women of Missouri during the Sixties. Compiled by Missouri Division, UDC. Jefferson City, MO: Hugh Stephens, n.d.

Report of the Proceedings of the Ex-Confederate Association of Missouri, in Its [Second–Ninth] Annual Meeting [title varies]. 1882-1891. Various publishers, 1882-1891.

Schurz, Carl. *The Reminiscences of Carl Schurz, 1852-1863.* Vol. 2. London: John Murray, 1909.

———. *The Reminiscences of Carl Schurz, 1863-1869.* Vol. 3. New York: McClure, 1908.

Siddali, Silvana R., ed. *Missouri's War: The Civil War in Documents.* Athens: Ohio University Press, 2009.

Souvenir and Official Programme of the 21st National Encampment Grand Army of the Republic St. Louis, Mo., Sept. 28, 29, 30, 1887. N.p.: N.p., 1887.

Souvenir of the Missouri Legislature. 39th General Assembly. Vol. 1. Sedalia, MO: Sedalia Printing Company, 1897.

Stone's Hannibal City Directory, 1897-98. Hannibal, MO: H. N. Stone, 1897.

The War of the Rebellion: A Compilation of the Official Records of the Union and Confederate Armies. Series 1–3. Washington, DC: Government Printing Office, 1880–1901.

Articles

Beilein, Joseph M., Jr. "The Guerrilla Shirt: A Labor of Love and the Style of Rebellion in Civil War Missouri." *Civil War History* 58, no. 2 (June 2012): 151-179.

Boyd, Miller W., III. "'The Free People, Who Have Bought Themselves, Are Not Much Inclined to It, but the Others Are in Favor of It': Patterns of Black Enlistment in Civil War Missouri, 1863-1865." *Missouri Historical Review* 111, no. 1 (October 2016): 1-24.

Burkhardt, Patrick. "The Lost Cause Ideology and Civil War Memory at the Semicentennial: A Look at the Confederate Monument in St. Louis." *The Confluence* 2, no. 2 (Spring–Summer 2011): 16–25.

Greene, Lorenzo, Antonio F. Holland, and Gary Kremer. "The Role of the Negro in Missouri History, 1719-1970." In *Official Manual of the State of Missouri, 1973-1974*, 1-11. Jefferson City: Missouri Secretary of States' Office, 1974.

Guitar, Sarah. "Monuments and Memorials in Missouri." *Missouri Historical Review* 19, no. 4 (July 1925): 555-603.

Hacker, J. David. "A Census-Based Count of the Civil War Dead." *Civil War History* 57, no. 4 (December 2011): 307-348.

Hulbert, Matthew C. "Constructing Guerrilla Memory: John Newman Edwards and Missouri's Irregular Lost Cause." *Journal of the Civil War Era* 2, no. 1 (March 2012): 58-81.

———. "How to Remember 'This Damnable Guerrilla Warfare': Four Vignettes from Civil War Missouri." *Civil War History* 59, no. 2 (June 2013): 143-168.

Kirkpatrick, Arthur Roy. "The Admission of Missouri to the Confederacy." *Missouri Historical Review* 55, no. 4 (July 1961): 366-386.

Klein, Kerwin Lee. "On the Emergence of *Memory* in Historical Discourse." *Representations* 69 (Winter 2000): 127-150.

Meinig, Donald W. "American Wests: Preface to a Geographical Interpretation." *Annals of the Association of American Cartographers* 62 (June 1972): 159-184.

Nora, Pierre. "Between Memory and History: *Les Lieux de Mémoire*." *Representations* 26 (Spring 1989): 7-24.

Pfeifer, Michael J. "The Ritual of Lynching: Extralegal Justice in Missouri, 1890-1942." *Gateway Heritage* 13, Issue 3 (Winter 1993): 22-33.

Phillips, Christopher. "The Crime against Missouri: Slavery, Kansas, and the Cant of Southernness in the Border West." *Civil War History* 48 (March 2002): 60-81.

Primm, James N. "The G.A.R. in Missouri, 1866-1870." *Journal of Southern History* 20, no. 3 (August 1954): 356-375.

Sheridan, Richard B. "A Most Unusual Gathering: The 1913 Semi-Centennial Memorial Reunion of the Survivors of Quantrill's Raid on Lawrence." *Kansas History* 20, no. 3 (Autumn 1997): 176-191.

Smith, George W. "New England Business Interests in Missouri during the Civil War." *Missouri Historical Review* 41, no. 1 (October 1946): 1-18.

Sutherland, Daniel E. "Sideshow No Longer: A Historiographical Review of the Guerrilla War." *Civil War History* 46, no. 1 (March 2000): 5-23.

Weber, David J. "Turner, the Boltonians, and the Borderlands." *American Historical Review* 91 (1986): 66-81.

Whites, LeeAnn. "Forty Shirts and a Wagonload of Wheat: Women, the Domestic Supply Line, and the Civil War on the Western Border." *Journal of the Civil War Era* 1 (March 2011): 56-78.

Theses and Dissertations

Boccardi, Megan B. "Remembering in Black and White: Missouri Women's Memorial Work, 1860-1910." PhD diss., University of Missouri, 2011.

Boyd, Miller Williams, III. "The Exigencies of War: Black Military Service, Free Labor, and Education in Civil War Missouri." PhD diss., University of Mississippi, 2016.

McConachie, Alexander S. "The 'Big Cinch': A Business Elite in the Life of a City, St. Louis, 1895-1915." PhD diss., Washington University, 1976.

McKerley, John W. "Citizens and Strangers: The Politics of Race in Missouri from Slavery to the Era of Jim Crow." PhD diss., University of Iowa, 2008.

Myers, Amanda M. "'Glory Stands beside Our Grief': The Maryland United Daughters of the Confederacy and the Assertion of Their Identity." MA thesis, University of Mississippi, 2010.

Books

Anderson, Benedict. *Imagined Communities: Reflections on the Origin and Spread of Nationalism*. New York: Verso, 2006.

Ankesheiln, Wade F. *The Heart Is the Heritage: The Story of the Founding of the Confederate Home of Missouri*. Coral Springs, FL: Llumina Press, 2007.

Arenson, Adam. *The Great Heart of the Republic: St. Louis and the Cultural Civil War*. Cambridge, MA: Harvard University Press, 2011.

Aron, Stephen. *American Confluence: The Missouri Frontier from Borderland to Border State*. Bloomington: Indiana University Press, 2006.

Astor, Aaron. *Rebels on the Border: Civil War, Emancipation, and the Reconstruction of Kentucky and Missouri*. Baton Rouge: Louisiana State University Press, 2012.

Athearn, Robert G. *The Mythic West in Twentieth-Century America*. Lawrence: University Press of Kansas, 1986.

Axtell, James. *The Invasion Within: The Contest of Cultures in Colonial North America*. New York: Oxford University Press, 1985.

Ayers, Edward L., et al. *All Over the Map: Rethinking American Regions*. Baltimore: Johns Hopkins University Press, 1996.

Beilein, Joseph, Jr. *Bushwhackers: Guerrilla Warfare, Manhood, and the Household in Civil War Missouri*. Kent, OH: Kent State University Press, 2016.

Berger, Henry W. *St. Louis and Empire: 250 Years of Imperial Quest and Urban Crisis*. Carbondale: Southern Illinois University Press, 2015.

Billington, Ray Allen. *Westward Expansion: A History of the American Frontier*. New York: Macmillan, 1967.

Blair, William A. *Cities of the Dead: Contesting the Memory of the Civil War in the South, 1865-1914*. Chapel Hill: University of North Carolina Press, 2004.

Blight, David. *Race and Reunion: The Civil War in American Memory*. Cambridge, MA: Belknap Press of Harvard University Press, 2001.

Blum, Edward J. *Reforging the White Republic: Race, Religion, and American Nationalism, 1865-1898*. Baton Rouge: Louisiana State University Press, 2005.

Boman, Dennis K. *Lincoln's Resolute Unionist: Hamilton Gamble, Dred Scott Dissenter and Missouri's Civil War Governor*. Baton Rouge: Louisiana State University Press, 2006.

Bradshaw, Michael. *Regions and Regionalism in the United States*. Jackson: University Press of Mississippi, 1988.

Brownlee, Richard S. *Gray Ghosts of the Confederacy: Guerrilla Warfare in the West, 1861-1865*. Baton Rouge: Louisiana State University Press, 1958.

Brundage, W. Fitzhugh. *The Southern Past: A Clash of Race and Memory*. Cambridge, MA: Belknap Press of Harvard University Press, 2005.

Buck, Paul H. *The Road to Reunion, 1865-1900*. New York: Vintage, 1937.

Burke, Diane Mutti. *On Slavery's Border: Missouri's Small-Slaveholding Households, 1815-1865*. Athens: University of Georgia Press, 2010.

Carmichael, Peter S. *The War for the Common Soldier: How Men Thought, Fought, and Survived in Civil War Armies*. Chapel Hill: University of North Carolina Press, 2018.

Cayton, Andrew R. L., and Fredrika J. Teute, eds. *Contact Points: American Frontiers from the Mohawk Valley to the Mississippi, 1750-1830*. Chapel Hill: University of North Carolina Press, 1998.

Christensen, Lawrence O., and Gary R. Kremer, *A History of Missouri*, vol. 4, *1875-1919*. Columbia: University of Missouri Press, 1997.

Cook, Robert J. *Civil War Memories: Contesting the Past in the United States since 1865*. Baltimore: Johns Hopkins University Press, 2017.

Coski, John M. *The Confederate Battle Flag: America's Most Embattled Emblem*. Cambridge, MA: Belknap Press of Harvard University Press, 2005.

Coulter, Charles E. *"Take Up the Black Man's Burden": Kansas City's African American Communities, 1865-1939*. Columbia: University of Missouri Press, 2006.

Cox, Karen L. *Dixie's Daughters: The United Daughters of the Confederacy and the Preservation of Confederate Culture*. Gainesville: University Press of Florida, 2003.

Dean, Eric T., Jr. *Shook over Hell: Post-Traumatic Stress, Vietnam, and the Civil War*. Cambridge, MA: Harvard University Press, 1997.

Dearing, Mary R. *Veterans in Politics: The Story of the G.A.R.* Baton Rouge: Louisiana State University Press, 1952.

Deverell, William, ed. *A Companion to the American West*. Malden, MA: Blackwell, 2004.

Dorsett, Lyle W. *The Pendergast Machine*. New York: Oxford University Press, 1968.

Durkheim, Émile. *The Elementary Forms of Religious Life*. Translated by Karen Fields. New York: Free Press, 1995.

Earle, Jonathan, and Diane Mutti Burke, eds. *Bleeding Kansas, Bleeding Missouri: The Long Civil War on the Border*. Lawrence: University Press of Kansas, 2013.

Epps, Kristen. *Slavery on the Periphery: The Kansas-Missouri Border in the Antebellum and Civil War Eras*. Athens: University of Georgia Press, 2016.

Erwin, James W. *Guerrilla Hunters in Civil War Missouri*. Charleston, SC: History Press, 2013.

Etcheson, Nicole. *Bleeding Kansas: Contested Liberty in the Civil War Era*. Lawrence: University Press of Kansas, 2004.

Fahs, Alice, and Joan Waugh, eds. *The Memory of the Civil War in American Culture*. Chapel Hill: University of North Carolina Press, 2004.

Faragher, John Mack, ed. *Rereading Frederick Jackson Turner: "The Significance of the Frontier in American History" and Other Essays*. New Haven, CT: Yale University Press, 1994.

Faust, Drew Gilpin. *This Republic of Suffering: Death and the American Civil War*. New York: Vintage, 2009.

Fellman, Michael. *Inside War: The Guerrilla Conflict in Missouri during the American Civil War*. New York: Oxford University Press, 1989.

Foley, William E. *The Genesis of Missouri: From Wilderness Outpost to Statehood*. Columbia: University of Missouri Press, 1989.

Foster, Gaines M. *Ghosts of the Confederacy: Defeat, the Lost Cause, and the Emergence of the New South, 1865 to 1913*. New York: Oxford University Press, 1987.

Fussell, Paul. *The Great War and Modern Memory: The Illustrated Edition*. New York: Sterling, 1974.

Gallagher, Gary W. *Causes Won, Lost, and Forgotten: How Hollywood and Popular Art Shape What We Know about the Civil War*. Chapel Hill: University of North Carolina Press, 2008.

———. *The Union War*. Cambridge, MA: Harvard University Press, 2011.

Gannon, Barbara. *The Won Cause: Black and White Comradeship in the Grand Army of the Republic*. Chapel Hill: University of North Carolina Press, 2011.

Geiger, Mark W. *Financial Fraud and Guerrilla Violence in Missouri's Civil War, 1861–1865*. New Haven, CT: Yale University Press, 2001.

Gerteis, Louis S. *The Civil War in Missouri: A Military History*. Columbia: University of Missouri Press, 2012.

———. *Civil War St. Louis*. Lawrence: University Press of Kansas, 2001.

Goodrich, Thomas. *Black Flag: Guerrilla Warfare on the Western Border, 1861–1865*. Bloomington: Indiana University Press, 1995.

Gordon, Lesley J., and John C. Inscoe, eds. *Inside the Confederate Nation: Essays in Honor of Emory M. Thomas*. Baton Rouge: Louisiana State University Press, 2005.

Greene, Lorenzo J., Gary R. Kremer, and Antonio F. Holland. *Missouri's Black Heritage*. Columbia: University of Missouri Press, 1980.

Halbwachs, Maurice. *On Collective Memory*. Translated and edited by Lewis A. Coser. Chicago: University of Chicago Press, 1992.

Handley-Cousins, Sarah. *Bodies in Blue: Disability in the Civil War North*. Athens: University of Georgia Press, 2019.

Hattaway, Herman. *Gettysburg to Vicksburg: The Five Original Civil War Battlefield Parks*. Columbia: University of Missouri Press, 2001.

Hausladen, Gary J., ed. *Western Places, American Myths: How We Think about the West*. Las Vegas: University of Nevada Press, 2003.

Hernando, Matthew J. *Faces Like Devils: The Bald Knobber Vigilantes in the Ozarks*. Columbia: University of Missouri Press, 2015.

Hulbert, Matthew C. *The Ghosts of Guerrilla Memory: How Civil War Bushwhackers Became Gunslingers in the American West*. Athens: University of Georgia Press, 2016.

Hurt, R. Douglas. *Agriculture and Slavery in Missouri's Little Dixie*. Columbia: University of Missouri Press, 1992.

Janney, Caroline E. *Burying the Dead but Not the Past: Ladies' Memorial Associations and the Lost Cause*. Chapel Hill: University of North Carolina Press, 2012.

———. *Remembering the Civil War: Reunion and the Limits of Reconciliation*. Chapel Hill: University of North Carolina Press, 2013.

Jordan, Brian Matthew. *Marching Home: Union Veterans and Their Unending Civil War*. New York: Liveright, 2014.

Kammen, Michael. *Mystic Chords of Memory: The Transformation of Tradition in American Culture*. New York: Knopf, 1991.

Kelman, Ari. *A Misplaced Massacre: Struggling over the Memory of Sand Creek*. Cambridge, MA: Harvard University Press, 2013.

Kremer, Gary R. *James Milton Turner and the Promise of America: The Public Life of a Post–Civil War Black Leader*. Columbia: University of Missouri Press, 1991.

———. *Race and Meaning: The African American Experience in Missouri*. Columbia: University of Missouri Press, 2014.

Limerick, Patricia Nelson. *The Legacy of Conquest: The Unbroken Past of the American West*. New York: Norton, 1987.

Marshall, Anne. *Creating a Confederate Kentucky: The Lost Cause and Civil War Memory in a Border State*. Chapel Hill: University of North Carolina Press, 2010.

Marten, James. *Sing Not War: The Lives of Union and Confederate Veterans in Gilded Age America*. Chapel Hill: University of North Carolina Press, 1992.

McCandless, Perry. *A History of Missouri*, vol. 2, *1820 to 1860*. Columbia: University of Missouri Press, 1972.

McConnell, Stuart. *Glorious Contentment: The Grand Army of the Republic, 1865-1900*. Chapel Hill: University of North Carolina Press, 1992.

McLaurin, Melton A. *Celia: A Slave*. New York: Harper Perennial, 1993.

McPherson, James. *Battle Cry of Freedom: The Civil War Era*. New York: Oxford University Press, 1988.

Mering, John Vollmer. *The Whig Party in Missouri*. Columbia: University of Missouri Press, 1967.

Merk, Frederick. *Manifest Destiny and Mission in American History, A Reinterpretation*. New York: Knopf, 1963.

Monaghan, Jay. *Civil War on the Western Border, 1854-1865*. Lincoln: University of Nebraska Press, 1955.

Nash, Gerald D. *Creating the West: Historical Interpretations, 1890-1990*. Albuquerque: University of New Mexico Press, 1991.

Neely, Jeremy. *The Border between Them: Violence and Reconciliation on the Kansas-Missouri Line*. Columbia: University of Missouri Press, 2007.

Neff, John R. *Honoring the Civil War Dead: Commemoration and the Problem of Reconciliation*. Lawrence: University Press of Kansas, 2005.

Nostrand, Richard L., and Lawrence E. Estaville, eds. *Homelands: A Geography of Culture and Place across America*. Baltimore: Johns Hopkins University Press, 2001.

Oertel, Kristen. *Bleeding Borders: Race, Gender, and Violence in Pre–Civil War Kansas*. Baton Rouge: Louisiana State University Press, 2013.

Parrish, William E., ed. *The Civil War in Missouri: Essays from the Missouri Historical Review, 1906-2006*. Columbia: State Historical Society of Missouri, 2006.

———. *A History of Missouri,* vol. 3, *1860 to 1875*. Columbia: University of Missouri Press, 1973.

———. *Missouri under Radical Rule, 1865-1870*. Columbia: University of Missouri Press, 1965.

———. *Turbulent Partnership: Missouri and the Union, 1861-1865*. Columbia: University of Missouri Press, 1963.

Phillips, Christopher. *The Making of a Southerner: William Barclay Napton's Private Civil War*. Columbia: University of Missouri Press, 2008.

———. *Missouri's Confederate: Claiborne Fox Jackson and the Creation of Southern Identity in the Border West*. Columbia: University of Missouri Press, 2000.

———. *The Rivers Ran Backward: The Civil War and the Remaking of the Middle American Border*. New York: Oxford University Press, 2016.

Rash, Nancy. *The Painting and Politics of George Caleb Bingham*. New Haven, CT: Yale University Press, 1991.

Reddig, William M. *Tom's Town: Kansas City and the Pendergast Legend*. Columbia: University of Missouri Press, 1986.

Richardson, Heather Cox. *West from Appomattox: The Reconstruction of America after the Civil War*. New Haven, CT: Yale University Press, 2007.

Richter, Daniel K. *Facing East from Indian Country*. Cambridge, MA: Harvard University Press, 2001.

Robinson, Michael D. *A Union Indivisible: Secession and the Politics of Slavery in the Border South*. Chapel Hill: University of North Carolina Press, 2017.

Romeo, Sharon. *Gender and the Jubilee: Black Freedom and the Reconstruction of Citizenship in Civil War Missouri*. Athens: University of Georgia Press, 2016.

Rosenburg, R. B. *Living Monuments: Confederate Soldiers' Homes in the New South*. Chapel Hill: University of North Carolina Press, 1993.

Schirmer, Sherry Lamb. *A City Divided: The Racial Landscape of Kansas City, 1900-1960*. Columbia: University of Missouri Press, 2002.

SenGupta, Gunja. *For God and Mammon: Evangelicals and Entrepreneurs, Masters and Slaves in Territorial Kansas, 1854-1860*. Athens: University of Georgia Press, 1996.

Shaffer, Donald R. *After the Glory: The Struggles of Black Civil War Veterans.* Lawrence: University Press of Kansas, 2004.

Shortridge, James R. *Kansas City and How It Grew, 1822–2011.* Lawrence: University Press of Kansas, 2012.

———. *The Middle West: Its Meaning in American Culture.* Lawrence: University Press of Kansas, 1989.

Silber, Nina. *Gender and the Sectional Conflict.* Chapel Hill: University of North Carolina Press, 2008.

———. *The Romance of Reunion: Northerners and the South, 1865–1900.* Chapel Hill: University of North Carolina Press, 1993.

———. *This War Ain't Over: Fighting the Civil War in New Deal America.* Chapel Hill: University of North Carolina Press, 2018.

Smith, Henry Nash. *Virgin Land: The American West as Symbol and Myth.* Cambridge, MA: Harvard University Press, 1950.

Smith, Ronald D. *Thomas Ewing, Jr.: Frontier Lawyer and Civil War General.* Columbia: University of Missouri Press, 2008.

Stanley, Matthew E. *The Loyal West: Civil War and Reunion in Middle America.* Urbana: University of Illinois Press, 2017.

Stevens, Walter Barlow. *Centennial History of Missouri: The Center State, 1821–1915.* Vol. 4. St. Louis: S. J. Clarke, 1915.

Stiles, T. J. *Jesse James: Last Rebel of the Civil War.* New York: Knopf, 2002.

Sutherland, Daniel. *A Savage Conflict: The Decisive Role of Guerrillas in the American Civil War.* Chapel Hill: University of North Carolina Press, 2009.

Walker, Steve, and David F. Riggs. *Vicksburg Battlefield Monuments: A Pictorial Record.* Jackson: University Press of Mississippi, 1984.

Warren, Robert Penn. *The Legacy of the Civil War.* Lincoln: University of Nebraska Press, 1961.

West, Elliott. *The Last Indian War: The Nez Perce Story.* Oxford: Oxford University Press, 2009.

White, Richard. *"It's Your Misfortune and None of My Own": A New History of the American West.* Norman: University of Oklahoma Press, 1991.

———. *The Middle Ground: Indians, Empires, and Republics in the Great Lakes Region, 1650–1815.* New York: Cambridge University Press, 1991.

Whites, LeeAnn, and Alecia P. Long, eds. *Occupied Women: Gender, Military Occupation, and the American Civil War on the Border.* Lawrence: University Press of Kansas, 2013.

Zelinsky, Wilbur. *The Cultural Geography of the United States.* Englewood Cliffs, NJ: Prentice-Hall, 1973.

Web Sources

Ayers, Edward. "American Regionalism." University of Virginia. xroads.virginia.edu/~drbr/ayers_in.html.

Bott, Celeste. "City, Missouri Civil War Museum at Odds over Who Owns Confederate Monument." *St. Louis Post-Dispatch,* June 15, 2017. https://www.stltoday.com/news/local/govt-and-politics/city-missouri-civil-war-museum

-at-odds-over-who-owns/article_5c861934-f70f-54ea-a82b-ee9528a072e6.html.

Chadde, Sky. "We Won, You Know?" *St. Louis Post-Dispatch*, January 4, 2018. https://www.stltoday.com/news/local/govt-and-politics/we-won-you-know-st-louis-senator-wants-to-put/article_dbf17162-bd0b-5b73-ba55-ee2101ad4b4b.html.

"Confederate Flags Return to Graveyard." *Los Angeles Times*, June 2, 2003. http://articles.latimes.com/2003/jun/02/nation/na-flag2.

Deal, Kenneth. "Confederate Lives Matter, Too." *St. Louis Post-Dispatch*, May 16, 2015. http://www.stltoday.com/news/opinion/mailbag/confederate-lives-matter-too/article_45549244-5977-5943-8ae3-85d0e1b930eb.html.

"Flags at the Confederate Home." Confederate Memorial State Historic Site, Missouri State Parks. https://mostateparks.com/page/55052/flags-confederate-home.

"General Information at Confederate Memorial State Historic Site." Missouri State Parks. http://mostateparks.com/page/54952/general-information.

"Group Seeks to Fly Confederate Flag at Higginsville Cemetery." KMBC (Kansas City), May 12, 2014. http://www.kmbc.com/news/group-seeks-to-fly-confederate-flag-at-higginsville-cemetery/25935578.

"History of the National Home for Disabled Soldiers." National Park Service. http://www.nps.gov/nr/travel/veterans_affairs/History.html.

Horsley, Lynn, and Max Londberg. "Daughters of the Confederacy Monument Removed Friday from Ward Parkway." *Kansas City Star*, August 25, 2017. https://www.kansascity.com/news/politics-government/article169288407.html.

Levings, Darryl. "How William Quantrill Wound up with Three Graves." *Kansas City Star*, October 3, 2011. http://civilwar150.kansascity.com/articles/how-quantrill-wound-up-with-three-graves/.

"Lynching in America: Confronting the Legacy of Racial Terror." Equal Justice Initiative, 3rd Edition, 2017. https://lynchinginamerica.eji.org/report/.

McCarthy, Harry. *Missouri, Bright Land of the West.* Montgomery: Schreiner and Son, 1861. http://library.duke.edu/digitalcollections/hasm_conf0048/.

McDermott, Kevin. "Forest Park Confederate Monument Must Go, Says Krewson, but No Plan Yet on Who Pays." *St. Louis Post-Dispatch*, May 17, 2017. https://www.stltoday.com/news/local/govt-and-politics/forest-park-confederate-monument-must-go-says-krewson-but-no/article_170de254-e8d8-563d-838e-0c3825fb48b0.html.

"Missouri Officials Take Down Confederate Flags after Gephardt Complaint." Fox News, January 14, 2003. http://www.foxnews.com/story/2003/01/14/missouri-officials-take-down-confederate-flags-after-gephardt-complaint.html.

"Missouri Removes Rebel Flag at Historic Sites." *New York Times*, January 16, 2003. http://www.nytimes.com/2003/01/16/us/missouri-removes-rebel-flag-at-historic-sites.html.

O'Neil, Tim. "Everything You Need to Know about the Confederate Monument in Forest Park." *St. Louis Post-Dispatch*, May 30, 2017. https://www.stltoday.com/news/local/govt-and-politics/everything-you-need-to-know-about-the-confederate-monument-in/article_bf090beb-965c-5f8b-bef1-e84fcc8646a6.html.

Pekarsky, Michelle. "United Daughters of the Confederacy Says Monument on Ward Parkway Will Be Removed." Fox4 WDAF-TV Kansas City, August 20, 2017. https://fox4kc.com/2017/08/20/confederate-memorial-monument-on-ward-parkway-will-be-removed/.

Sacco, Nick. "The Contested Memories of General Nathaniel Lyon in St. Louis." *Muster*, May 28, 2019. https://www.journalofthecivilwarera.org/2019/05/the-contested-memories-of-general-nathaniel-lyon-in-st-louis/.

———. "A Free Country for White Men: The Legacy of Frank Blair Jr. and His Statue in St. Louis." *Muster*, July 28, 2017. https://www.journalofthecivilwarera.org/2017/07/free-country-white-men-legacy-frank-blair-jr-statue-st-louis/.

Schmitt, Will. "No Punishment for Missouri Lawmaker Who Says Hanging Comment Was Blown out of Proportion." *Springfield News-Leader*, January 4, 2018. https://www.news-leader.com/story/news/politics/2018/01/04/no-punishment-missouri-rep-warren-love-who-says-hanging-comment-blown-out-proportion/1005570001/.

Schuessler, Ryan. "In Missouri, Flames of the Civil War and Fires of Ferguson Are Linked." Aljazeera America, January 10, 2015. http://america.aljazeera.com/articles/2015/1/10/in-missouri-the-flamesofcivilwarandthefiresoffergusonarelinked.html.

Serhan, Yasmeen. "St. Louis to Remove Its Confederate Monument." *The Atlantic*, June 26, 2017. https://www.theatlantic.com/news/archive/2017/06/st-louis-to-remove-its-confederate-monument/531720/.

"Should Confederate Memorial Be Removed from Forest Park?" *St. Louis Post-Dispatch*, April 22, 2015. http://www.stltoday.com/lifestyles/columns/joe-holleman/should-confederate-memorial-be-removed-from-forest-park/article_ba334819-f41c-53c3-854f-614bbcaa0d8c.html.

"A Soldier's Dream: The History of Lincoln University and the Men of the 62nd and 65th Colored Infantry." Video file. Missouri State Archives, 2010. http://www.sos.mo.gov/mdh/soldiersdream/.

Suntrup, Jack. "Critics Demand Missouri Lawmaker Resign after Saying Vandals Should Be 'Hung from a Tall Tree with a Long Rope.'" *St. Louis Post-Dispatch*, August 31, 2017. https://www.stltoday.com/news/local/govt-and-politics/critics-demand-missouri-lawmaker-resign-after-saying-vandals-should-be/article_ce20f2a9-41e1-547c-a3ba-7fe380923905.html.

"Vandal Throws Paint on Confederate Statue in Springfield." KY3, August 30, 2017. https://www.ky3.com/content/news/Vandal-throws-paint-on-Confederate-statue--442257183.html.

Velez, Denise Oliver. "'Show Me' Missouri Racism." Daily Kos, August 17, 2014. http://www.dailykos.com/story/2014/08/17/1321204/--Show-Me-Missouri-racism.

Wicentowski, Danny. "Civil War Museum to Krewson: See You in Court." *Riverfront Times*, June 16, 2017. https://www.riverfronttimes.com/newsblog/2017/06/16/civil-war-museum-to-krewson-give-us-the-confederate-monument-or-get-sued.

Index